Friends of Calvin

IEAN CALVIN, DE NOYON
EN PICARDIE, PASTEVR DE L'E-
GLISE DE GENEVE.

I. CALVIN.

John Calvin, engraving by Pierre Cruche. From the *Icones* of Beza

Friends of Calvin

Machiel A. van den Berg

Translated by

Reinder Bruinsma

WILLIAM B. EERDMANS PUBLISHING COMPANY

GRAND RAPIDS, MICHIGAN / CAMBRIDGE, U.K.

Originally published in Dutch under the title *Vrienden van Calvijn*
Copyright © 2006 by M. A. van den Berg
Published by Uitgeverij de Banier B. V., Utrecht, The Netherlands

This English edition © 2009 William B. Eerdmans Publishing Company
All rights reserved

Published 2009 by
Wm. B. Eerdmans Publishing Co.
2140 Oak Industrial Drive N.E., Grand Rapids, Michigan 49505 /
P.O. Box 163, Cambridge CB3 9PU U.K.

Printed in the United States of America

15 14 13 12 11 10 09   7 6 5 4 3 2 1

Library of Congress Cataloging-in-Publication Data

Berg, M. A. van den.
[Vrienden van Calvijn. English]
Friends of Calvin / Machiel A. van den Berg;
translated by Reinder Bruinsma.
p.   cm.
Includes bibliographical references and index.
ISBN 978-0-8028-6227-3 (alk. paper)
1. Calvin, Jean, 1509-1564 — Friends and associates.   I. Title.

BX9418.B3313   2009
284′.20922 — dc22
[B]
2009006932

www.eerdmans.com

Contents

Contents

vi

Introduction

C. S. Lewis, the English Christian philosopher, offered a unique description of true friendship. There may be many people who want to be "friendly," he said, but there are few "real friends." Friendship is sharing in the deepest interests of the other. It is the bond between souls who meet in "the same truth" and have "a common vision." Friendship even manifests a glorious likeness to heaven itself, where we will enjoy the presence of God that much more because we will share that special experience with others. In these words Lewis expresses his high praise for Christian friendship.[1]

To what extent was John Calvin able to enjoy such true friendships? At first glance, his great predecessor and model Martin Luther would appear to have possessed a much greater talent for the virtue of congeniality. In his *Table Talk* we meet him around his famous dining table, in the midst of his colleagues and friends and entertaining them with solemnity and humor. His friends are indispensable companions, and he would not be able to fulfill his profound calling without them. His conversation with them is clear proof of this: he tells them in all frankness what occupies and motivates him. He is the great Reformer of Wittenberg; but at the same time, seated with others around his simple kitchen table, he is just a friend of many.

---

1. See "Friendship," in Lesley Walmsley, ed., *C. S. Lewis on Love* (London, 1998), p. 20.

It is hard to imagine Calvin in the same way. When we look at his portraits, the first impression we get is not necessarily that of a very amiable person. We see an aristocratic and serious man, one who no doubt commanded the respect and admiration of those who looked up to him. But his portraits give the viewer a sense of distance. Calvin simply does not impress us as a homey person, one who could not do without friends.

But this first impression turns out to be totally false.[2] A close study of Calvin's career reveals that friendships were the joy of his life. When he said farewell to his Geneva colleagues — those who were also his brothers and friends — a few days before his death, he arranged for a common meal. There they celebrated their cordial collegiality in a final way. This says everything about how he shared his life with many others in true and deep friendship. It may well be that this cordial sharing was even more essential for Calvin than for Luther because the former had to do without a "helpmeet" during most of his life. His married bliss was of but short duration, and he never had a family. But his friends made up for this lack.

Friends often determine what one becomes in life. A well-known saying puts it this way: "Tell me about your friends, and I will tell you who you are." Another saying is: "The eyes of a friend are like a mirror." Getting acquainted with Calvin's friends can serve us as an illustration of that truth.

Concentrated Love for One's Neighbor

We need only take a look at Calvin's extensive correspondence to become convinced that he had a close network of friends.[3] And the content of his letters often shows the great warmth that characterized those friendships. He sympathized with his friends, communicating

2. One of the few authors who emphasizes this is N. J. Hommes, *Misère en Grootheid van Calvijn* (Delft, n.d.), pp. 132-39.

3. See the remark made by Fritz Büsser, *Calvins Urteil über sich selbst* (Zurich, 1950), p. 75: "Without friendship, there would not have been any Calvin-correspondence, that varied between everyday comments to highly political statements or church decisions or expositions about theological matters."

with them in joy and in sadness. Crucial issues about the Reformation would find their place next to all kinds of matters of everyday life and worries about health. Calvin was sincerely and deeply involved with the ups and downs in the lives of his friends.

His friends, in turn, were helpful to him: they offered a listening ear when he sometimes needed to cool down; they tempered his rather explosive temperament; and they provided the comfort of home to a man who was to enjoy only nine years of happy wedded and family life himself. They formed the spiritual circle he needed, meaning that he did not have to execute his mission in utter loneliness. For Calvin, friendships were a form of "concentrated love for one's neighbor," a place where cordiality and honesty met.[4] It was not enough that they were friends for the duration of his life on earth. The expectation that he would enjoy these friends in eternal life constituted a bond on an even deeper level. The way Calvin points this out to Melanchthon speaks for itself: "The distance in place cannot prevent us — content with the bond that Christ has established through his blood and has enclosed in our hearts through his Spirit — from holding on to the hope, of which your letter also reminds us, that we will in the end live together eternally and in eternal enjoyment of our love and friendship."[5]

Friendship was not a matter of flattery. Somewhere Calvin says: "Christians do not have friendships in order to smooth talk one another, but rather to focus on care for one another."[6] At times Calvin could be very direct and vulnerable when asking his friends not to spare him their criticism. The fact that they did what he asked of them helped form his character. Above everything else, Calvin saw friendship as a special token of God's goodness. God's covenant gives human friendship a deeper dimension, a dimension that the world is ignorant about. Friends who together live out of God's grace can be very close because they have been given by God to each other. No worldly friendship can ever match that.

In a sermon on 2 Timothy 1:3-5, Calvin says that the grace that

4. Büsser, *Calvins Urteil*, p. 76.

5. M. A. van den Berg, "Calvijn en Melanchthon, een beproefde vriendschap," *Theologia Reformata* 41 (1998): 78-102, 96.

6. *CO*, 16: 50.

God has given is the joy of the heart and is experienced in mutual friendship. He differentiates this from earthly congeniality when he says: "But Christian friendship exceeds this by far. Because, if we present ourselves before God and there say 'Our Father,' we simultaneously think of all with whom we have close ties and from whom we should never be separated."[7]

A Biographical Companion

Looking at Calvin through the eyes of his friends, we get a surprising insight into his person. This does not primarily apply to the assessment given by friends in their explicit remarks. We do not actually have very many statements about Calvin from the mouths of his friends. More important is the significance these friends had for Calvin in various periods of his life. For a shorter or longer period they were in intense contact with Calvin. Most of them remained his lifelong friends; however, in some cases the friendships ended unhappily. But all of them had their own influence on Calvin's development, and they form a colorful palette that illustrates the versatility of his life.

These twenty-four portraits have been published earlier as a series of articles in the *Gereformeerd Weekblad* (published by Bout in Huizen). They can be read separately, of course, but they also show a degree of cohesion. At times one friend moves us along to another friend. Each portrait offers a sketch of the main events of that friend's life, but the relationship to Calvin is the central focus. Since I wrote these as independent portraits, some repetition of central events and principles in Calvin's life has been unavoidable. The order in which the friends appear here is largely determined by the chronology of Calvin's life.

As far as it was possible, each chapter is accompanied by a portrait of the friend described in that chapter. Most of these have been taken from Calvin's successor Theodore Beza's *Icones*, published in 1580 with a view toward giving more visibility to the broad circle of kindred souls in the world of Renaissance and Reformation. That Beza regarded such a network so essential that he wanted to bring it to the attention of his

7. *CO,* 54: 19.

contemporaries is itself evidence of the importance of these relationships for Calvin. In those cases where no portraits of the person have survived, we have selected pictures of Calvin himself — from various phases of his life.

Thanks

Finally, a word of appreciation to those who have been of assistance to me as I wrote these sketches. I want to mention, in particular, Dr. Wulfert de Greef, who, with his wide knowledge of the literature by and about Calvin, was willing to provide criticism as only a friend can do. I also want to express my enormous gratitude to the modern "friends of Calvin," of the Institut de l'Histoire de la Réformation in Geneva. They have once again allowed me to enjoy their warm hospitality. They have assisted me in every possible way as I completed this book in their excellent library.

Geneva, January 2006

CLAUDE D'HANGEST

An Aristocratic Friend from His Youth

**Calligraphy by Chevallier de Berny (1772), in which Calvin
is referred to as "priest of Pont l'Éveque"**

The Friend from His Youth

In 1532 the young and erudite John Calvin, at the age of twenty-two, showed what he was worth. Youthful and ambitious as he was, he revealed his great talent by writing a humanist commentary on the Roman philosopher Seneca's *De Clementia* ("on mercy"), and thus presented himself to the scholarly world of his day.[1] As was customary for an author at that time, Calvin began his book with a dedication. Who received this honor in Calvin's debut piece of writing? It was Claude d'Hangest, the abbot of the St. Eloi's monastery in Noyon, the town where Calvin was born. Claude, writes Calvin, has deserved to "receive the first fruits of our harvest," because "whatever I am and have I owe to you."[2] Apparently, he saw his first substantial publication — "our commentary" — not just as the result of his own diligent work but as the fruit of a scholarly interest he shared with his friends, among whom Claude seemed to have occupied an important place.

Claude d'Hangest was a son of Adrien d'Hangest, one of the lords of the Montmor dynasty and the cousin of the bishop of Noyon. His family belonged to the highest nobility in Picardy, in the north of France, and it had close ties with the French royal house. The strong connection between John Calvin's father, Gérard Cauvin, and this noble family apparently enabled him to have his son accompany the d'Hangest sons to the school of the Montmors — the so-called "school of the Capets." This educational institution derived its name from a special "cappa," a cloak worn by the pupils, and it laid the foundation for Calvin's later humanist education.

Some of the students were dependent on scholarships, but we learn from Beza's *Life of Calvin* that John's school fees were paid for by his own father. This indicates that Gérard was not too poor to have his gifted son educated along with boys from a much higher social class. The incessant rumor about Calvin's poor background, which his opponents later used eagerly to undermine his status, thus lacks any substantiation.[3] Nonetheless, as Calvin himself said, he was very conscious

1. Ford Lewis Battles, ed., *Calvin's Commentary on Seneca's De Clementia* (Leyden, 1969).

2. Battles, *Calvin on De Clementia*, pp. 12-13.

3. See E. Doumergue, *Calvijn's Jeugd* (Kampen, 1986), p. 26.

Claude d'Hangest

of the privilege of moving — "as someone from among the common people" — in such high circles, where civilization and erudition set the tone. Even though he was not directly dependent on the parents of this friend from his youth in a financial way, he owed them a great deal with respect to culture.

The Son of a Noyon Citizen

Calvin's cradle rocked in the home of an ecclesiastical clerk in Noyon. His Cauvin ancestors came from Pont-l'Évêque, a village close to Noyon, and were, according to an old family tradition, simple folks who plied the river in their small boats. One biographer of the young Calvin suggests that this background explains their entrepreneurial spirit and their love of travel, characteristics that would later apply to the young John.[4] But John's father, Gérard, did not wish to follow in the footsteps of his forefathers and find his future on the river; instead, he looked ashore for a solid position with promising career possibilities. It seems that his family was not completely without means, for he certainly must have had a decent education in order to acquire the respectable clerical post that he found in Noyon. His successful career brought him in close contact with the bishop of Noyon, in whose service he was employed.

This prelate, Charles d'Hangest (1461-1528), belonged to a prominent noble family that in every respect occupied a central position in Noyon. Charles d'Hangest was one of the sons of Jean d'Hangest IV, Lord of Genlis. Charles's mother, Marie d'Amboise, was the sister of Cardinal d'Amboise, one of the most powerful men in the government of Louis XII. Thus there is no doubt that this family belonged to the most influential nobility at the French court and in the church in France.[5]

Calvin's father enjoyed a good relationship with his employer, and as a result he was able to ensure that his three sons would become the beneficiaries of chaplaincies in the church in Noyon. For that reason

---

4. Abel Lefranc, *La jeunesse de Calvin* (Paris, 1888), p. 1.
5. T. H. L. Parker, *John Calvin* (Tring/Batavia/Sydney, 1975), p. 4; Bernard Cottret, *Calvin* (Paris, 1995), p. 23.

John went through the motions of being ordained as a priest at the age of twelve — as well as receiving the tonsure. This simple fact did not by any means indicate that he would in time actually become a member of the clergy; but it did mean that he could get the funds that were connected with this position and use them to pay for his studies. On the other hand, this did not prevent Gérard from experiencing conflicts with the canon of the cathedral in his later years — to such an extent, in fact, that he would die in a state of excommunication. There is no doubt that this bitter experience influenced the attitude of his sons toward ecclesiastical authorities. Charles, John's oldest brother and himself a priest, continued the struggle of his father in Noyon, until he suffered a similar fate. It is likely that John's respect for men of the cloth was not enhanced by the way they treated his father and later his brother.

Gérard Cauvin was part of Noyon's establishment, officially obtaining his full civil rights in 1497. He also married into the right kind of family: his wife was the daughter of a wealthy retired innkeeper, Jean le Franc, who came from the neighboring city of Cambrai. Once the father-in-law had accumulated his fortune, he moved to Noyon and became Gérard Cauvin's neighbor. Eventually he was even granted the honorable position of city councilor.

Inherited Piety

Tradition has it that Calvin's mother, Jeanne le Franc, was a true beauty but also a singularly pious woman. She took her children, from their earliest years, with her when she would go on a pilgrimage, for instance, to the abby of Ourscamp. Much later Calvin would remember well how, as a small boy, he once was allowed to kiss the relic of St. Anna.[6] His mother died when he was only six years old, a time of life when a child cannot yet cope with life without the consolation of a mother. It may be too much psychological speculation to draw any conclusions about Calvin's future life from this intense loss. But the fact remains that, from

6. *Iohannis Calvini opera quae supersunt omnia*, ed. G. Baum, E. Cunitz, and E. Reuss (Brunswick and Berlin: Braunschweig, 1863-1900), 6: 452 (hereafter *CO*); *Traktaat over de relieken:* see Lefranc, *La jeunesse du Calvin*, p. 6, n. 2.

Claude d'Hangest

that time onward, Calvin never again experienced a warm family life, though his father soon remarried. This second marriage was also blessed with children, and John would have a good relationship with them. His half sister Marie, along with his brother Antoine, would later join him in Geneva in his exile.

It may well be that the situation in his parental home after his mother's death contributed to the fact that Calvin, without too much difficulty, found in another family what he may not have found in suffi- cient measure in his own home: the warm recognition of his own per- sonal and special giftedness. He did receive this in the castle of the d'Hangest family, where he became — partly through his father's influ- ence — a frequent visitor.

Adopted into the Circles of Nobility

Calvin's association with the Montmor family, who recognized an un- usual talent in him, left a significant mark on him. They took him into their home and allowed him to grow up along with his friends of the no- bility. Calvin at one point reminds his friend Claude of the time when, as children in the Montmor home, they tasted what would forever be the ultimate delight for Calvin: "the study of the essential elements of life and literature. . . ." He goes on to say that he was educated "in your home, introduced to the same study, together with you. I am indebted to your most noble family with regard to my earliest education in life and literature."[7]

A deep gratitude thus emerges from the memory of this friend- ship and the beneficent home of its origins. It provided him with the opportunity to become acquainted with the refined culture of a family of nobility in which love for science in the humanist tradition was highly valued. This home also supplied the roots for the ease with which Calvin later acquired a more or less natural aptitude to mingle with the great of the world. In spite of his personal modesty, which at times tended toward shyness, Calvin's personality also exuded a mea- sure of aristocratic sophistication. Even though he was but the son of a

7. Battles, *Calvin on De Clementia,* pp. 12-13.

citizen of Noyon, the friendship of his youth and a noble family's warm welcome ensured that he was well prepared for his later calling. Indeed, he was to become more than a respected scholar: as a Reformer of the church, Calvin was destined to play an important role in his contacts with the political leaders of his time. In God's providence, Calvin's friendship with Claude d'Hangest prepared him for the position where God would use him "alongside princes and authorities."

From time to time Calvin signed his letters — especially when he was writing to people he knew when he was young — with the pseudonym Charles d'Espeville. This was not just an arbitrary, made-up name. It is possible that he used this pseudonym in trying to assume a certain noble pretense in his social contacts, and it may refer to his links with the d'Hangest family, because the Espeville estate was part of their holdings.[8] Some of the proceeds from this estate's farmlands were part of the chaplaincy stipend that Calvin had been given as a twelve-year-old boy. By adopting this name, which was attached to an estate befitting a nobleman, he was able to create the impression that he belonged to the Picardian aristocracy — though in reality, of course, he lived as a junior clergyman partly on the proceeds from Espeville lands that were given to the church.[9] It is true that he was from Espeville, but he had no noble blood. Did Claude d'Hangest perhaps at some time honor him with this "title," the name of part of his family's estate? We will never know.

When we look at some early portraits of Calvin, it is difficult to escape the impression that the young scholar did not mind projecting an aristocratic image: he always seemed to resemble a nobleman rather than an ordinary citizen.

Roots of Culture and Erudition

The Montmor family sent their children to Paris for their further education because that is where the best colleges were in those days. Calvin followed them in 1523, when he was fourteen, and he studied alongside

8. Lefranc, *La jeunesse*, p. 186.
9. Lefranc, *La jeunesse*, p. 10.

Claude d'Hangest

Joachim and Yves d'Hangest. He found lodgings with his uncle, his father's brother Richard, a locksmith, who did not live far from Calvin's friends from his hometown. They probably even shared the same tutor. The investment of the Montmor family in this middle-class boy would prove to be very worthwhile. His exceptional aptitude, which they had already seen much earlier in his youth, would soon develop significantly.

History does not tell us very much about Calvin's friends in the d'Hangest family. The humble praise that Calvin expresses to Claude in the dedication of his first book, which is fully in line with humanist courtesy, would have been more apt if the roles had been reversed. Calvin applauds Claude's "vibrant and generous character of a nobleman," which is how Claude is known: "sharp and stable, with a good and trustworthy memory, well-versed in the study of the liberal arts." This humanist ideal may have meant even more to Calvin in 1532 than it would in later periods of his life. In those days he was still very much the promising scholar; in later years his great erudition would be enlisted in the knowledge of Scripture. However, his true inward nobility did profit, until the end of his life, from a noble *esprit* that he had been able to develop as the result of the hospitality of the family of Claude d'Hangest. The roots of culture and knowledge, planted in his youth, later produced rich fruit in his service to and enhancement of Christ's kingdom.

We should not ignore the small fact that Claude made arrangements for Calvin in 1529, when he was still a student in Bourges, to get the position of local priest in the village of Pont-l'Évêque ("bridge of the bishop"), the origins of the Cauvin family.[10] The proceeds from this ecclesiastical post served as a kind of educational grant, enabling him to complete his publication of the commentary on *De Clementia*. Therefore, the dedication to Claude may have also been an acknowledgment of services rendered.

Calvin's Influence on Others

One might well ask what influence Calvin, in turn, had on Claude and the d'Hangest family. We know but little about later contacts between

---

10. Battles, *Calvin on De Clementia*, p. 40.

the two schoolmates. But it does appear that members of the Montmor family were, in later years, rather positively inclined toward the ideas of their former protégé. During the wars of religion we meet some nobles from the d'Hangest family among the leaders of the Huguenot Party, and it may well be that they stayed in contact with the Reformer after he settled in Geneva. In any case, we do know that in 1547 a thirty-four-year-old son of the Montmor family (whose name remains unknown) sought refuge with Calvin in Geneva. Calvin tells another friend, the Lord of Falais, to whom he recommended this friend from his youth, that the latter was converted after a tempestuous and riotous youth.[11] Calvin had taken him in and was eager to find a stable position for him and to lead him to a good marriage. In this endeavor he was seeking the assistance of his important friends.

On the other hand, Calvin spoke quite negatively about Claude's youngest brother, François d'Hangest, in a letter to Bullinger in 1563. This nobleman, the Lord of Genlis, was part of the entourage of the Prince of Condé, the leader of the Huguenots, about whom, we should add, Calvin also had little good to say. According to Calvin, Condé was someone "one cannot rely on; not only is he weak and a coward, but he is also a conceited fool, who is totally preoccupied with his own lust." In short, "as long as Condé is able to hide himself in the skirts of immoral women, he believes he is king." François d'Hangest had enjoyed the favors of this prince, though "he had brought misery on his master through secret treachery."[12]

There appears to have been little, if any, basis for this extremely negative view of Claude's youngest brother. For a short while it seemed as though François would convert to the Catholic camp, but this "apostasy" was short-lived. He eventually became one of the most illustrious Huguenot leaders and as such played a role in the Spanish-Dutch Eighty Years' War, where he was distinguished by his bravery. In 1567, on behalf of Condé, he came to the rescue of the Prince of Orange in Brabant.[13]

11. Françoise Bonali-Fiquet, ed., *Jean Calvin, Lettres à Monsieur et Madame de Falais* (Geneva, 1991), pp. 168, 170.

12. *CO*, 21: 133.

13. Lefranc, *La jeunesse*, p. 188.

Claude d'Hangest

Another brother from this noble family of Noyon, Jean d'Hangest, Lord of Ivoy, also was a convinced Calvinist and Huguenot. He became one of the foremost lieutenants under Admiral de Coligny, the Protestant commander who enjoyed Calvin's fullest confidence. This nobleman took the city of Valenciennes from the Spaniards in 1570; but he was taken prisoner in 1572 by the Spanish, who strangled him to death in Antwerp. This brother of the young Calvin's friend Claude thus became a martyr in the Calvinist struggle for freedom in the Netherlands.

FRANÇOIS DANIEL

A Study Companion and Friend for Life

Calvin at age twenty-six

François Daniel

Many of Calvin's biographers cannot imagine that he was ever truly "young." The portrait they usually paint is one of a quiet, introverted young man who could not possibly have displayed a hint of cheerfulness. If this caricature were the true picture, one would have to conclude that he led a solitary life and had no real friends. It is true that Calvin somewhere refers to himself as a *subrusticus,* a term he uses to indicate his natural shyness about public duties.[1] But it did not indicate that he had no capacity for friendship or camaraderie. Calvin's correspondence provides unmistakable evidence of passionate friendships and loyalties. He had a number of friendships during his student days, and some of those lasted a lifetime.

Like Luther, Calvin had a father who badly wanted his son to study law. In contrast to his Wittenberg predecessor, however, John preferred the study of law to remaining in Paris for further theology training. His esteem for the values of biblical humanism conflicted with the scholastic severity of the University of Paris. So he was eager to attend the University of Orléans's faculty of law, which enjoyed an excellent reputation. There he became part of a group of close friends who studied together and shared the student life. One of those friends was François Daniel, and Calvin developed a very close friendship with him, as we learn from the correspondence that has survived.[2] These two student friends would value this relationship throughout their entire lives. This is quite remarkable when we consider that Daniel never was a convert, in the full sense of the word, to Calvin's ideas: in spite of his evangelical conviction, he remained loyal to the Roman Catholic Church. But Calvin never saw that as a reason not to recognize him as a "dear brother." Of course, he made repeated attempts to convince his friend of the need to free himself from the bonds of a church that obstructed the freedom to live in accordance with God's Word. Yet, even though François never did join the camp of the Reformation, that did not spoil their friendship.

1. The word means "a bit uncouth, reticent." *CO,* 31: 21.

2. For more about his friendship with Calvin, see Abel Lefranc, *La Jeunesse de Calvin* (Paris, 1888), pp. 72-85; E. Doumergue, *Calvijns Jeugd* (Kampen, 1986), pp. 132-38.

A Study Companion and Friend for Life

Another Hospitable Family

Who was François Daniel? His family lived in Orléans, and he grew up in that city. As some students still do today, he continued to live with his parents while being a student. Calvin's student lodgings were in the home of another friend, Nicolas Duchemin, but he was also a frequent guest in the Daniel home. His relationship with the family became so intimate that he even became privy to confidential family business. One of François's sisters wanted to enter a convent in Paris, and the family asked Calvin, when he happened to be in Paris, to have a talk with her about her motivations. John reported to his friend that he had done so and that the conversation had made it unmistakably clear that François's sister was extremely motivated to take her vows. Therefore, he writes, he had not tried to make her change her mind. Clearly, this letter of 1532 shows that Calvin did not yet have conscientious objections to the monastic vow, though he was critical of it because of his understanding of the gospel.[3] He writes that he spoke a few words to admonish her not to trust primarily in her own vow, but rather "to depend fully on the power of God, in whom we live and have our being." The fact that Calvin asks his friend in this letter to give his warm greetings to his mother and another sister — and he continued this practice in all of his letters throughout the years — shows that he felt accepted as a son and brother in the Daniel family. Just as in Noyon, Calvin found in this city of his student life a family with whom he could feel truly at home.

Along with his friends Daniel, Duchemin, and Connan, Calvin belonged to a circle of students who were under the influence of French evangelical humanism. But they all remained loyal to the mother church. When Pierre de l'Estoile, their law professor — also a member of the clergy and a devout follower of the Church of Rome — was attacked by a colleague, these students wrote a pamphlet in defense of their beloved teacher. Calvin wrote the preface; it was his first official publication.[4] The fact that de l'Estoile was vehemently opposed to the new teachings of Luther apparently did nothing, as yet, to diminish the

---

3. Calvin, *Epistolae* (Geneva, 2005), 1: 71-74 (letter dated June 27, 1533).

4. Praefatio in Nic. Chemini Antapologiam, *CO*, 9: 785-86. See W. de Greef, *Johannes Calvijn, zijn Werk en Geschriften,* 2nd rev. ed. (Kampen, 2006), pp. 99-100.

François Daniel

loyalty of his students. At that time Calvin had not yet taken the decisive step toward the reformation of the church. At the end of 1533, François was still writing to his friend John about the possibility of the latter's getting a legal job in the church.[5] A bishop who came from the region of Calvin's birthplace had arrived in Orléans, and he might, on the recommendation of the Daniels, be able to help Calvin get this position. We read nowhere that Calvin indignantly rejects this offer. Imagine, though, what might have happened had he accepted it. He would have become a local, conservative canon lawyer. What a difference in how the history of the church — and even the entire cultural and political history of the West — might have turned out!

Animated Exchange of News

The letters between Calvin and Daniel show how lively and harmonious their relationship was. They wrote about anything that came to their minds. It could be about an overcoat that Calvin had borrowed and that he now returned with a word of appreciation.[6] (Showing a somewhat pedantic side, the young humanist tries to impress his friend by letting him know that he knows several words for such a coat, including the Latin and Greek words for it.) Or it might be a promise that Calvin would bring some good wine along. At another time it might be a recommendation of a skillful doctor.[7] Calvin was apparently concerned, from a young age, about health — both his own and that of his friends. Naturally, the letters between Daniel and Calvin also touched on their mutual love of literature and the books they could recommend and send each other.

Calvin often used pseudonyms. Was this only based on an understandable caution, or did it also betray a degree of playfulness? Sometimes, for instance, he signed his letters "Martianus Lucanius": when one rearranges the letters of this last name, one discovers that they are an anagram for Calvinus, the Latinized name he had adopted for him-

---

5. *Epistolae,* 1: 87-89 (letter dated December 27, 1533).
6. *Epistolae,* 1: 39-42.
7. *Epistolae,* 1: 84-86.

self, according to the student fashion of the time. And he continued to use "Charles d'Espeville" to sign his letters to Daniel.

That Calvin was not a stranger to the world around him is clear from another letter to Daniel, in which he gives his friend the latest news from Paris, news that he assumes will, through Daniel, also reach his other friends. In a short note accompanying this dispatch we find a sample of Calvin's sense of humor.[8] He writes that another friend, Framberge, should not share in his greetings. "With keeping silent, with flattery and with admonishment," Calvin says, he has tried to get something from Framberge — but with no success. Furthermore, one of Framberge's brothers, whom Calvin had recently met, did not even bring a greeting along for his friend! That Calvin is so (mock) indignant about this points to the loyalty and warmth he expects from friendship, because these are qualities that he himself offers. But he does allow Daniel to share the content of the letter with his sisters, so that he will not have to laugh alone.

In that particular letter Calvin goes on at some length about the commotion that had arisen concerning the sister of the king, Marguerite of Navarre, who belonged to the circle of the evangelicals.[9] He talks about a critical drama (in a way that suggests he has actually seen it himself) in which Marguerite and the court chaplain, Gérard Roussel, have been portrayed rather maliciously. The play caused quite a sensation. Calvin also refers to a protest of Catholic theologians against an evangelical book by Marguerite. Fortunately, the king had protected his sister. From Calvin's letters to Daniel it appears that there was great interest in everything related to the evangelical renewal in France among this circle of young students. However, this did not mean that they had embraced the much more radical teachings of Luther.

The way the two friends interacted also left room for self-mockery. In March of 1534, Calvin had to leave Paris, and he found himself "in exile" in the home of Louis du Tillet, the canon of Angoulême. There, in the excellent library of his host, he found the peace and quiet to study undisturbed. He wrote his friend François with considerable self-irony:

8. *Epistolae*, 1: 81-83.
9. *Epistolae*, 1: 75-80.

François Daniel

"With you I can chat or fill a page without having a given subject, but why would I want to spend time on useless things? It seems to suffice that I tell you only what you are truly interested in, that is, that I am well and that, in spite of my indolence, my studies are progressing. Even the slowest and most slothful individual must inevitably be stirred to work by the friendliness of my protector."[10]

Of course, Calvin was not really lazy. The opposite was true: eating and sleeping seemed like unnecessary interruptions of his constant labor. His motto was: *Terar dum prosim* ("I may be consumed as long as I am useful"). His remarks in the letter to François probably reflect the way his friend had always detected the opposite of laziness in him. His young student friends had great admiration for the substantial talents and energy of the young lawyer who stood head and shoulders above them. And it may be that François would occasionally joke with John about his laziness, while he naturally meant the exact opposite.

Reformed Friends

The intimate bond between François Daniel and John Calvin was not lost when their student days were over. After the two friends went their separate ways, they stayed in touch. François became a legal clerk in the service of the church, and he did not make the same faith choice that John did: that is, he remained within the Roman Catholic Church. He was a humanist who, though he was influenced by French evangelicalism, did not experience the breakthrough of the Reformation. By contrast, Calvin became the Reformer of Geneva. He tried to bring his friend to the same understanding with respect to the kingdom of Christ; unfortunately, he did not succeed. But their friendship did not suffer as a result. Until the end of his life, Calvin called himself François's "humble brother and loyal friend."

It may be that, at the beginning of his real calling in life — becoming the Reformer of Geneva — Calvin had greater expectations for Daniel than ever were realized. Most likely, he hoped his friend would exhibit the same measure of passion and zeal for the Reformation of the

10. *Epistolae*, 1: 92-94.

church that he had, which we may perhaps deduce from a letter that Calvin wrote in October 1536.[11] After a lengthy apology for not having written for such a long time (three full months) and notations on his health problems, Calvin informs his friend about a religious dispute in which he had become involved in Lausanne, and about the calling that he had sensed in Geneva. The way he writes about the collapse of idolatry, which should first of all take place in the human heart rather than in the churches, gives the impression that Calvin believes he is conversing with someone with a kindred (i.e., Reformed) mind. This impression is further strengthened by what follows: "There are so many 'lazy bellies' where you are, that are content to enjoy their chatter in the shadow. If their positive disposition would be as extensive as their flood of words, they would immediately hurry here to accept a share in the burden. There is such a shortage of servants of the Word, there are so many congregations that are in need of shepherds — if there are some who have a heart, let them come." It must have been a terrible disappointment to Calvin that his friend's life was not caught up with the same fire. François and John would not become fellow Reformers, but they remained friends.

A Fatherly Friend

We see special evidence of the lifelong friendship in the year 1559, the most critical year in the history of the French Reformation. The peace treaty of Cateau-Cambrésis, which France had concluded with Spain, might well have become the beginning of a total eradication of everything evangelical in Europe. However, in the providence of God, King Henri II, the successor of Francis I on the French throne, died as a result of an accident in a tournament. With his death began a long period of political sparring, during which the powers of the Reformation and of Rome were more or less in balance at the French court. The number of Reformed churches in France increased sharply. Yet many of the Reformed also left France for the border town of Geneva, from which they intended to continue serving the cause of Christ's kingdom in France.

11. *Epistolae*, 1: 134-38.

François Daniel

Among the many young Frenchmen who left France in 1559 was the son of Calvin's friend from Orléans. François Daniel, Jr., had left home because he refused to start with his law studies, as his father had wanted him to do. His move to Geneva, where he knew that the friend of his father's youth was living, was partly inspired by his desire to study theology. Calvin thought positively about the motives of this young man, and he argues on his behalf in a letter to François, Sr.[12] Calvin does not excuse the young man's disobedience to his father as such; yet he says that Daniel should not fault his son for "esteeming God's command above the contentment of his father." Thus the friend of the father becomes a fatherly friend to the son, and takes care of him in this foreign city. But François Daniel, Sr., should not, says Calvin, see this as a way for Calvin to help strengthen the opposition of the son to his father. On the contrary, he says, he is willing to do anything that might help to reconcile the son with his father.

But Calvin does not let this letter go without a certain amount of criticism of his old friend. Should father Daniel not have made a clearer choice in favor of the Reformation? You have taught your son in the teachings of the gospel, Calvin writes, and now he draws the conclusion that you, up till now, have always avoided. Your son should be an example to you, to finally free yourself. In other words, Calvin does not doubt the spiritual sincerity of his friend, but he disapproves of the fact that Daniel keeps his evangelical convictions hidden by outwardly remaining in the fold of the mother church.

Yet, remarkably enough, in his coaching of the young François Daniel, Calvin places himself in support of the father's wishes. He attempts to persuade the youth not to simply discard the study of law. God also needs good, God-fearing lawyers in a country that suffers under the corruption of justice, he says. Considering the fact that Calvin was desperate to find enough pastors to respond to the urgent requests from France, this is even more remarkable. Nonetheless, he did not steer the young Daniel on a course toward theology so that he might return to France as a preacher. He respected the father's wishes so much that he only wanted to coach the son in the spirit of his father. It is also

12. *CO*, 17: 585-86.

A Study Companion and Friend for Life

noteworthy that Calvin writes his friend that, whatever his son will choose as his life's calling, the most important thing remains that he be well schooled in the true faith.

The elder Daniel appears to have more or less resigned himself to the fact that his son would stay in Geneva, where he had sought refuge with Calvin, because he sent the latter money for his son's upkeep. Calvin managed these funds and reported on the expenses. In one letter he says that the son's coat was stolen in Lyon, but that they had been fortunate enough to buy a new one for a reasonable price.[13] It awoke a distant memory of the student years when Calvin once borrowed Daniel's coat for a journey home.

After a few months the "prodigal son" returned to his father. He still had little enthusiasm for his law study, Calvin writes, but father François must now care for further motivation.[14] Meticulous as he was, Calvin gave Daniel a financial account of the money he had sent for his son's expenses. Calvin was reimbursed, but he indicates that this was not necessary, "since I was in your debt from the old days." He ends his letter by saying that he is sending along two gold coins for Daniel's two daughters as a New Year's present.

What cordial attachment is apparent in Calvin's correspondence with the elder Daniel! At one point François, Jr., in a letter to Calvin, writes that his father burns with an eagerness to travel to Geneva to see his old friend once again. That probably never took place. What remained was a lifelong friendship that was never broken, despite the fact that these two friends went their separate ways. The secret was that both friends, from beginning to end, continued to recognize each other as students of Holy Scripture.

13. *CO,* 7: 680-81.
14. *CO,* 18: 16-17.

François Daniel

NICOLAS COP

A Friend in the Reformed Resistance

Portrait of Calvin in his youth

When was Calvin converted? Many have asked that question, but no one has been able to pinpoint the moment when Calvin was called from darkness to the light of the liberating gospel of grace. It was a gradual development, but some special moments do stand out. Calvin has always been very reticent about it himself: "I do not like to talk about myself," he once wrote.[1] But in the preface to his commentary on the Psalms, he lifts the veil a bit. There he tells of how God pulled him from his humble beginnings and elevated him to the most honorable office of herald and servant of the gospel. "I tried to do my very best [in my career as a humanist lawyer], but God eventually directed my course in another direction through the reign of his providence." Calvin says that God, by means of a sudden conversion *(subita conversio),* subjected his heart to obedience, and that he then acquired "the taste of true piety" in such measure that, though he did not completely relinquish his law studies, he gave priority to his study of Holy Scripture.[2] It sounds almost arrogant — though that is not the case — when he says that, within a year of that conversion, many of those who longed for the pure teachings asked him to teach them, even though he himself was only a beginner.

Nicolas Cop (ca. 1505-1540) was quite possibly one of those "students." It appears that Calvin became such an important counselor to this friend that Cop, in his famous rectorial discourse in Paris, offered a clear plea for the Reformation. The relationship with Cop, who we might call a "friend in the Reformed resistance," sheds light on Calvin's development from a humanist Catholic — following in the footsteps of a circle of French lovers of the Bible who were influenced by Erasmus — to biblical Reformer in the school of Luther.

The Son of the King's Personal Physician

Nicolas Cop was the son of a famous father, Guillaume Cop, the personal physician to the king of France. Originally from Basel, Guillaume Cop was an important figure in a group of leading humanists in Europe

---

1. "De me no libenter loquar," in a letter to Cardinal Sadolet. *CO,* 5: 89.
2. *CO,* 31: 21.

Nicolas Cop

and was a personal friend of Erasmus. Erasmus once wrote about Cop: "I love Cop so much that just hearing his name already makes me happy."[3] The senior Cop was so famous that, according to Erasmus, both France and Germany wanted to claim him for his knowledge. In France, Cop belonged to the group assembled around Lefèvre d'Étaples, who favored a renewal of biblical humanism in France — without actually breaking with Rome.

Calvin was also a frequent visitor in the home of this important courtier, and Cop's sons, Nicolas, Jean, and Michel, were friends that he had come to know during his studies in Paris. Later Michel would become one of his colleagues in Geneva. Nicolas, approximately four years older than Calvin, already occupied a prestigious position in Paris — despite his youth — as the rector of the university. In this capacity he caused a significant stir when he gave his rectorial inauguration an unambiguous Reformed accent.

It appears that Calvin and Cop met as they moved in the circle of the evangelical humanists in France. As noted above, Calvin had sent his friend François Daniel a sparkling report on the agitation that had boiled up concerning Marguerite of Navarre, the sister of the French king, Francis I.[4] Marguerite was very sympathetic toward the humanist party in France and was herself a talented writer. One of her books, *Speculum animae peccatricis* ("The Mirror of a Sinful Soul"), had been put on the list of forbidden books, condemned by theologians at the conservative Sorbonne as "heretical." In this book she directed the sinner far too explicitly toward Christ — to live on the basis of his grace. This flew in the face of the Roman Catholic Church's general thinking with respect to the intercession of the saints and the performance of good works.

The king was far from pleased with the Sorbonne's action against his dear sister. The faculty would have to be called to account; they would have to give reason for their criticism of this book. The rector of the university, the young Nicolas Cop, was given the responsibility of leading the investigation. He called a meeting of the Sorbonne's four

3. E. Doumergue, *Calvijn's Jeugd* (Kampen, 1986), pp. 108, 109.
4. *CO*, 10/2: 27-30.

A Friend in the Reformed Resistance

21

faculties — the arts, theology, canonical law, and medicine — and he gave Marguerite's critics a strong piece of his mind. Who had given them the authority, he asked, to voice their criticism in the name of the university? And he threatened them with the anger of the king. But the theologians of the Sorbonne did not go down without a fight. One of them admitted that the king was, of course, not to be criticized in matters of faith. Instead, he placed the blame on the king's entourage, who had wanted to blemish the noble soul of the king and had attempted to discredit the holy faculty of the Sorbonne. This response reveals that the conservative religious powers in France were highly suspicious of the increasing evangelical influence at the court of Francis I. The affair ended with the university's decision, arrived at under the fervent leadership of Rector Cop, that there was nothing in the book by Marguerite of Navarre that needed to be censored. It appeared that the reform-minded party in Paris could celebrate a triumph.

All Saints' Day, 1533

It stands to reason that in 1533 the evangelicals in France were hopeful about the chance for renewal. Church and university seemed to be open to a new spirit, and even the king appeared to be supportive of those who wanted reform. Could this sense of optimism have been part of the explanation for an even more daring action of Nicolas Cop? Did Cop, along with Calvin, see an opportunity to take the next step to ensure that the defeat of the Sorbonne would be followed by a victory of the evangelical teachings? We do not know precisely what the two friends discussed, and whether it was a matter of deliberate tactics; but a short time after his first action as rector, Cop offered an even more public manifestation of his reform-minded spirit. On November 1, 1533, All Saints' Day, the rector gave his traditional address to mark the beginning of the new academic year in the Church of the Cordoliers. Cop was a medical doctor rather than a theologian, yet his address was more like a sermon. And it had a very courageous message: in no uncertain terms he aligned himself with those who, in the steps of Luther, longed for an evangelical renewal of the church and its preaching. Here, on the same day that Martin Luther had come forward with his Ninety-five Theses

Nicolas Cop

sixteen years earlier, a "French Luther" spoke before the forum of the intellectual and spiritual leaders of his day.

The content of his speech is a clever combination of the new evangelical ideas with a subtle transition from the Erasmian humanist influences to the more radical position of the Lutherans, who until that time had been persecuted in France.[5] Cop took his point of departure from the *Philosophia Christiana,* the Erasmian concept that emphasized the central meaning of Christ for human salvation without immediately implying that the veneration of Mary, for example, be discontinued. The introduction of the address still ends with the customary *Ave Maria*. But then Cop began to introduce more specifically Lutheran ideas: the theme of "Law and Gospel"; grace rather than merits; the gospel instead of the useless sophists — the rallying themes of the reform-minded renewers over against the conservative Catholics.

The Manifesto of the French Reformation
Cop's explanation of the Beatitudes forms the most important part of his academic address. He clearly had been inspired in the preparation of his speech by his reading of the sermons of Luther and Bucer. His speech openly pleads for a gospel of free grace: the justification of the sinner through the grace of Christ. When dealing with the last beatitude, "Blessed are you when people insult you, persecute you and falsely say all kinds of evil against you because of me," Cop passionately takes a stand for the true believers of his time who were being persecuted by fire and sword: "Heretics, tempters, liars and slanderers — those names are often given by the world and by evil men to those who simply, honestly and seriously, want to plant the gospel in the hearts of the believers; those who believe that they must be obedient to God."[6]

Cop's rectorial address almost seems like a French parallel of Luther's Ninety-five Theses, a public manifesto of the Protestant faith in opposition to Catholic orthodoxy. What contribution may Calvin have

5. *Concio Academica, nomine rectoris universitatis parisiensis Nicolai Copi scripta et recitata Cal.* November 1533. *CO,* 10/2: 30-36; Bernard Cottret, *Calvin* (Paris, 1995), pp. 85-89.
6. *CO,* 10/2: 36.

made to this address? It is a fascinating question that is difficult to answer. However, we do know that after Calvin's death, Beza found a copy of part of this address in Calvin's own handwriting. A complete copy — that of Cop himself — was discovered in Strasbourg.[7] But the manuscript found in Geneva is a remarkable discovery that could mean one of two things. Calvin may have been so impressed by the Reformational testimony of his friend that he copied part of his address to keep for the rest of his life. We might conclude from this that Cop was a friend who may very well have assisted Calvin on his journey from Rome to the Reformation. In this view, Calvin was dependent in part on Cop for his conversion journey. But the reverse could also have been true: Calvin, the theologian and "teacher" of Cop, may very well have provided the medical doctor with the relevant arguments. Some even think that Calvin wrote the text of the rectorial address, which explains why the text of it has been incorporated in an academic edition of Calvin's writings.

This latter view has much to commend itself. Keeping Calvin's autobiographical remark in mind — that many sought him out because of his knowledge[8] — we might assume that Cop, when preparing his address, profited from Calvin's reading of and experience with the writings of such Reformers as Luther and Bucer. The theological content of the address may be linked to Calvin, but Cop would still be the author of the actual text. It would seem less likely that Calvin copied Cop's speech because he regarded it as such an important document. It is debatable whether Calvin would have needed a copy if he wanted to remember the content, since he had an excellent — even photographic — memory. Whatever the case, the fact that Calvin and Cop were both intimately involved in the composition of this extraordinary Reformation manifesto is not only proven by the two extant copies in Geneva and Strasbourg, but also by the way they both reacted to the disturbance that erupted subsequent to the address. The beginning of the 1533 academic year gave them both good reason to flee in great haste!

7. See J. Rott, "Documents strasbourgeous concernant Calvin," *Revue d'Histoire et de Philosophie* 44 (1964): 290-335.
8. *CO*, 31: 21.

Nicolas Cop

How the Tides Are Turning

Cop's address about reform lit the fuse, but the explosion had an effect that differed from what the reform-minded agitators were expecting. Instead of blowing up the conservative bulwark at the Sorbonne, it detonated in the circle of those who supported the new teaching. Fierce opponents lodged a complaint against Cop with the parliament, and the rector had to appear in person. Undaunted, he donned his official garb and, escorted by the heralds and registrars of the university, he went to the court. Cop's public action confirmed that this was a new phase in the Reformation in France. The evangelical party was planning to no longer keep quiet, as the "Nicodemites" had (something Calvin later found so difficult to deal with); henceforth, they openly defended their cause. The risk, however, was greater than they had perhaps surmised.

Perhaps Cop was still taking courage from the positive outcome of his earlier strategy, when, with a measure of support from the king, he had been able to successfully withstand the theologians of the Sorbonne. But now he could no longer count on the king. At the moment of the parliamentary inquiry, the king was not only absent, but his attitude toward the evangelical party had also become more and more dismissive. Of course, this had to do with the broader political picture. King Francis wanted to see his son married to the niece of the pope, and this brought him increasingly into the anti-Lutheran camp. A significant sign of this change in climate was that the fiercest enemy of French evangelicalism, Noël Bédier, whom Francis I had earlier sent from Paris into exile, was able to return triumphantly in December 1533.

In any case, great danger loomed for Cop and his friends. He might be the rector of the university, but the dignity of that office would not protect him in a heresy trial, which could, with little doubt, end in his death. The very moment Cop was to enter the Parliament building, he received a warning message from a member of parliament who was favorable toward him: "Make sure to get away, for inside you will face a certain death." Though Cop was a courageous man, he was also a realist. He immediately understood that his situation was hopeless and that there was no way he could win his case. He ran into an alley without delay, changed his clothes, and fled from the city. The parliament contacted the king, who was in Lyon, and the latter signed a royal order calling for the capture of Cop and the eradication of the entire Lutheran sect. The order set a reward of 300 pounds on Cop's head. But Nicolas Cop succeeded in safely reaching his ancestral city of Basel, where he was given asylum in 1534.

How was Calvin affected by this drama? Some fifty of Cop's sympathizers were arrested in Paris, but Calvin was not among them. However, like his friend Cop, he fled Paris. Calvin may not have needed to flee the country right then, because the young humanist was not as well known as Cop was. But it was just as well that he did, because police officers soon searched the room where he lived and confiscated his correspondence, among other things. They no doubt found a link between Calvin and Cop and friends, and so they knew which camp Calvin belonged to. For that reason he felt that it was prudent to escape from the city. The story is that he had to do so very hastily, climbing through a window and letting himself down by means of sheets that were tied together — just as the apostle Paul once had to escape. Later, of course, he would become the most prominent French refugee.

We know little about Calvin's friendship with Cop from that point on. They were certain to have met from time to time, and Calvin would point to Basel as a place of refuge for many supporters of reform. But their friendship was certainly significant. At a crucial period in Calvin's life, Cop's courage contributed to the determination with which his younger friend, the future Reformer of Geneva, accepted the consequences of his conversion. The legal proceedings between the reform-minded people and the defenders of the Roman Catholic power were not just a matter of words; they had become a matter of life and death. The antagonism from the Sorbonne must have made a considerable impression on the somewhat timid personality of the twenty-four-year-old youth. But now there was no turning back. The gospel could not remain a hobby of an elite group of humanists who were allowed a degree of liberty as long at they did not operate in public. Calvin learned from Cop that standing up for the cause of the Reformation was a calling one could not turn away from, even if it would cost everything.

The Cop affair in Paris had made it clear that a settlement was no longer possible. The hostility of the persecutors was irreconcilable.

Nicolas Cop

Confronted with this, the young Reformer saw that there was no other form of courage in this spiritual battle than openly witnessing to the gospel of free grace. The die had been cast. From that point onward, Calvin's life would be shaped by his Reformational calling. His flight was not an attempt to avoid further struggle. He used the time he was in hiding for study, so that he would be armed for future combat. Very soon he would no longer circulate his ideas via the writings of friends but by means of his own publications.

LOUIS DU TILLET

A Friend Who Turned Away

Portrait of Calvin in his youth on a medallion

As we saw in the preceding chapter, things had gotten too hot for Calvin in Paris after the disturbance caused by Nicolas Cop's rectorial address. It was time to disappear into anonymity for a while. He could not have found a better safe house than that of a former fellow student he had come to know in Paris, Louis du Tillet (ca. 1509-?).[1] This friend had become a priest in the village of Claix and was the canon of the cathedral in Angoulême in the Saintonge region in the south of France. His father had been the vice president of the auditor's office. Louis was the youngest of four brothers, and his older brothers all occupied important positions: one of them was the highest clerk of the court; another was the personal secretary of the king; and the third later became the bishop of Meaux.

In addition to a safe house, Louis provided Calvin with access to the kind of place where the young scholar preferred to be: the family's library, which must have contained a magnificent collection of books for that time. Some sources mention three to four thousand books, of which many were ancient manuscripts. No doubt this paradise for humanists also had volumes by many church fathers on the shelves, as well as the books of reform-minded contemporaries. Calvin wrote to his friend François Daniel about the abundant favor his benefactor had bestowed on him. In that letter he adds that this may have had more to do with his scholarship than with his person. Whatever the case may have been, nothing was too much for Louis to ensure that his guest felt comfortable. Calvin was overjoyed. This was a wonderful asylum where he could study in peace and quiet, while others were on the run and did not know where to turn. Beyond all expectation, he received this blessing "as out of the hand of the Lord."[2]

Calvin's compensation to Louis, in return for the hospitality, was to teach his benefactor the Greek language. He even got the nickname "the little Greek of Claix."[3] It was apparently quite unusual to know

1. E. Doumergue, *Calvijn's Jeugd* (Kampen, 1986), pp. 348-63; Bernard Cottret, *Calvin* (Paris, 1995), pp. 87-89; Olivia Carpi-Mailly, "Jean Calvin et Louis du Tillet, entre foi et amitié, un échange révélateur," in *Calvin et ses contemporains,* ed. Olivier Millet (Geneva, 1998), pp. 7-19.

2. Calvin, *Epistolae,* 1: 92-94.

3. Doumergue, *Calvijn's Jeugd,* p. 356.

A Friend Who Turned Away

biblical Greek at that time, and Louis was quite proud that, thanks to his friend, he was now among those who were known as experts in this language.

Calvin's stay in Claix was undoubtedly one of the factors that had a decisive influence on the writing of his best-known work, *The Institutes of the Christian Religion.* One of his biographers says that the du Tillet library was the smithy where the weapon of the Reformation was forged.[4] The first edition was published in 1536.

For years du Tillet was Calvin's inseparable traveling companion. Wherever John went, he took Louis with him. For instance, from Claix they visited Poitiers, where Calvin preached in the cave of Saint-Bénoit, outside the city, and where he also celebrated the Lord's Supper in a Reformed fashion. Next they both went to the well-known Orléans, where Calvin wrote his book about the sleep of death, *Psychopannychia.*

The Affair of the Placards

In Calvin's time, students were more eager to travel than they are today; they frequently went on long journeys to visit famous scholars and renowned universities. But the reason the two friends John and Louis embarked on a trip in October 1534 was less motivated by this common interest than it was by the critical situation in which the evangelical renewal in France now found itself. The so-called "Affair of the Placards" and its immediate consequences seemed to have been their motivation for leaving France.

A storm of indignation was sweeping through all of France in October 1534. There had been a daring attempt to launch a direct attack against the heart of the Roman Catholic faith, the holy sacrifice of the mass. Placards had been displayed throughout the country dismissing the sacred mass as idolatry, advancing the Lutheran conviction without any reservation. A copy of this offensive from the reform-minded party was even found posted on the king's bedroom door, in his castle in Amboise.

---

4. Doumergue, *Calvijn's Jeugd,* p. 357, refers to a contemporaneous biography by Florimon de Raemond, someone from the camp of Calvin's opponents.

This time the "heretics" had clearly gone too far, and the measures against them were severe. Several strongly worded decrees were issued, and many of the Reformed faced martyrdom in the early months of 1535. A recent study has shown that, in the French context, an attack on the holy sacrament (the firm assurance of salvation) was considered an assault on the king himself.[5] The spiritual order and the sociopolitical order were so intertwined in the kingdom of France that people could not help concluding that a rejection of the sacrifice of the mass would inevitably lead to total anarchy in all areas of life. Therefore, the posting of the placard on the king's bedroom door was considered a crime against the supreme power of the state. In any case, the Affair of the Placards destroyed what remained of the consideration that the reform-minded might still have been able to expect from the authorities. From that moment on, all supporters of reform were seen as enemies of France who had to be exterminated. It is against the background of this threat that we see Calvin and du Tillet depart from France.

Two Travel Companions
The journey did not go as smoothly as they might have hoped. The prosperous Louis cared for the travel budget, and two servants accompanied the young travelers. But when one of the servants discovered in Metz that this was not a study trip from which they would soon return, he decided to relieve his masters of their money and possessions. Fortunately, the other servant still had a few crowns in his pocket, and that money allowed them, though almost destitute, to reach Strasbourg, where they received a hospitable reception from the pastors Capito and Bucer. But Strasbourg was not their actual destination, so after a short stay they traveled to Basel in January 1535.

In this city, situated on the Rhine River, the two traveling companions once again met their Parisian friend Nicholas Cop, which gave them great pleasure. They undoubtedly shared with each other the seri-

5. Christopher Edwood, *The Body Broken: The Calvinist Doctrine of the Eucharist and the Symbolization of Power in Sixteenth-Century France* (New York/Oxford, 1999).

ous news about the brethren who were suffering oppression in Paris. Indeed, Calvin was in Basel when the news came to him that his friend and protector Etienne de la Forge had been burned alive in Paris on February 16, 1534.

Little is known about this sojourn in Basel. Calvin certainly would have met many with whom he was to share the future calling of a Reformer, those Reformation leaders who were preaching the gospel freely in this city. In that sense, his visit there was of crucial importance. Furthermore, in Basel he found a publisher for the first edition of the *Institutes*. He also met two men who would be his future colleagues in Geneva: William Farel and Pierre Viret. And he found time for study in Basel. Yet his stay there only lasted a little more than one year. In March 1536, Calvin and du Tillet took up their travel gear again and departed for Ferrara. Renée, a French princess who had married an Italian Renaissance prince, lived in that Italian principality in the Po Valley. Her court had become a meeting place for reform-minded humanists from France. However, Renée and her guests experienced great problems when her hostile husband detected the true interests of these French friends and wanted to send the Inquisition after them. After a few weeks Calvin and du Tillet once again had to flee on short notice. They returned to Basel.

Upon arriving in Basel the second time, John left his friend Louis behind and continued to France, because the situation there was less dangerous for about six months. A royal decree had seen to that: exiles who were planning to abjure their heresy were allowed to return. This was most certainly not Calvin's plan, but he used the opportunity to take care of some family business. He planned to sell his remaining possessions in Noyon, and he intended to take his family along with him into exile. He did not need Louis du Tillet for that, so he left him behind in Basel. The next time they were to meet was the most decisive moment of Calvin's life, the time when he unexpectedly visited Geneva.

"By Chance" in Geneva

Louis du Tillet seems to have found his place of refuge in Geneva. This city, on the border of Switzerland and France, had — under Farel's passionate leadership — decided to exchange the yoke of Rome for the freedom of the gospel of Christ. There, to his great surprise and joy, he would see his friend John again.

However, it had not been Calvin's plan to visit Geneva at all. After he had arranged his affairs in Noyon, he had intended to travel with his brother Antoine and half sister Marie to Strasbourg to find a quiet place where they could stay, now that the situation in France had become risky once again. But the normal route from Noyon to Strasbourg had become too dangerous because of the fighting between the German emperor and the French king. Hence they had to make a detour to the south to reach the capital of the Elzas, and thus in the month of July they arrived in Geneva unexpectedly, and were looking for a place to stay for just one night.

The two inseparable friends, John and Louis, enjoyed a very joyous reunion. But what du Tillet did next would not have been what Calvin intended at all. Louis did not keep quiet about his French friend's visit, but immediately notified Farel of the unexpected reunion. Farel, in turn, knew exactly what he had to do: he hurried to Calvin's lodgings and appealed to him with the greatest seriousness that it was his destiny to be in Geneva. Calvin was not prepared to accept this "call to Geneva" right away; on the contrary, his preference was to continue his studies in a quiet, peaceful town and to lead the life of a scholar. But Farel went so far as to threaten Calvin with God's wrath from heaven if he were to retreat from the task for which his immense capacity made him so suitable. As a consequence, Calvin drastically changed his plans, allowing himself to be drawn into the service of proclaiming the Word of God in a city that so badly needed to be taught in it. He thus owed his call to Geneva, at least indirectly, to his friendship with Louis du Tillet. This is quite remarkable considering that some years later it would be this same friend who would express his doubts regarding Calvin's calling to be a servant of the Word. But that was only after he himself had left Geneva for France, where he would eventually return to the Church of Rome.

A Friend Who Turned Away

Pangs of Conscience

It must have been a dramatic change for Louis du Tillet, the former priest from Claix, to serve as a servant of the Word in Geneva. At first it seemed as if he felt totally at home in the circle of the Genevan Reformers. He wanted the people to call him Lord of Haultmont (De Alto Monte), and we regularly come across that name in letters between him and Calvin, correspondence in which the most intimate friends pass on and receive greetings. No one could have noticed that a nagging doubt remained in his mind whether he had indeed followed the path of God. Now that he was no longer able to continue his travels with Calvin — because the two friends had to take up their work in the Lord's vineyard — du Tillet felt homesick and was plagued by his conscience. These feelings became so strong that in August 1537 he left Geneva and, via Strasbourg, went back to France.

A Calling Assailed

At first it was not clear that this move would eventually mean du Tillet's complete return to the fold of the Roman Catholic Church, including a return ultimately to the office of parish priest. Part of the correspondence in French between Calvin and du Tillet has survived. Du Tillet emphasizes that he can no longer see his departure from the mother church as a calling from God, and in these letters he also tries to infect Calvin with this doubt. But in that endeavor he was entirely unsuccessful.

It appears that initially Calvin did not suspect that his friend would eventually return to the church he had left. It must have been a severe blow for him to discover that Louis had not only joined the "Nicodemites," who were halfheartedly hiding their Reformational convictions under an outward observance of Roman Catholic practices, but also that he had returned to his parish as priest and had openly recanted his reform-minded beliefs. In the preface to his commentary on the Psalms in 1557, Calvin still cannot hide his indignation: there he refers to du Tillet as "a person who scandalously turned around and returned to the papists."[6]

6. *CO,* 31: 32.

At first Calvin was afraid that he himself, because of his "uncivilized rudeness," had been the reason his friend, whose "joyous presence" he genuinely missed, had become estranged from him.[7] His words indicate a humble self-knowledge that evidently was part of his nature. The letters suggest that du Tillet must have possessed a much gentler and more doubting personality; he may well have looked up to Calvin and felt unable to respond to his arguments. And perhaps he only dared to distance himself from Calvin after he had left Geneva. He does so at length in his letters, in which he tells Calvin of his pangs of conscience. In short, the letters from du Tillet wish to make clear that leaving the Roman churches cannot be God's way because, as long as the church maintains the offices, which have been instituted by Christ and which are present in the ministration of the Word and the sacraments, one is not allowed "to leave the churches."

It is noteworthy that du Tillet speaks of "churches" in the plural (*églises*) here.[8] Nowhere does he point to Rome with her authority and teachings. Nonetheless, he is clearly of the opinion that the path Calvin had traveled — to become a pastor in a Reformational city, the path along which Louis allowed himself to be taken — was not according to God's will. In fact, du Tillet accuses Calvin of causing a "schism." But Calvin emphasizes, in response, that, though there may still be "remnants of God's blessing" in the Roman Catholic churches, the sheep in those churches cannot listen to the voice of the Shepherd anymore without obstruction. How, then, can such a church be called "a pillar of the truth"?[9]

No Turning Back

On July 10, 1538, Calvin wrote to du Tillet about his expulsion from Geneva, not knowing at that time to what extent his friend had already returned to Rome. No doubt the "*echec* in Geneva" must have been a fierce temptation for Calvin. Had he really been called to be a servant of

7. *Epistolae*, 1: 310-18
8. *Epistolae*, 1: 148, 166.
9. *Epistolae*, 1: 315.

the Word? He remained convinced that he was, though he had become very conscious of the mistakes he had made in Geneva. But why should this good friend, du Tillet, in his reply to Calvin, seize on the latter's interruption of his ministry in Geneva to express doubts about his calling? Should Calvin consider everything that God had wrought in that city to be "works of man"? In that letter the friend who has returned to the Catholic priesthood goes on at some length to convince Calvin of that, and that only in the church that values apostolic succession can one find a true calling to ecclesiastical office.

It may well be that in all of this du Tillet tried to link his own pangs of conscience to the temptations Calvin experienced. Wouldn't the rejected Reformer of Geneva also do better to return to France, the country they both loved so deeply? Of course, du Tillet still did believe — along with Calvin — that there were many scandalous practices in the Church of Rome that needed reform. But that conviction did not legitimate, for du Tillet, the radical decision Calvin had made: to leave his home country and the mother church for the sake and the service of the gospel.[10]

Calvin responded in October 1538, shortly after he had been confirmed once more as pastor, now in the church in Strasbourg.[11] With his new sense of calling, which came to him via Bucer, he was convinced, despite all his inner struggles, that God wanted him to remain a servant of the Word. Even a generous offer of financial assistance from a wealthy friend did not entice him to return to the noncommittal existence of humanist scholar. Calvin admonishes du Tillet, in all seriousness, not to sit in judgment from the peace and quiet of his study over those who are in the midst of the battle.

In the end, the friend who initially was the means by which Calvin was called to be a servant of the Word in Geneva, and who, after his disappointing return to the Roman Catholic Church, was the person who expressed strong doubts about Calvin's calling — he was just the one who reinforced Calvin's conviction that he was indeed following the path of God. This is clear from what he now writes to du Tillet: "I believe

10. *Epistolae*, 1: 446-53.
11. *CO*, 10/2: 269-72.

you thought that our oppression would be sufficient to bring me to utter despair, even to the point that I would deny everything there was up till now [in terms of conviction and calling]. It is true that I have experienced severe inner struggles, but not to the extent that I would say, *Nescio ubi sint viae Domini* ['I do not know where to find the ways of the Lord']. And therefore, these temptations [to give up everything] have, as far as I am concerned, been in vain."[12] In the final analysis, in his attempts to sow doubt, the friend who turned back to Catholicism only fortified Calvin's determination never to depart from the ways of the Lord.

12. *CO*, 10/2: 272.

A Friend Who Turned Away

PIERRE ROBERT OLIVÉTAN

A Biblical Relative and Friend

Dutch portrait of Calvin in his study

Pierre Robert Olivétan

We know that Calvin needed but little sleep. He worked late into the night and would begin his work again early the next morning. Was that perhaps a common characteristic of his family? This question comes up when we realize that one of his second cousins even owed his name to this trait. His name originally was simply Pierre Robert (1506-1538), and his father, like Calvin's father — who was his cousin — was a lawyer in the chapter of Noyon.[1] Pierre often worked so late that people began calling him Olivétan — the man of the "oil lamp" — because it was still burning when most people had long retired for the night. The nickname stuck.

Indeed, they might have better called him "the man of light," for despite all his modesty, his accomplishments were of great significance for the French Reformation. Aided by his thorough knowledge of the original biblical languages and inspired by his deep passion for the gospel of free grace, he translated the Bible into French, and that first French Protestant translation of the Bible came to be named after him: the Bible of Olivétan. But before he accomplished this great work, he was involved in an endeavor that also proved to be invaluable. According to his earliest biographers, his contemporaries and friends Beza and Colladon, Pierre Robert Olivétan was the man who could show his cousin and friend the way to the Light: as a result of his testimony, the darkness receded from Calvin and made room for the precious light of the gospel of Jesus Christ. Spurred by Olivétan's inspiring example, Calvin became a student of Scripture.[2] Therefore, when we read the words *Post Tenebras Lux* ("after the darkness the light") on the famous monument of the Reformation in Geneva, which gives such a central position to Calvin, we should not forget Olivétan's oil lamp.

A Study Companion and Inspirer

Calvin must have known his cousin from the time they were small boys growing up in Noyon, though we have no record of their contact. No cor-

1. Abel Lefranc, *La Jeunesse de Calvin* (Paris, 1888), pp. 27-31; E. Doumergue, *Calvijns Jeugd* (Kampen, 1986), pp. 111-21.
2. *CO*, 21: 29 (Beza); 54 (Colladon).

respondence between John and his cousin-friend Pierre Robert is extant; in fact, we know only a little about his short but productive life (Olivétan was only thirty-two years old when he died). Nonetheless, when he was in the prime of his life, he was a great blessing to the church of Christ, much more than his relative anonymity would suggest. Though we know more about many of the other French Reformers and friends of Calvin, what we know about Olivétan tells us that he was a model of true evangelical servanthood. We can see a young man who unconditionally put his life in the service of the Word of the God: the Word rather than the servant received the attention. It was his deepest desire to offer his French brothers and sisters the same gift that Luther had given the Germans, a Bible in the vernacular, so that believers of all walks of life could have the Bible in their hands and in their hearts, and could "hear the voice of God himself." That was the purpose of his existence, and he gave his life for it. He died in Italy in 1538 under mysterious circumstances. One rumor suggested that he had been poisoned by his opponents.

We do not know very much about where and how the personal interaction between Calvin and Olivétan took place. But their joint interest in the publication of Olivétan's Bible translation indicates that there was a close bond between them. Calvin wrote two introductions to the Olivétan translation, and those were the first truly Protestant products of his pen.[3]

It is likely that they also met as students in Paris. Pierre Robert, who was a little older than John, may have been the acquaintance who was able to bring the new student from Noyon into contact with other young humanists. There is no doubt that Olivétan was, already at an early date, under the influence of the evangelical-humanist movement of renewal, part of a group gathered around the biblical scholar Lefèvre d'Étaples. We do not know whether the two students from Picardy met very frequently, but we do know that Olivétan was in Orléans in 1528, when Calvin had just begun his law studies there, after having been

---

3. A Latin preface, *CO,* 9: 787-90; and a French preface for the New Testament, *CO,* 9: 791-822. See W. de Greef, *Johannes Calvijn, zijn Werk en Geschriften* (Kampen, 2006), pp. 105-10.

forced to leave Paris when the favorable climate for the reform-minded had turned hostile. Was his choice for this city on the Loire River partly inspired by the fact that Olivétan was there? That remains a matter of speculation. But we can see that Olivétan was a friend and brother to him in Orléans as well as in Paris.

Olivétan's Reformational conviction made it impossible for him to stay on in France any longer, so he departed from Orléans for Strasbourg during the same year that Calvin left for that city. There he was further equipped for his life's work, the translation of the Bible, which he would complete in 1535. His love and zeal was so infectious that we can see in Calvin the same intense longing to study the original languages of Scripture in order to be able to learn about and explain the background of the text. We may well perceive Olivétan as a precursor, as someone who prepared the way for Calvin. It is significant that the latter would subsequently appear in the very cities where Olivétan had gone before: Strasbourg, Basel, and even Geneva. In each of those places, Olivétan was already there — or had already been there — when Calvin arrived. The subsequent impact of the younger Calvin would have been unthinkable without his older cousin, whom God used to prepare his destined path.

A Bible Teacher

As we have seen, Olivétan left Orléans for Strasbourg in 1528. There he entrusted himself to the care of Bucer, who referred to him in a letter to Farel as "a young man from Noyon" who had been forced to leave Orléans because of the persecution and had come to Strasbourg to study Greek and Hebrew. He was prompted in this by his aspiration to be able to translate the Bible.[4]

By 1531, Olivétan occupied the position of schoolmaster in Neuchâtel. It was certainly not due to a lack of theological skills that he did not feel the call to be a servant of the Word. His great modesty, which bordered on shyness, was the reason he eschewed the public role

4. A. L. Herminjard, *Correspondance des Réformateurs dans les Pays de Langue Française,* 9 vols. (Geneva/Basel/Lyon/Paris, 1878-1897), 2: 112.

A Biblical Relative and Friend

of a Reformer and preferred a more unassuming position as teacher and scholar. In that capacity he used his knowledge in an extremely productive way by writing a small textbook for children, *Instructions des enfants,* which not only taught the alphabet but also used hundreds of Bible passages to instruct children in the main tenets of the faith. This little book was important for the children in his school in Neuchâtel, and it was also later used for catechetical instruction in Geneva.[5]

For a short time during 1532, Olivétan served as a private teacher in the home of Jean Chautemps, a prominent citizen of Geneva, who opened his home as a hospitable guesthouse for those who wanted to serve the Reformation. This was a tense and turbulent period of transition, one during which Geneva was still being won over to the gospel. There is a story that the shy Olivétan once was audacious enough to get into a public debate with a monk who was vilifying the teachings of Luther. Even making such a public appearance would seem to have been at odds with his modest personality, let alone that the debate was said to be the reason he had to leave Geneva. We do not know whether that was really the cause for his departure from the city where his cousin John would later rise to such an important position. But we do know that he left Geneva in 1532 for the Piémont valley, where he was to become the evangelist of the Waldenses.

Olivétan's great devotion to the service of the Word also had its melancholy side in his personal life. In Neuchâtel, Olivétan fell in love with Jeanne, the sister of a pastor, and she responded to his feelings. But there was to be no marriage, for Olivétan was unable to justify combining his dangerous missionary calling with matrimonial life. Jeanne waited for Pierre Robert for some years, but in vain. The only place he had left for her was in his last will and testament: he bequeathed her half of his possessions. When her name no longer appeared in a later version of the will, the two other beneficiaries, Calvin and his brother Antoine, thought that it must be a misunderstanding. Therefore, they took steps to share the inheritance with her. John Calvin's portion of the bequest was seventy books, a formidable treasure in those days. He

5. Hans J. Hillerbrand, *The Oxford Encyclopedia of the Reformation* (New York/Oxford, 1996), 3: 174-75.

Pierre Robert Olivétan

sold them all, except one — a Hebrew Bible. However, the true legacy of Olivétan, this faithful servant of the gospel, was of inestimable value: the Bible in the everyday language of the people.

The Nightingale and the Crow

The conviction that a love for the treasure of the Word must cost something is probably what gave the passionate William Farel the boldness to start a fund-raising campaign in the Piémont valley to raise the money for a translation of the Bible. That there was an intense hunger for God's Word among the Waldenses is evident from the fact that Farel was able to raise over 800 ecus. In those days that was an astronomical figure, and most of it was given by poor farmers. We also need to realize that the Waldenses themselves spoke a dialect rather than the French that Olivétan gave them in his translation of the Bible. The French Reformation thus owes its Bible to the generosity of the Waldenses, who donated funds adequate to pay for the translator and to completely finance the printing of it.

Thus was Olivétan put to work. Calvin writes in his first preface to the Bible translation how Farel and Viret (whom he refers to with the strange pseudonyms Chusemeth and Chloretes) had to go to great lengths to overcome Olivétan's modesty. And before the translation was published, Calvin sought to protect his friend against the inevitable criticism his translation might possibly evoke. "It is easy to be critical," Calvin says, "but just try it yourself."

For Olivétan, the task of translating the Bible from the original languages into French seemed almost impossible. He was so excited about the "eloquence" of the original Hebrew and Greek that he thought his own language sounded "barbaric" by comparison.[6] He used a striking metaphor to illustrate the challenge of translating: teaching the "sweet nightingale" to sing like a "husky crow." Nonetheless, he went about his work with all his skills and love, because France needed to hear the saving Word. "Hear, O heavens! Listen, O earth, for the Lord hath spoken." These words from Isaiah 1 are quoted on the ti-

6. See Bernard Cottret, *Calvin* (Paris, 1995), pp. 108-12.

A Biblical Relative and Friend

43

tle page of the translation and form the basis for the work. According to Olivétan, God also speaks through the French tongue, even though it might be a coarse language. Calvin had a much less negative assessment of his mother tongue. In later editions of this translation he found, by way of a mild criticism of Olivétan, who had by then died, that the translator in the end had not done full justice to the beauty of the French language.

The Treasure of Christ's Bride

Olivétan's own *Defense of the Translation* is proof in itself that he was able to write in beautiful French.[7] It is a passionate text in which he merges love for the Word and for the church. While most authors tend to dedicate their work to their individual benefactors, Olivétan dedicates his work to the Waldenses as a group, those poor farmers who had given so generously to make his project a reality. He refers to them as "Christ's poor little church that, as a bride, was looking for her Groom with burning desire." As the translator, he has the privilege of returning her dowry to her. He wants to water and nurture "the small flowers of our hope, which have been withered and burned by the fire of our miserable ignorance."

It has been suggested that his style seems to be somewhat akin to that of the great French author Rabelais, whose books he did possess. We discover, for example, in his enthralling review of the tortures suffered by the church of Christ, a flood of words and horrifying images that almost allow us to see the suffering of the believers before our very eyes: "Ye, who are insulted, reviled, routed, jeered at, cursed, robbed, imprisoned, thrown in hell, exiled, denounced, spit out, mutilated, have your ears cut off, have been squeezed with tongs, have been branded, plucked, drawn, toasted, roasted, stoned, burned, drowned, beheaded, quartered, and have received similar glorious and wonderful titles of the kingdom of heaven." To this church of martyrs, and to it alone, he dedicates his translation!

7. *Apologie du Translateur.* See G. Casalis and B. Roussel, eds., *Olivétan, Traducteur de la Bible,* Actes du Colloque Olivétan (Noyon, May 1985), pp. 169-89.

Pierre Robert Olivétan

In 1535, Olivétan's translation of the Bible into French, in process for years, came off the press in the print shop of Pierre de Vingle in Neuchâtel. It was not a fully original translation, but one that was built on an earlier translation of Lefèvre d'Étaples; but that translation had not been based on the original languages. The entire Old Testament was translated from the Hebrew — and that was brand-new. The New Testament was a revision of an earlier translation, and thus it was of a different quality. Olivétan had urged his cousin Calvin to correct this translation for him; but that had not been possible in the first edition. In a letter to Christopher Fabri after the first edition had been published, Calvin writes that he had promised his assistance but that the edition was ready before he had been able to start with the revision.[8] Subsequently, Calvin would be involved many times in the revision of this Bible translation, a project with which he had been connected from its very inception. The Olivétan translation remained the basis for the Protestant Bible in French for centuries to come.

Two Prefaces

It is difficult to tell exactly how much Calvin contributed to his cousin's life's work. It is clear that Olivétan regarded his younger friend as very important for the presentation of his work, because he asked him to provide two prefaces for his translation.

The first one, which Calvin wrote in Latin, is, remarkably enough, a preface of the kind that Olivétan seemed to have rejected in his own dedication. Olivétan did not see the need to dedicate his work to the high and mighty, but that is exactly what Calvin does: he dedicates the French Bible translation to the emperors, kings, princes, and all those who are subject to the rule of Christ.[9] His intention, however, was not to ensure that this dedication would solicit appreciation or honor for the work itself. How would that ever be possible, since this work is not the work of man — not a new book that needs human approbation. It is

8. Calvin, *Epistolae*, 1: 115-18.
9. "Ioannes Calvinus caesaribus, regibus, principibus, gentibusque omnibus Christi imperio subditis salutera." *CO*, 9: 787.

"the prophetic word, the eternal truth, from the most elevated king." Why, Calvin asks, would there be reason to be afraid — like the "rabbis" — to allow simple people to hear God speak to them through his Word? Putting the Bible in the hands of ordinary people, men and women, does not make it a source of heresy, as had been argued, but rather the best instrument to fight against heresy. For it is the Word of God himself, Calvin says, through his Holy Spirit. Denying that a pure translation is useful is an offense to the Holy Spirit.

The second preface by Calvin is a letter to "all who love Jesus Christ and his gospel."[10] It is a cordial and pastoral letter (in French), and it is more or less the first theological piece of writing by Calvin. Here the young theologian (no more than twenty-five years old) gives a very bright summary of the content of God's Word. For people who quite possibly had a complete Bible in their hands for the first time in their lives, it must have been a revelation to read so much more in it than they would have surmised from the poor biblical instruction and liturgical practices of the Roman Catholic Church.

The Bible: The Light from Christ

Calvin knew that the Word of God, through the Spirit, spoke for itself. It did not need his introductory remarks. Yet it might be useful to give some assistance. He provides a short summary of the entire salvation history of the Old and the New Covenant, and at its center, Jesus Christ and him crucified. In all of the Old Testament the focus was already on Jesus, in the promises that were to receive their glorious fulfillment in the New Covenant. Calvin writes: "Without the gospel all of us are useless and nothing; without the gospel we are no Christians; without the gospel all riches are poverty and wisdom foolishness in the eyes of God." Lack of knowledge is the misery that causes people to be lost; for if they miss the Word of God, they will never attain salvation.

Olivétan, the Bible translator, was the man of the small oil lamp, the man of the light. His love for his Lord and Master, and for those who also love him, prompted Olivétan to give his life in the service of the gos-

---

10. "A tous amateurs de Iésus Christ, et de son S. Evanhile, salut." *CO*, 9: 791.

Pierre Robert Olivétan

pel. "Olivet" is also a name linked to olive oil: before olives can provide light, they must first be pressed into oil. Jesus first went to the garden on Mount Olivet so that, through his night of suffering, the light of his cross and resurrection would radiate. Olivétan was a man who was privileged to serve that Light. For this reason his cousin-friend and brother in Christ ends his preface to the Olivétan Bible with these words: "The Lord of all Light wants, by his Holy Spirit, through this holy and saving gospel, to teach the ignorant people, strengthen the weak, and give light to the blind, and to let his truth rule over all nations, so that the entire world will only know one God, only one Savior, one faith and one gospel. Amen."

RENÉE DE FRANCE

A Royal Friend

Renée de France

"If God had given me a beard around my chin, and I had been a man, all would have been my subjects. That would have been so at this very moment, were it not that the Salian law [which prohibited succession to the throne along the female line] had blocked that road for me."[1] This was the reaction of the Duchess of Ferrara when she was criticized for wasting money on poor French refugees at her Italian court by giving them a hospitable reception. For she was Renée of France (1510-1575), and had she been a man, she would have ruled as king over France. Her father, Louis XII, died without sons; therefore, in accordance with the Salian law, her brother-in-law, Francis I, who was married to her older sister, became king. Renée was given in marriage to Hercules d'Este, the Duke of Ferrara, in 1528.

Things could have gone quite differently via the matrimonial market of that day. In 1527 the chancellor of England, Cardinal Woolsey, had indicated his interest in seeing Renée become the bride of Henry VIII of England. However, this marriage did not materialize because Henry had become interested in Anne Boleyn in the meantime. Referring to the sad fate of this second wife of the English king (she was beheaded when she was unable to provide her husband with a son, after having been accused of adultery — falsely, in all likelihood), one historian observes: "Thus Renée escaped her death verdict."[2]

How different history would have been had she been a man, and had she been able to rule her country as its monarch in accordance with her evangelical conviction! During this most crucial phase of European history, France would have been governed by a queen who was convinced of the principles of the Reformation, which is something breathtaking to ponder. But we have to deal with the facts and the way history unfolded in reality. Faith in God's providential rule persuades us that things had to happen the way they did and not otherwise. Yet we cannot help thinking how close the influence and spirit of the Reformation came to the throne of one of the greatest powers in Europe. France could have become the center of the Reformation of the church in Eu-

1. Quoted by E. Doumergue, *Calvijn in het Strijdperk* (Kampen, 1986), p. 36.
2. Sam Wellman, *John Calvin: Father of Reformed Theology* (Uhrichsville, OH, 2001), p. 117.

rope. A Reformed France, in cooperation with a Lutheran Germany, could have delivered a decisive blow to the power of Rome, could have set the entire Christian church free toward a genuine renewal in accordance with God's Word.

That may have been Calvin's deepest aspiration. Of all the Reformers, he had the most realistic perception of the political tensions and relationships of his time. Was this perhaps one of the reasons why, throughout his life, he tried to extend his influence to the palaces of kings? It is remarkable to see how the son of a simple church clerk from the provinces corresponded with great ease with those who belonged to the highest circles. His spiritual nobility and immense scholarship made him a welcome guest at several courts, especially with women, who were eager to benefit from his extraordinary knowledge. For example, he had a special bond with Marguerite of Angoulême, the sister of Francis I. But even closer — and also more spiritual — was his enduring association with Renée of France.

A French Place of Refuge in the Po Valley

Renée made her court in Ferrara into a place of refuge for all who loved France and were deeply interested in the cause of Reformational renewal in their homeland. While that new spirit of reform was not fully out in the open — outwardly everyone at the Ferrara court remained loyal to Rome — the conversations and encounters were filled with the desire for a Bible-based renewal of church and life. Doumergue writes: "At the court of Renée, 'French' meant the same as 'won for the gospel.'"[3]

In the early spring of 1536, the two young friends John Calvin and Louis du Tillet crossed the Alps on their way to sunny Italy, planning to stay in Ferrara in the Po Valley. In his biography of Calvin, Beza says that Calvin left Basel as soon as the two young friends had finished the first edition of the *Institutes,* in order "to greet Italy from a distance."[4] Never had he been so close to Rome, and he would never be this close again. How could he venture into a country where he knew the power of the

3. Doumergue, *Calvijn in het Strijdperk,* p. 37.
4. "Simulque Italiae veluti procul salutandae desiderium." *CO,* 21: 125.

Catholic Church to be even stronger than in France, from which he had more or less fled? Wasn't he being audacious, unnecessarily putting his head into the lion's mouth?

With appropriate prudence, he did not use his own name but pretended to be a young French nobleman by using his old pseudonym Charles d'Espeville. There is a portrait by an unknown Dutch painter from this period of Calvin's life that depicts the young scholar as a distinguished seigneur.[5] In particular, the viewer's eye is caught by the lifted finger of his left hand, which holds his elegant gloves. There is a glittering ring on this finger, and he radiates the nobility of his refinement and erudition. This is the figure that Renée must have first seen when Calvin arrived in Ferrara from France.

What had, in fact, brought Calvin to Ferrara was the Duchess Renée. When she married her Italian duke in 1528 in Paris, Calvin was living as a young student in that city. She was a contemporary of Calvin, only a year younger, and it may well be that they had met at the court of Princess Marguerite, the sister of King Francis I, who, like Renée, invited those who favored the reforms into her court. If the risk of persecution had now made it too dangerous to stay at the court of Marguerite in France, there was always the possibility of taking refuge with Renée, who had made her court into a piece of France outside its borders.

In any case, Calvin had the opportunity to see some friends from Paris who had already taken refuge in Ferrara before he arrived: Jehannet, the singer, and Clement Marot, the well-known writer of psalms who had been forced to flee after the Affair of the Placards. Along with others in this court, including some ladies from the household of the duchess, they formed a group of gospel-minded people who encouraged one another from the Word of God. Publicly, they still followed the Roman Catholic practices that they were expected to adhere to. But their shared love for France, and their hope that the light of the gospel would soon break through in their beloved home country, united all who were part of Renée's circle at her court.

5. E. Doumergue, *Iconographie Calvinienne* (Lausanne, 1909), pp. 19-21.

A Royal Friend

Mutual Affection

Undoubtedly, Renée and her guests must have known about the extraordinary erudition of Calvin, and it made him an attractive guest to have. The duchess regularly had heart-to-heart talks with the young Reformer in her private quarters until late in the evening, and it appears that a mutual feeling of attraction developed. The few weeks Calvin stayed in Ferrara — the only period during which he actually met his gracious hostess — would result in a lifelong bond of spiritual friendship. Beza even writes that Renée "from that time onwards felt for [Calvin] a measure of love."[6] One might almost conclude that the sentiments these two had for each other — in all purity — amounted to more than just a shared love for France and for the gospel. Except for Idelette van Buren, the woman who became Calvin's wife and heart's companion in 1540, there was no other woman for whom Calvin ever felt more respect and deeper care than Renée. After Calvin's death, Beza dedicated a collection of a few of his pamplets, the *Opuscules* ("small works"), to the duchess, saying, "I know in what high esteem you were held by the deceased, since he had the opportunity to teach the gospel to you, and confirmed you in its doctrines."

Calvin's arrival in Ferrara came at a crucial time for Renée: at that moment she felt that she needed special spiritual counsel because the atmosphere for those who were reform-minded was quickly deteriorating at the court of Hercules d'Este. Initially, the duke had given his wife permission to invite whomever she wished. But because he was facing pressure from Rome, which very much feared the "Lutheran influences" in Italy, he began taking steps to purge his court of Protestant influences. He dismissed Renée's lady-in-waiting, Madame de Soubise, a kindred spirit and confidante. It was just then that Calvin, who was to become Renée's spiritual counselor in a special way, arrived. However, the joy of this friendship was of short duration: a few weeks after his arrival in Ferrara, Calvin had to leave again in great haste.

6. *CO,* 21: 125.

Persecution

Would Calvin and his friend Louis du Tillet have undertaken their long and hazardous journey across the Alps if they had known that their stay in Ferrara would be cut short after just a few weeks? Probably not, but the journey and the stay proved to be extremely valuable, considering the lasting friendship between Calvin and the duchess. However, it could also have meant the end of the promising career of a young Reformer, because a few weeks after they arrived there, a real persecution of reformists at the court in Ferrara suddenly broke out. The direct cause was a demonstrative action by one of the French courtiers: on Good Friday, April 14, 1536, Jehannet dramatically left the church when the service reached its climax, the solemn veneration of the cross. This action led to his arrest. When he was put on the rack, he told the inquisitor that all the French people at Renée's court were followers of the new teaching. The inquisitor and the duke then decided to put a radical end to this "heresy." More arrests followed. Calvin and du Tillet did not wait for their turn to be arrested, but left the palace head over heels and fled the city where they had only stayed for a few weeks. It was reported that Renée provided them with the money they needed for their journey, before she bade them goodbye with deep regret.

The subsequent situation became almost unbearable for Renée herself. Under pressure from Rome, the court made every attempt to force the "heretical" duchess to denounce her evangelical conviction. Courtiers with kindred minds were exiled from her entourage. She was herself surrounded by inquisitors, and she became more or less a prisoner in her own palace. Unfortunately, much of Calvin's correspondence with his contacts at the court of Ferrara has not survived; but it is clear that he stayed in touch with the duchess. He did whatever he could to ensure that kindred souls would be able to visit and support Renée. He wanted to protect her against the power of Rome, and he sent several counselors. His extant letters, particularly those written in his later years, show the depth and cordiality of their tie.

Return to Rome

How difficult it must have been for Calvin to hear that, in the end, Renée was not able to withstand the pressure of the Inquisition. In 1554, Renée was freed from the convent where she had been basically held prisoner and isolated from all the people she loved. She was freed from the convent because she had made her confession and participated in the mass; the result was that she was considered rehabilitated. Her status changed from prisoner back to that of respected duchess.

Had she finally become a "Nicodemite"? We know how difficult it was for Calvin to deal with those who, because of the pressures from their environment, kept their evangelical conviction hidden behind outward conformity to Roman Catholic practices. Remarkably enough, it was precisely during his short stay in Ferrara in 1536 that Calvin had written two letters in which he criticized former friends for this deception and conformity.[7] He warned his friend Duchemin against continued participation in Roman Catholic practices: it is high time, he says, for him to leave the Egypt of his spiritual imprisonment. Had France not become such an Egypt? He would not condone any compromise with idolatry. Should Duchemin not follow a route of exile — similar to Calvin's — for the sake of his belief in the gospel? He also sent a letter from Ferrara to Gérard Roussel, who had become the bishop of Oleron, and that epistle was even sharper. The brotherly friendship, Calvin writes, is ended, for as a bishop, Roussel collaborates in the idolatry by which Christ is, as it were, crucified anew. Expressing sharp accusations, Calvin, who was in exile for the sake of Christ, distances himself from his friend who had chosen to become a bishop.

One would thus expect Calvin to have been very critical of Renée when she eventually gave in to the pressure from Rome. But that was not the case, though, from the letter Calvin wrote her after her apparent return to the fold of Rome, we can sense how much it pained him.[8] The letter seems to show that he somewhat blames himself for not being able to assist her better in her spiritual need. In his letter he actually

---

7. Published separately as *Epistolae duae de rebus hoc seculo cognitu apprime necessariis* (Basel, 1537); *CO,* 5: 233-312.

8. *CO,* 15: 417-19.

finds it difficult to believe that she has relapsed, and though he cannot but condemn her action, he in no way rejects her. On the contrary, with his heart full of passion, he points her to the grace of Christ, which even provides forgiveness for such a weakness as this. And between the lines, Calvin believes that in her heart Renée has not changed, which we can surmise when he appeals to her — by referring to his earlier correspondence — to keep her home pure in accordance with the gospel. He apparently knew her too well after all.

The Good Duchess

The Duke of Ferrara died in 1559. On his deathbed he made his wife swear that she would never again correspond with Calvin. It appears that it had always been clear to him, to his great frustration, that Calvin was the source of his wife's perseverance in her reformist convictions. Therefore, by means of this spiritual blackmail, he tried to trap his wife in an impossible promise. She promised what her husband asked, but she regretted it immediately. We can see Calvin's pastoral skills when he let her know that she could not be expected to keep a promise that so blatantly went against the will of God.[9] In other words, he was saying, she did not need to feel guilty for staying in contact with Calvin.

Her position at Ferrara, however, became untenable. Her son Alfonso forced her to make a choice: renounce her faith or return to France. Calvin counseled her to choose the second option because she could probably serve God better in France than in an Italian prison. So she moved to her castle in Montargis in 1560. Calvin rejoiced about this, both for the salvation of her soul and for the honor of God — as he wrote her. In her own castle she could live in freedom according to her own evangelical conviction; she could even hire her own pastors. At one point she even appears to have interfered in the affairs of the church. One of her pastors, Morel, complained to Calvin that she wanted to have her say on the church board when matters of discipline were at stake. But when Calvin explained to her that this fell outside of her call-

9. *CO,* 18: 147, 148.

ing, she willingly accepted his argument. She followed the judgment of Calvin, her Reformational confessor, *con amore*.

As *la bonne Duchesse* ("the good duchess"), she transformed her castle in Montargis into a place of refuge for those in the persecuted church of Christ. When her son-in-law, the Duke of Guise, who was then acting as a Catholic leader, gave her an order to surrender Huguenots to him during the religious wars, she did not deliver the candidates for slaughter into his hands. She stepped into the breach on behalf of the persecuted people who had found refuge within her walls, and Calvin praised her and deemed it an honor that her castle, contrary to what might be expected of a royal house, might be called a "hospital."

On January 24, 1564, a few months before his death, Calvin wrote his longest letter — and the last one that has survived — to his friend Renée.[10] He wrote because there had been a tragedy in her family: that same son-in-law, the Duke of Guise, had been killed by an assassin. The French reformists were jubilant about the death of this Catholic tyrant. But to Renée, he was still her son-in-law, the husband of her own daughter, and she found it difficult to accept this euphoria. In a long pastoral letter under these circumstances, Calvin tells her that he would not go as far as those pastors who regarded the assassination of De Guise as a confirmation of God's rejection of him. Calvin says that he has prayed at times himself that God would halt the violence from the persecutor; but he also, so he writes, personally thwarted a conspiracy against this duke. Calvin's words breathe a sense of reality and are full of restraint: the judgment belongs to God. It goes too far to affirm that the duke is damned when there is no absolutely certain evidence that God has rejected him. What mildness is there in Calvin's judgment! Who could ever dare accuse the Reformer of Geneva of a cold and pitiless judgment when this deadly enemy of all who loved the gospel could be the object of his prayer?

Renée survived Calvin by eleven years. She remained a protector of the Huguenots during the years when France was engulfed in the wars of religion. She even lived to experience the gruesome St. Bartholomew Massacre of 1572. Her castle remained an asylum for the servants of the

10. *CO*, 20: 244-49.

gospel of free grace. In 1575, this royal lady friend of Calvin, who was never allowed to rule over her beloved France because she was a woman, entered into the bliss of the kingdom of Christ — to rule forever with all his saints.

JOHN SINAPIUS

A Friend in Love

Calvin portrayed as a nobleman by an unknown Dutch painter

John Sinapius

Who would ever have expected to encounter John Calvin as a marriage broker? He does not immediately strike us as an expert in matters of the heart, and he only experienced nine years of married happiness himself. For the most part, it would seem that Calvin's attention was directed toward "higher matters" than brokering a marriage.

Therefore, it is quite astonishing to read in a letter from Simon Grynaeus, Calvin's friend and colleague from Basel, an urgent request for him to assist in arranging the marriage of a mutual friend. Grynaeus's worries concerned a German doctor who was so in love with a lady-in-waiting at the Ferrara court that he could no longer do his work. John Sinapius (1505-1560) was this amorous man who was unable to concentrate on anything as long as he could not hold the object of his passionate affection in his arms. Grynaeus hopes that Calvin can actually do something because the latter does know the lady in question, and he might be willing to put in a good word to her on behalf of Sinapius — so that a marriage might ensue.

A Greek Teacher Becomes a Doctor

The life narrative of John Sinapius (a Latinized form of the German name Senf, or "mustard") is typical of that of a biblical humanist in the first half of the sixteenth century.[1] He was born on December 12, 1505,[2] in the German city of Schweinfurt, on the Main River, where his father was one of the city councilors. As a young boy he went to the Latin school and then continued his studies in Erfurt. The Greek language, one of three specialties in "the new science" of humanism, became his scholarly passion. He was tutored in the language by Melanchthon in Wittenberg, among others. In those days students were quite mobile and were inclined to move to wherever they could find good teachers. Thus, soon after his stay in Wittenberg, he landed in Heidelberg, where

1. On the life of Sinapius, see John I. Flood, *Johannes Sinapius (1505-1560): Hellenist and Physician in Germany and Italy* (Geneva, 1997); Peter G. Bietenholz, *Contemporaries of Erasmus: A Biographical Register of the Renaissance and Reformation,* 3 vols. (Toronto, 1987), 3: 254-55; E. Doumergue, *Calvijn in het Strijdperk* (Kampen, 1986), pp. 49-56.

2. We know this date from a horoscope that was made for him.

Grynaeus became his teacher and friend. When Grynaeus left for Basel in 1529, Sinapius succeeded him as professor of Greek at the University of Heidelberg.

What made Sinapius, the Hellenist (an expert in the Greek language and culture), decide to study medicine? The climate of hostility toward humanists at the University of Heidelberg likely played a role. The conservative theologians there did not trust all the attention that was being paid to the ancient languages, which naturally cast a new light on Scripture. Sinapius defended these new insights with enthusiasm. He wrote *Defensio Eloquentiae* ("defense of eloquence") to underscore that it is impossible to properly understand God's Word without a knowledge of the original languages. When, to his disappointment, he continued to experience too much opposition, he decided to leave for Italy and to embark on medical study.

An intense personal experience may also have contributed to his choice of a new profession. In his student years Sinapius went through a period of severe illness: he suffered from syphilis, the venereal disease that took many victims at the beginning of the sixteenth century (similar to today's AIDS epidemic). Syphilis was not only a life-threatening disease, but it also had its morally objectionable dimension. The lifestyle that would cause someone to be infected would hardly seem congruent with the serious life of a humanist. But humanists, it is clear, were not always puritans. Like all humans, they were definitely sinners who were no strangers to the struggle between the willingness of the spirit and the weakness of the flesh. The young Sinapius was not the only scholarly victim of this disease. Ulrich von Hutten, the well-known humanist and friend of Luther, died of it. A special therapy, which Sinapius regarded as a gracious miracle of God, had restored him to full health. May this personal experience have perhaps played a role in his choice to henceforth use his talents in the service of healing the body?

Apart from the above considerations, the transition from the study of Greek to that of medicine was not uncommon. This was true because the study of medicine was done in the context of humanism, particularly in the discovery and interpretation of the medical sources from classical antiquity, which were written mainly in Greek. As long as the knowledge of this language was absent from Western culture, many of the valuable books remained inaccessible. Now these sources were being rediscovered and eagerly studied. After his medical study in Italy, Grynaeus was called to Basel by Oecolampadius to teach Greek and medicine.

Erasmus was the one who advised Sinapius to go for further study to Ferrara, where Giovanni Manardo, one of the greatest medical authorities in Europe at the time, was a professor. The gracious introduction from the great humanist Erasmus obviously opened many doors for Sinapius; Professor Manardo even invited him to come and live in his home. When he had completed his studies in 1532, he became a professor himself. He also entered into the service of Hercules d'Este and Renée of France as their personal physician. In addition to being the doctor of the duke and duchess, he served as the private tutor of their children. It appeared that he had found his destination: a prestigious position at one of the most renowned medical institutions in Europe and a respected member of the humanist entourage at the Ferrara court. What more could he wish for? The German doctor from Schweinfurt had become a distinguished scholar with a bright future.

Ferrara, however, would offer him more than just the honor and glory of a humanist. Two encounters at the court, both with persons from France, would enrich and broaden his life to a greater extent than all the medical science could offer him. At Ferrara he met the love of his life, and he also became acquainted with Calvin. As we shall see, these encounters were not unrelated.

Meeting Calvin

Sinapius was in Ferrara during Calvin's short stay at the court, and there he met the young Frenchman whose fame had already preceded him. We do not get the impression that this first meeting immediately led to a friendly relationship. It would seem that, for Sinapius, Calvin was just one of the many compatriots of Duchess Renée, while Calvin may have regarded Sinapius as simply a German humanist in the tradition of Martin Luther. On the other hand, it would not have been strange if the two had a special interest in each other from the very beginning: Sinapius would have seen Calvin as an expert in Greek; furthermore, friendship with a medical doctor would have been an interesting proposition for a man like Calvin, who continuously struggled with his health. These interests may have played a role in the development of their relationship, but there is no evidence to that effect. Later correspondence between the two also fails to reveal any learned passages about Greek or medicine.

A later letter does reveal that, when they first became acquainted, Sinapius had no clear idea who Calvin was. Looking back on Calvin's stay at Ferrara, Sinapius writes: "You were hidden to me as a Silenus of Alcibiades."[3] For those familiar with classical Greek literature, the meaning of this allusion would have been abundantly clear: in the style of a humanist scholar, Sinapius is referring to the passage in Plato's *Symposion* ("The Meal") in which Alcibiades, one of the participants in the conversation, compares Socrates to a Silenus figurine. Looking at the outside, one can only see a drunken satyr playing the flute; but when one opens the figurine, one discovers a much more valuable statuette of a god. Hence, a Silenus of Alcibiades is someone who hides a treasure beneath a much less ostentatious exterior. With the use of this metaphor, Sinapius seems to be saying that when he met Calvin, he did not initially discover the treasure of heavenly wisdom that this young Frenchman had hidden in himself.

Sinapius's observation is an important one, and it provides us with a good picture of Calvin's stay in Ferrara. Those who believe that Calvin's presence in Ferrara had an openly missionary character are mistaken.[4] Sinapius recognized in Calvin a pious and erudite young man, but he did not yet see the Reformer that Calvin already was deep in his heart. Calvin's desires in Ferrara were the same as they were in Geneva shortly thereafter, when he was "arrested" by Farel: his convictions were not ambiguous, but he preferred the work of a scholar studying Scripture to a public role as Reformer. It was only later that Sinapius

---

3. Letter sent from Ferrara, September 1, 1539. A. L. Herminjard, *Correspondance des Réformateurs dans las Pays de Lungue Française,* 9 vols. (Geneva/Basel/Lyon/Paris, 1878-97), 6: 3-6 (cited hereafter as Herminjard).

4. See Jules Bonnet, "Calvin à Ferrare," *Bulletin de la Société de l'Histoire du Protestantisme Français* 41: 13; Charles Dardier, "Voyage de Calvin en Italie," in *Musée Historique de la Réformation Calviniana* (Geneva), 4/2.

John Sinapius

fully discovered how a divine treasure of wisdom had been hidden in this "Silenus." The woman whom Sinapius came to love so passionately likely played a role in this discovery.

Hopelessly in Love

Eventually Sinapius wanted to settle in Germany again, where he had been offered an excellent position; but he was unable to detach himself from Ferrara. In a visit to his old master and friend Grynaeus in Basel in 1537, he gave the latter a view into a heart paralyzed by love. A French lady, Françoise de Boussiron, who had originally come from Poitou, had stolen his heart; as a result, he could no longer do his normal work. This was why Grynaeus, as an assistant and friend of the lovesick medic, picked up his pen to put in a good word for him to Calvin, the only person Sinapius and he believed could present a favorable plea to the passionately desired "bride." Grynaeus writes that it would be a terrible loss if their mutual friend would no longer be able to pursue his "necessary studies" because of his hopeless infatuation.[5] Calvin's intervention would thus enhance both Sinapius's happiness in love and his scholarly output.

What made Calvin so suitable as a marriage broker was the unique spiritual bond that had developed between Françoise and him. Ever since his stay at Ferrara, the two had been involved in regular correspondence. (It is a great pity that none of these letters has survived.) For instance, she was the one who informed Calvin of the death of his cousin Olivétan in Italy.[6] The fact that they had an exchange of letters points to a special bond, and that bond is also seen in the fact that Françoise was the person at the court of Ferrara who acted most closely in the spirit of Calvin. That even landed her in some difficulties with her mistress, Renée, as we shall see when the story unfolds.

In any case, Sinapius knew of the close contact between Calvin and Françoise, and he expected Calvin to have a strong influence on her. One

5. Herminjard, 4: 205.
6. And not vice versa, i.e., that Calvin informed *her* about Olivétan's death, as Doumergue incorrectly deduces from Herminjard, 5: 228.

might even suspect that Sinapius may have regarded Calvin as a possible rival in love. Might the young Françoise not prefer the elegant Charles d'Espeville (Calvin's pseudonym in Ferrara) to a German doctor from Schweinfurt? Whether he mentioned these suspicions to Grynaeus or not, there was no doubt in the mind of his Basel friend that Sinapius was truly in love. He writes to Calvin: "Sinapius's choice is truly immutable, not from fantasy but through serious consideration." He adds: "He has already known her for quite some time." It was not a whim inspired by Françoise's beauty, but a love that he felt deeply. This kind of depth of affection was quite an anomaly at a time when most marriages were no more than matters of business, politics, or convenience. In fact, Grynaeus had been aware of this affection for some years, for he also wrote about it to his friend Blaurer in 1535.[7] In the same year that he had interceded with Calvin (1537), Grynaeus devoted yet another letter to the subject.[8] Once more he asked Calvin to persuade Françoise to say yes, because Sinapius's love was "so powerful, pure and constant" that it deserved to develop into the delight of marriage.

Françoise's Choice

Françoise eventually said yes to her German admirer, but we do not know what arguments Calvin used to help her make that decision. In a poem that was written in honor of her marriage, there is a somewhat awkward reference to the fact that she had earlier been engaged to a French nobleman. Could it be that she hesitated to respond to Johannes Sinapius's love because she believed she had to remain available to her countryman? And might that have been someone with whom she could have served the cause of the Reformation in France? We do not know, but if that had been the case, Calvin's counsel must have carried considerable weight, because she had great confidence in him as her spiritual adviser.

Françoise's spiritual choice for the reformist way was what caused a controversy with her mistress. At one point she was no longer willing

7. Herminjard, 4: 205.
8. Herminjard, 4: 205.

John Sinapius

to attend mass, and this was at a time when such a refusal was still un-acceptable to Renée. An evangelical conviction was fine — even more than that — but breaking with the liturgical practice of the Church of Rome was still not negotiable. Thus did Françoise's "Calvinistic deter-mination" get her into trouble. Fortunately, Calvin came to her rescue. In a letter to Renée he voices his opposition to her court chaplain, a cer-tain Richardot, who played a dubious role in this matter.[9] This so-called friend of Calvin was a two-faced individual, and Calvin did not think highly of him. He said that Richardot sold the "little bit of Bible knowl-edge" that he had to rich people, making sure that his preaching sat well with his benefactors.

It appears that Françoise poured out her troubles to Calvin, thereby unmasking the treacherous Richardot, who would later move to the Netherlands and, as Granvelle's confidant, become the bishop of Arras. In this role he developed into a cruel prosecutor of those who were of the same mind as those whom he had earlier called his "friends." Unfortunately, his successor at Renée's court, the notorious Bolsec, would also prove to be a disloyal "friend" — and would give Cal-vin no end of trouble. Françoise probably saw through this false preacher as well. He, in turn, was the reason that she once again fell from favor with Duchess Renée and eventually could not stay at the court of Ferrara.

This may have been a reason why Calvin took a favorable view of a marriage between Françoise and Sinapius. Indeed, her husband would be able to take her with him to Germany, where the spiritual climate would be more sympathetic to them than it was in Ferrara, where the In-quisition sought to suppress all reformist influences.

A Pure and Holy Life

In a letter to Calvin of September 1, 1539, Sinapius writes how grateful he is that, as a result of Calvin's intervention, the desire of his heart has turned into reality.[10] Along with his wife, he is eager to share in a life-

9. Herminjard, 6: 1058.
10. Herminjard, 6, no. 813: 3-6.

long friendship with Calvin. At first Sinapius was not a Calvinist; rather, he was a humanist who came from a Lutheran milieu.[11] But through Françoise he must have come to understand better and better what the Reformational views of his friend would mean in everyday life. His statement at the close of this letter to Calvin speaks for itself: he writes that he and his wife want to live as Christians, as they should, "pure and holy *coram Domino*," and that they wish to conform as little as possible to the flesh and to the world. We can recognize Calvin's emphasis on the *meditatio futurae vitae,* the contemplation of the life to come, as a sanctifying power in this earthly life.

Sinapius and Françoise left Ferrara in 1545 because it had become increasingly difficult for them to live in accordance with their evangelical convictions. In a letter dating from 1553, Calvin reminds Sinapius of the evil role Bolsec played in raising suspicions about his wife, including stooping so low as to try to ruin Renée's reputation with her husband in an attempt to earn his favor.

Like a Lonely Sparrow on the Roof

Back in Germany, Sinapius found employment as personal physician at the court of the prince-bishop of Würzburg. This seems peculiar — a friend of Calvin in the service of a Roman Catholic ruler — and it may indicate that Sinapius did not wish to be openly known as a follower of Calvin in Germany. He continued to be a friend of Erasmus, who had returned from Italy. The latter, in spite of his reformist tendencies, did not see much of a problem in his being in the service of a humanist Catholic Church leader. As the servant of the prince-bishop, Sinapius even negotiated with Emperor Charles V during a time of political tension in Germany.

Sinapius's dear bride, Françoise, died on June 28, 1553. On De-

11. Cornelis Augustijn, Christoph Burger, and Frans P. van Stam, "Calvin in the Light of the Early Letters," in *Calvin Praeceptor Ecclesiae,* ed. Herman J. Selderhuis (Geneva, 2004), pp. 139-57, refer to Sinapius too easily as "Calvin's co-religionist." Like Calvin, Sinapius was a humanist in the tradition of Erasmus; but his religious roots were Lutheran. Through his wife, who most certainly was a kindred spirit with Calvin, he became a friend of the latter, yet without becoming an outspoken Calvinist.

John Sinapius

cember 5 of that year, as Sinapius writes to Calvin, "one can hear the thunder of the canons."[12] Germany was being torn apart by the Schmalkaldian War, and his beloved ancestral city Schweinfurt, whose history he had himself chronicled, became a ruin. But the worst was that his "honest and most loyal wife" had been taken from him. He never fully recovered from the loss. For the remainder of his life he would refer to his great sorrow in all his letters. Françoise had contracted measles, a common illness in children, but life threatening for adults. She died peacefully in his arms: "She did not struggle, as dying people usually do, but only asked me to pray to God for her," Sinapius writes to Calvin. Then he asks the Reformer to pray not only on behalf of his one daughter, Theodora, but, surprisingly, to pray for his deceased wife. The Roman Catholic practice of praying for the dead was apparently so ingrained — but also so acceptable — that, as late as 1553, he saw nothing wrong with making this request of Calvin.

Sinapius's own health deteriorated quickly. On January 4, 1557, he says in a letter to Calvin: "I lead a lonely life, as a hermit or a lonely sparrow on the roof, a sick and old widower. Hardly able to lift my own legs, as a living corpse."[13] Just before the end of his own life he had to witness the murder of his master. On December 13, 1560, one day after his fifty-fifth birthday, the doctor died, a man who owed the love of his life to his wife's spiritual friend. Doumergue rightly concludes: "The sad reality of life removed the poetic veil that covered the life in Ferrara."[14]

12. Letter dated December 5, 1553. *CO*, 14: 688-89.
13. *CO*, 16: 374-77.
14. Doumergue, *Calvijn in het Strijdperk*, p. 56.

SIMON GRYNAEUS

An Exegetical Friend

Grynaeus, from Beza's *Icones*

Dedicating a piece of writing to someone is simultaneously a way of giving attention and asking for attention. The dedication is a gesture of appreciation from the author that emphasizes how much the recipient of the honor has contributed to the creation of the book. But an unproven author may also try to get the attention of his potential readers by dedicating his book to someone of some authority in the subject area of the new publication. Viewed in that way, a dedication may well be regarded as a tactical maneuver to ensure as positive a reception as possible via the support of another authority.

In about ten of his publications, Calvin wrote a dedication to a private individual.[1] He dedicated his first Bible commentary, the exposition of the Epistle to the Romans, to Simon Grynaeus (1493-1541), and he had a special reason to do so. This Reformer from Basel, who Calvin had befriended during his first visit to that city on the Rhine, became a teacher and a friend par excellence of the young evangelical humanist from France. He shared with Calvin his ideas about the hermeneutics of Holy Scripture.

Grynaeus was about sixteen years older than Calvin, and initially at least, he must have been primarily his teacher. Yet, in the relatively short period they knew each other (Grynaeus died at forty-eight of the plague), a close and personal fondness developed. This friendship was rooted in their common passion for the exegesis of Scripture, which they saw as the main raison d'être and calling of the Reformation. Thus we might call their relationship an "exegetical friendship."

The Son of a Farmer Becomes a Scholar

Simon Grynaeus was born as Simon Griner in 1493 in the southern German city of Veringen. One of his biographers characterized his pedigree and future rather poignantly when he said that Grynaeus "was honored elsewhere, but forgotten in his country of birth." He was one of the many German humanists who did not find a place for their calling in their own country, but who earned much respect in other places.

1. See Jean-François Gilmont, *Jean Calvin et le Livre Imprimé* (Geneva, 1997), pp. 259ff.

Simon came from a farmer's family that apparently had some means, because at the age of fourteen, as the youngest son, he was given the opportunity to attend the famous Latin school in Pforzheim. There he met Melanchthon, who was four years his junior, and they remained friends for life. The spirit of the renowned Johannes Reuchlin (Melanchthon's uncle) made this school an important breeding ground for a love for the classics — the sources of Latin, Greek, and Hebrew literature — that was being reawakened during this time of humanism.

After he had finished his first examination in the classical languages in 1511, Grynaeus registered at the university of Vienna, and after four years he graduated as *Magister Artium* (he earned this title after completing a general academic education, comparable to a master's degree). The young Simon developed into a multifaceted and promising scholar. He not only became proficient in the languages, with Greek as his specialty, but also in mathematics, philosophy, physics, and medicine. Initially, Grynaeus moved even further east, to the Hungarian city then known as Ofen (today known as Budapest), where in 1520 he was offered the position of rector of a school. Part of the Hungarian capital's attraction for him may well have been its royal Corvina Library, which was regarded as one of the largest and finest book collections in Europe at that time. It was a Mecca for young humanists. But there may well have been other reasons to leave Vienna, such as an outbreak of the plague, or possibly the hostile intellectual climate toward those who were favorably inclined not only toward humanism but also toward Luther's thought. Clearly, Simon Grynaeus was one of those influenced by the new movement that exerted its reformist influence from Wittenberg.

Via Wittenberg to Heidelberg

In Ofen, Grynaeus's "heretical" ideas soon got him into trouble. The Dominicans saw to it that this reform-minded humanist was put in prison. Fortunately, he was able to regain his freedom through the intervention of a few noblemen; but there was no doubt that life in Hungary had become too dangerous for him. Therefore, he decided to seek refuge in Wittenberg, which at the time was "the capital of the Reformation." The presence of his friend Melanchthon probably played an important role in this move. Following a humanistic custom, he changed his German name Griner into Grynaeus, which, according to Vergil, was one of the names of the Greek deity Apollos. In Wittenberg he met Luther, and his reformist bent was no doubt further strengthened during his short stay there. But he also met Andreas Karlstadt, who would later cause him endless trouble in Basel. In 1523 he paid a visit to his family in Veringen, and there he married Magdalena Spirensis. (He remarried after her death, and only much later, in 1539, did his second wife give birth to his only son, Samuel.)

In 1524, Grynaeus was invited to teach Greek at his famous alma mater, the University of Heidelberg. But the university paid its professors so poorly that he became overworked because of the odd jobs he had to take to survive. "My health has been inexpressibly weakened," was his complaint to the university senate. In addition, his evangelical ideas isolated him from the others. The scholastic theologians were still in the majority, and they did all they could to exterminate all reform-minded renewal. His views on the Lord's Supper were similar to the Swiss opinion: that is, that the words spoken by Jesus when he instituted the Lord's Supper had only a spiritual meaning. This also put him in an isolated position.

A Miraculous Rescue

In his commentary on the book of Daniel, Melanchthon tells the story of how Grynaeus was miraculously rescued through the intervention of an angel.[2] This occurred during the well-known Diet of Spiers, when the evangelical princes submitted their *Protestatio* (to which Protestants owe their name) to Emperor Charles V. Grynaeus was one of the many visitors there, along with Melanchthon, his close friend.

At one point Grynaeus made a critical remark to Johannes Faber, the bishop of Vienna, as they were leaving the church. He courageously called the bishop to account for the sermon the latter had just

---

2. G. Baum and E. Cunitz, eds., *Histoire Ecclesiastique des Églises Réformées au Royaume de France: Corpus Reformatorum* (Paris, 1883), 13: 906-7.

An Exegetical Friend

preached. How could such a learned man of the church, he asked, preach such heresy that was contrary to the Word of God? And he asked that question publicly. Faber did not care for a public discussion of the matter, so he kindly asked Grynaeus whether he would be prepared to discuss the matter quietly on some other day. He invited Grynaeus to come for a visit, and the latter agreed.

Immediately after this conversation at the church, Grynaeus went to see his friend Melanchthon, and during the meal told him what had happened. At some point during their discussion, Melanchthon was called away briefly from the dining room. Someone wanted to talk to him. It was, Melanchthon says with great astonishment in his commentary, not someone he knew, but "an old, grey man with a very serious face, who had a remarkable way of speaking and was dressed in a strange fashion." This rather bizarre man said that soldiers were on their way to Melanchthon's home, sent by the emperor to take Grynaeus prisoner. Immediately after having extended his kind invitation to Grynaeus, Faber had gone to the imperial authorities to accuse him of dangerous heresy. The old stranger urged Grynaeus to leave the city without delay, and immediately after he delivered his message, he disappeared. Melanchthon took the warning with utter seriousness, and he escorted Grynaeus out of the city to the Rhine River as quickly as possible, where he was ferried across to safer territory. When the Melanchthon party returned, they heard that soldiers had arrived to arrest Grynaeus as soon as they had left the house. Melanchthon concludes that "Grynaeus would have died had he not been protected by angels." The strange old man who had come to warn him was clearly an angel from God.

Freedom for God's Word

Not long after this incident, Grynaeus left Heidelberg to continue his work in Basel, where humanist scholarship had established a solid base. Led by Oecolampadius, the city had clearly taken sides with the Reformation not long before that. And that's where Grynaeus would stay — with a few short interruptions — for the rest of his life. The famous Greek professor was eagerly welcomed to Basel, and things went better for him than they had in Heidelberg. Oecolampadius had tried to entice the scholar with the promise of a good salary, a pleasant climate, and the excellent printing facilities that could be found in Basel. These amenities may all have played a role in his decision to relocate, but the decisive argument must have been what Grynaeus wrote in his positive response: "I want, more than anything else, to be in a place where freedom for the Word of God is adequately ensured." And that, apparently, was the case in Basel.

A Prominent Humanist

In Basel, Grynaeus received a prominent position as a humanist scholar in accordance with his great qualities. His main task was teaching Greek, but he was also involved in a search for unknown sources from classical literature that might merit a new edition. Philosophy was also one of his scholarly interests. Stimulated by Erasmus, he worked on a new edition of the works of the Greek philosopher Aristotle, and he discovered five unknown books of the Latin historian Livy, which he prepared for publication.

Humanists were constantly searching the libraries for undiscovered writings in their endeavors to enrich the knowledge of Western culture from these sources. With this ideal in mind, Grynaeus traveled to England at one point. Through Thomas More, the friend of Erasmus and chancellor of England, he even met King Henry VIII. It appears that the cordial relationship between Grynaeus and More was not hindered by that fact that More remained an orthodox Catholic, while Grynaeus was favorable toward the new teachings. Henry VIII was involved in the process of divorcing his first wife, and he even asked Grynaeus to inquire about the position of the Swiss theologians on this matter. Grynaeus did what he could to ensure that this royal request would receive an answer. The Swiss agreed that the divorce would be legitimate; but Thomas More's conscientious objections to it would eventually result in his execution.

Was Grynaeus in Fact a Theologian?

Strictly speaking, Grynaeus was not a theologian: like Calvin, he did not possess a formal degree in theology. Nonetheless, after the death of Oecolampadius, he was given the title of professor in theology. He started his theological lectures with an exposition of the Epistle to the Romans. During the final years of Grynaeus's life, Karlstadt — the troublemaker who had been expelled from Wittenberg and had moved to Basel, where he had acquired the position of rector of the university — publicly disputed whether Grynaeus had the right to call himself a theologian. He should first graduate as a doctor in theology, said this radical purist, and only then should Grynaeus be allowed to serve the church in this teaching office. This convinced the city council to withdraw the title of professor in theology from Grynaeus.

It is significant that Calvin returned to Basel precisely during this period when Grynaeus had to cope with the bitterness over the unreasonable council decision. It was Calvin's second visit to the city, from May until September 1538, after he had himself been banished by the authorities from Geneva, where he had served for two years as instructor in Holy Scripture and preacher of the Word of God. Like Grynaeus, he was not an official theologian, and he likewise experienced opposition from the city council because of his reformist activities. There is little doubt that the recognition and sharing of this bitter experience would have brought the two friends even closer than they already were.

The First Encounter with Calvin

Three years earlier, Grynaeus and Calvin had become acquainted when Calvin, having fled from France, found in Basel a safe haven and a place where he could devote himself to the study of the classics and Scripture.[3] He arrived in the illustrious city of scholars with his friend Louis du Tillet. Here he found the peace to complete his *Institutes,* which was then published by the renowned print shop of Platter. He lodged with a

3. See E. Doumergue, *Calvijns Jeugd* (Kampen, 1986), pp. 447-64; Alexander Ganoczy, *The Young Calvin* (Edinburgh, 1987), pp. 91-102; Cornelis Augustijn, Christoph Burger, and Frans P. van Stam, "Calvin in the Light of the Early Letters," in *Calvin Praeceptor Ecclesiae,* ed. Herman J. Selderhuis (Geneva, 2004), pp. 145-47.

woman named Catharina Klein, and he used the pseudonym Lucianus (which contained all the letters of the name Calvinus).

Calvin's first stay in Basel was of great importance to him, and not least because of his relationship with Grynaeus. The latter had begun a new series of lectures on the Epistle to the Romans in the autumn of 1535, and there is no doubt that Calvin attended those lectures. And the letter with which he dedicates his first exegetical study to Grynaeus (in 1539) confirms that the exchange of ideas with this exegete — as Calvin will remember after three years — exerted a major influence on his views of the exegesis of Scripture.[4] The two had much in common: neither was a trained theologian; rather, they were philologists, interpreters of classical texts in the humanist tradition. Both had a great love for the Greek language, and together they studied Hebrew with Sebastian Münster. We may well assume that Calvin's friendship with Grynaeus contributed to his desire to also become an exegete — not only of classical writings, but particularly of Scripture.

How Is the Bible to Be Interpreted?

Calvin remembers in his letter how fully they agreed that it is extremely important for exegetes to abide by the rule to be clear and brief: the *perspicua brevitas* ("perspicuous brevity") is much to be preferred to long-winded excurses by the exegete, which detract from the "intention of the author." This is true for exegesis in general, but even truer in the exegesis of Scripture. This does not imply that Calvin sat in judgment of other exegetes who did not use his method and gave a much more elaborate treatment. But he defended the legitimacy of a short and closely text-based exegesis that stays close to what the original author wanted

---

4. A. L. Herminjard, *Correspondance des Réformateurs dans las Pays de Langue Française*, 9 vols. (Geneva/Basel/Lyon/Paris, 1878-97), no. 838 (cited hereafter as Herminjard); see also W. de Greef, *De Ware Uitleg* (Leyden, 1995), pp. 194f.; W. Balke, *Calvijn en de Bijbel* (Kampen, 2003), pp. 54-56; Nicole Kuropka, "Calvins Römerbriefwidmung und der Consensus Piorum," in *Calvin im Kontext der Schweizer Reformation*, ed. Peter Opitz (Zurich, 2003), pp. 147-67; Christoph Burger, "Calvins Beziehungen zur Weggefährten in der Schweiz, 1536-1538," in Opitz, *Calvin im Kontext der Schweizer Reformation* (Zurich, 2003), pp. 50-55.

to say. However, Calvin also pleaded for diversity in exegesis. It would have been rather pedantic for a thirty-year-old beginner to prescribe the method he chose after his dialogue with Grynaeus as the only valid option.

While working on his exegetical debut, Calvin acknowledged that one might ask whether another commentary on Romans was necessary — to be added to the many good ones that already existed. Yet, even though he showed a degree of modest hesitation, he decided to do his part in the long exegetical tradition. And it was precisely because he believed the Epistle to the Romans to be, in fact, the key to a proper understanding of the whole of Scripture. Thus it was no coincidence that he began his exegetical work with this book of the Bible.

Calvin compared his method with those of three of his colleagues, whom he greatly appreciated but from whom he also greatly differed. Melanchthon wrote a commentary on Romans; but in it he merely deals with the major points and does not follow the text verse by verse. Bullinger likewise deserved much praise, because he excelled in combining scholarship with clarity. Bucer was so sharp and erudite that he could not be surpassed by anybody. Nonetheless, Calvin found him too elaborate: Bucer did not know when to stop, and this makes it difficult to grasp the essence of the text if one has many other things to do.

Calvin more or less indicates that he does not intend to write an original commentary that is fully independent of the work of his predecessors. On the contrary, standing on their shoulders, he makes his contribution with all modesty but also with clear determination. He voices an intense desire that, in spite of the diversity that existed in method and talent, a fundamental unity would emerge among those who interpret Scripture. In any case, it was this unity that Calvin remembers with great joy about his association with Grynaeus. Writing three years after he has left Basel, he still has a vivid recollection of their exegetical discussions.

An Amiable Friend

Grynaeus was a very amiable friend to Calvin. But at times the professor from Basel would try to temper his Genevan colleague with mild criticism. Sometimes Calvin could be rather sharp and overzealous, especially when he got together with the ardent Farel. The reader of Calvin's letter to Grynaeus about Caroli, who had dared to accuse the Geneva Reformer of nonorthodox views on the Trinity, sees a fuming Calvin, one who does not stand for any nonsense.[5] Fortunately, Calvin — with his brethren — was absolved of all suspicion, and Caroli was deposed. Grynaeus clearly supported his Geneva colleagues in this matter.[6]

In another matter, one involving the Bernese preacher Kuntz, Grynaeus felt that he had to disapprove of Calvin's approach.[7] Kuntz was a sincere and devout preacher, and whatever difference of opinion there might be between him and Calvin, Grynaeus believed, should not be something to get overly excited about. Calvin should remember that Kuntz came from a simple farmer's family in a Swiss valley, while he was a Frenchman and, with his refined culture and great erudition, was on a different level. Apparently, Calvin's sharp personality could at times get carried away in his personal relationships.

In this way his friend from Basel supported Calvin with counsel and action, particularly in his early years in Geneva. He comforted Calvin during the perplexities that the latter experienced in those difficult years. He was, in fact, the person who directed Calvin toward Strasbourg after he had been expelled from Geneva. There Bucer took him under his wing and offered him a pastoral position in the church of French refugees. While in Basel — where he stayed in Grynaeus's home — Calvin may have intended to fully return to a life of scholarship. The crisis in Geneva had, as we have seen, raised doubts about his calling. Should he remain a pastor? Grynaeus thought so, and he helped Calvin go to Strasbourg. Grynaeus may have been, more than he himself recognized, the instrument that saved the young scholar for the church. This friendship certainly contributed to the fact that Calvin became one of the most blessed exegetes of Scripture.

5. Herminjard, 6: 634.
6. Herminjard, 6: 681.
7. Herminjard, 6: 691.

An Exegetical Friend

WILLIAM FAREL

A Passionate Friend

William Farel, from Beza's *Icones*

Some have the impression that the friends of Calvin and Farel (1489-1567) must have breathed a loud sigh of relief when these two insepara-ble brethren in the service of the Lord were robbed of their geographical proximity.[1] It was not that their friends were happy about the reason for the separation, which in itself was serious enough. It was a tremendous shock — felt far beyond the confines of the city — when Geneva fired its two ministers point-blank, along with the blind evangelist Couraud, and sent them into immediate exile. After Farel and Calvin had been insepa-rable for almost two years, and had fought shoulder to shoulder for the cause of the Reformation, they were now forced to go their separate ways. Their cordial relationship was to continue through the years, though not without occasional troubles; their extensive correspondence bears witness to this. But never again were they to serve together in the same congregation.

Why did the Strasbourg Reformer Bucer, a mutual friend, regard the separation of these two passionate friends in-arms as a much needed and useful consequence of this painful exile?[2] He explains his reasons in a letter he sent to Calvin after the latter's return to Basel and the quietness of his beloved studies. The Reformer from Strasbourg writes that he, along with other friends of Calvin, was of the opinion that it would not be in the best interests of the church — nor in Calvin's best interests — if the latter would leave Basel and join his colleague Farel, who in the meantime had become a minister in the Swiss city of

1. For information about Farel, see D. Nauta, *Guillaume Farel, in Leven en Werken Geschetst* (Amsterdam, 1978); Frances Bevan, *Het Leven van Willem Farel* (Aalten, 2001). On Calvin and Farel, see E. Doumergue, *Calvijn in het Strijdperk* (Kampen, 1986), esp. pp. 84-156; David N. Wiley, "Calvin's Friendship with Guillaume Farel," in *Calvin Studies Society Papers,* 1995, 1996, ed. David Foxgrover (Grand Rapids, 1998), pp. 187-204; Heiko A. Oberman, "Calvin and Farel: The Dynamics of Legitimation in Early Cal-vinism," *Journal of Early Modern History* 2 (1998): 32-60; Cornelis Augustijn, Christoph Burger, and Frans P. van Stam. "Calvin in the Light of the Early Letters," in *Calvin Praeceptor Ecclesiae,* ed. Herman J. Selderhuis (Geneva, 2004), pp. 139-58, esp. pp. 150-57; Frans P. van Stam, "Farels und Calvins Ausweisung aus Genf am 23. April 1538," *Zeitschrift für Kirchengeschichte* (1998): 209-28; Cornelis Augustijn, "Farel und Calvin in Bern 1537-1538," in *Calvin im Kontext der Schweizer Reformation,* ed. Peter Opitz (Zu-rich, 2003), pp. 9-23.
2. Augustijn et al., "Calvin in the Light of the Early Letters," p. 150.

A Passionate Friend

Neuchâtel. Calvin's relationship with Farel was so close that he felt no inhibition in promptly sharing with him this friendly — but also unmistakably critical — warning from Bucer.[3] It may well be that they both understood and accepted what their friends had observed: when they were together, their "chemistry" operated in such a way that the passion in their characters could become an uncontrollable fire. (I should note that in those days it was quite customary to let others read the letters that one received within a network of contacts and friends.)

Still, it is quite remarkable that Calvin, without any token of disapproval, communicated Bucer's concern to Farel. Farel and Calvin were very sensitive about this criticism, for they had been blamed for the problems that had caused their departure from Geneva. But they insisted to everyone that they were not, in essence, the cause of the disarray in the church in Geneva that had forced them to leave. Though they were certainly aware that they had their own weaknesses, and though they recognized that they were imperfect servants of God, they maintained that justice in the matter would reveal that they had not caused the bomb in Geneva to explode.

At the same time, Calvin understood what Bucer was trying to say. Farel's passionate nature did not always influence his development as a spiritual leader in a positive way. And exactly because Calvin could also be, under the surface of his restrained behavior, rather passionate and impetuous — and at times rather touchy — the contagious influence of a fire-eater like Farel was not always desirable. Bucer was correct in his observation. And it was the miraculous way of divine providence that Calvin, who had been won to the service of the church of Christ through a direct intervention by Farel, could now, with Farel some distance away, grow into the Reformer of Geneva and far beyond.

In Evangelical Circles

William Farel was older than Calvin by twenty years. He was born in 1489 in the small city of Gap in the French Dauphiné. His parents belonged to the established citizenry and were financially well off. Father

3. *CO*, 10/2: 228-30.

William Farel

Farel was a solicitor. William had two older brothers, who would later also warmly support the Reformation.

It is noteworthy that Farel's parents had planned a military career for young William. They may have early on regarded his tempestuous and intrepid nature as suitable for a career as a soldier. In the area where he was born — the border region of France and Italy, which frequently turned into a battlefield — there was a constant demand for young men with ambitions for the military. But William had no interest in that direction whatsoever. He would indeed become a soldier, but on a totally different kind of battlefield than that of the European conflicts of his times. He would become a dedicated soldier in the army of the kingdom of Christ.

Serving the church was a second option, but that was not his ambition either. His dislike for the priesthood was too great, and he shrank from the holy mystery of the sacrament of the mass. And so, for the time being, he followed his third option: he went to Paris for further study. In the year of Calvin's birth he set out on his long journey from home to the great city, where he would dedicate twelve years of his life to the study of literature and theology.

During this period of study, he came into contact with the evangelical circles surrounding the biblical humanist Lefèvre d'Étaples, and a special tie developed between the young William Farel and the father of the French evangelical movement. Farel experienced the same kind of relationship with Lefèvre d'Étaples that Luther enjoyed with his father confessor, Von Staupitz. As his spiritual coach, d'Étaples taught him that our relationship with God is not based on our own achievements but on grace alone. In the circle in which he now found himself, Farel soon became acquainted with the writings of Luther, which would have a decisive impact on him. Around 1521 we find Farel in the group that surrounded the reform-minded bishop Briconnet of Meaux. He resigned from his teaching post at a prestigious college and from that time forward became a preacher of the gospel. Farel filled his new calling, mostly as an itinerant preacher, with all the fervor he possessed. His radical ideas soon created a distance between himself and his friends, who were firmly determined never to leave the church for the sake of the gospel. At one point, a passionate sermon Farel preached against the worship of Mary and the saints had major consequences: he was forced to leave France and find refuge in Basel.

On Fire for the Gospel

Farel's life may be summarized in a single sentence: He led the uncertain existence of an itinerant preacher who was willing to dispose of everything for the sake of the gospel of free grace. Those with a less favorable impression of his character have called him a "Reformational agitator,"[4] a troublemaker, or a street preacher who caused problems wherever he appeared. But others have regarded him as a fiery preacher who was not afraid of anything or anyone when it came to defending the grace of his master Jesus Christ in the face of everything opposed to it. This often meant that he encountered physical abuse; a few times, in fact, he was mistreated to the extent that his life was in danger. Farel was not a quiet and docile teacher, but a fierce and zealous activist for the gospel. Calvin once compared him to the apostle Paul. If we read Paul's catalogue of his sufferings, we will find many things that remind us of Farel's life.

Farel arrived in Basel in 1524, and with Oecolampadius he organized a debate about the doctrine of free grace. He was allowed to teach and preach, though Oecolampadius was mildly crictical of him and urged him not to misuse the pulpit for polemics. It seemed that this had a positive result, because Farel became more aware of the fact that meekness and the gospel fit together. Nevertheless, Farel's sermons prompted the Basel magistrates to send him away. For Basel was also the city of Erasmus, and the famous humanist was clearly no friend of Farel. The latter did not mince words in his preaching, and he expressed his irritation with Erasmus's mild criticism of the Catholic ecclesiastical practices. He went so far as to refer to the prince of the humanists as a "Bileam." This was unacceptable to the Basel city fathers, and Farel had to leave.

Farel went from Basel to Strasbourg, where he became acquainted with Bucer and Capito. Eventually he entered the territory of Bern, the

4. As Augustijn called him in "Farel und Calvin in Bern 1537-1538," p. 9.

most powerful city of Switzerland, and he adopted the pseudonym Ursinus (Latin for "bear"). Bern appointed him preacher of the Word in Aigle; in addition, as the minister of Bern, he was charged with serving the Reformation in all the places that fell under the jurisdiction of the city. In Bern he also came into contact with Zwingli, who, like so many others who had become acquainted with Farel, urged him to proceed in his enthusiastic endeavors with prudence and meekness. In 1530, Farel gave the deciding push to the Reformation in Neuchâtel.

In 1530 we meet Farel, along with Olivétan and some others, in the region of the Waldenses. He later traveled to France, where he visited Gap, the town where he was born. Still later, he visited Geneva for the first time to encourage his fellow believers, and he narrowly escaped the city with his life. Yet a year later he would, under the powerful patronage of Bern, return to Geneva, where he would become the Reformer. This did not happen initially because of his own preaching and efforts — however important those may have been — but via his "arresting" in the memorable year 1536 of his colleague John Calvin, who was twenty years his junior.

Post Tenebras Lux: After Darkness, Light

The Reformation of Geneva will always be linked with the name of William Farel. The city was seething with unrest during the years before his arrival: discontent with and opposition to the clergy and the civic rulers were providing a fertile ground for the freedom struggle that was going on. A few other Swiss cities were viewing this development with mounting concern. Freiburg did all it could to keep Geneva in the Roman Catholic camp; but Bern wanted to strengthen the influences of reform. That is why Farel, as the agent of Bern, ventured into this arena of conflict — a move that would nearly cost him his life. "Throw this Luther into the Rhone," the Roman Catholic party shouted. They even tried to fire guns at him, but the ammunition exploded in the hands of the marksman, and Farel remained unhurt. In the end, the civil authorities arrested Farel to save him from the furious clergy, and they sent him into exile.

But by 1533 he was back in Geneva. He was determined not to be chased away again until the light of the gospel would shine in its full splendor over the city. In 1535 the city council ordered the minting of a new coin for Geneva with the legend *Post Tenebras Lux* ("after darkness, light"). Geneva was free. Partly due to the rivalry among Bern, France, and Savoy, the city was able to acquire its independence, even though it had to lean to a large extent on the protective arm of powerful Bern, which — somewhat against its own preference — had to allow Geneva its freedom.

Now it was important to fortify the religious as well as the civic freedom that had been won. One might question whether the impatient Farel was the right person for that task. Doumergue has good reason to argue that his passionate character made him more suitable to conquer than to rule.[5] Who was to guide the process of allowing the blazing fire of the gospel to develop into a quiet and warming light? At the very moment when this emerges as a burning question, "this Frenchman" passes through the city intending to spend only one night there. It was to be much longer than he could have imagined.

A Passionate Appeal

Picture that traveling Frenchman on a summer night in July 1536 as he sought rest in an inn in Geneva. Suddenly a man with a reddish beard stormed in through the door, creating a somewhat wild impression. As soon as he opened his mouth, he reinforced that impression. Without any beating around the bush, this sudden visitor told the young traveler that he has been the appointed person to serve God in this city, a place to which he had merely wished to pay a brief visit. The sudden visitor was William Farel, a man in the prime of his life, and he challenged the young French scholar, twenty years younger than he, to get involved in a struggle that the latter had always, because of his shy personality, tried to avoid. Calvin objected forcefully, but to no avail. More than twenty years later, he remembered Farel's challenge as if it had happened the day before: how the older man had erupted in anger when Calvin told him that he would rather devote his life to study. Calvin remembered Farel exclaiming, in "holy indignation," "And I declare, in the name of

5. Doumergue, *Calvijn in het Strijdperk,* p. 130.

almighty God, that your studies are just a pretense. If you refuse to give yourself together with us to the service of the Lord, God will curse you, for you are seeking yourself rather than Christ."[6] This was simply too much for Calvin. He relented and allowed himself to be hired as a teacher of Scripture. Farel knew what kind of person Calvin was; and he knew and admired the *Institutes.* He realized that Calvin would be much better equipped than he himself was to provide more content and greater depth to the Reformation in Geneva through his teaching.

Two exciting years followed, during which both preachers happily cooperated. One of Farel's great qualities was that he knew his own limitations. If there was one thing that was never uppermost in the mind of this preacher of the gospel, it was his own honor and reputation. And this meant that he had no difficulty in allowing Calvin, who was so much younger and had not shared the heat of the day and the cold of the night during the Reformation in Geneva, to take the lead. However, it would be stretching things to say that Farel handed all authority completely over to Calvin.[7] His name remained closely tied to the reform-minded party in Geneva, who liked to be called "Guillermins," after Farel's first name, Guillaume (William). Recent research on the events and publications in the years 1536-1538 shows that Farel remained the point man, even though he greedily and gratefully used what Calvin gave him in terms of content. Farel's fierce and daring confrontations with the city council are clear evidence of this.

At times Calvin had to warn his older colleague and friend not to get involved in the dirty work of his fanatical supporters. But they worked together inseparably to defend the freedom of the church in the face of a government that tried to block the measures that were necessary to keep the Word pure. In the end, it would be the conflict regarding the authority of the church to exercise discipline that, in April 1538, would prevent the friends from continuing their work in Geneva.[8]

6. Calvin mentions this in his preface to his commentary on the Psalms.

7. We find this common opinion with Bevan, as well as in G. P. van Itterzon, "Guillaume Farel," in *Christelijke Encyclopedie* (Kampen, 1958), pp. 18-19. Van Stam, "Calvin in the Light of the Early Letters," shows that Farel continued to be in charge to a greater extent than has often been assumed.

8. See Oberman, "Calvin and Farel."

A Passionate Friend

Lasting Friendship

Even though Calvin and Farel would no longer serve in the same congregation, they would remain "the most precious friends." They met regularly and corresponded frequently to share everything important; they discussed the state of the church and the political situation with cordial unanimity; they kept no secrets from each other and did not hesitate to share the most personal matters. They also did not spare each other their honest criticism, in a way that is only possible between true friends.

As a minister in Neuchâtel, Farel remained a regional Reformer, despite his evangelistic travels to Switzerland and France. Partly as the result of Calvin's international experience between his first and second stays in Geneva, experience he gained during the religious disputes in Germany, he developed into the most important European Reformer — with Geneva as his operational base.

Farel visited Geneva from time to time, and he continued to receive the recognition he deserved as the Reformer of that city. For good reason, his statue stands today next to Calvin's as part of the Reformation monument in Geneva. He, rather than Calvin, provided pastoral care to Servetus, the "blasphemer" who was condemned to death, on his way toward his execution. The following Sunday, he had again returned to his normal self in the Church of Sainte Pierre, where he chastised the young people of Geneva in such a way that he was subsequently called before the city council to give account.

Along with Pierre Viret, whom we shall meet later in these pages, Farel belonged to a small group of Calvin's dearest friends. Calvin underscores the close relationship of this Reformational trio in the introduction to his commentary on Paul's Epistle to Titus: Viret in Lausanne, Farel in Neuchâtel, and Calvin in Geneva. Calvin refers to himself as a Titus who was privileged to build on the foundational work of Paul, whom he used as a symbol for Farel.[9]

9. *CO*, 13: 477-78.

Strange Fire

Were these friends ever at loggerheads with one another? Most certainly they were. They once had a major disagreement because Calvin thought Farel had been far too lenient with an unreliable colleague.[10] But there was another moment, in 1558, when Calvin felt that his relationship with Farel was at a breaking point. It is quite remarkable how their frequent correspondence suddenly stopped after 1558.[11] The reason was Calvin's total bewilderment over an utterly "strange fire" that had taken hold of Farel. At one point the sixty-nine-year-old Farel approached Calvin asking whether he was willing to conduct his wedding service. Throughout his itinerant existence, Farel had lived without a wife, but at his advanced age he had decided to marry. That in itself was not the cause for Calvin's fury. But when Farel told him that his bride was going to be a girl of seventeen, Calvin believed that he had become senile. A widow had fled from France and had come to Farel's home, along with her daughter, to find refuge. Farel had fallen in love, not with the mother — which might have been somewhat acceptable — but with her young daughter. Everyone was astounded, and Calvin thought it might bring great disgrace on the gospel. But Farel was not to be deterred in any way. Calvin refused to conduct the wedding ceremony, but he did urge Farel to marry as quickly as possible so as to avoid further gossip. This marriage even resulted in the birth of a boy, who lived just a few years. Farel named his son Jean, after John Calvin, which raises the question whether, after all that had happened, Farel still wanted to express his appreciation to his friend.

This shameful affair unfortunately cast a heavy shadow over the friendship between the two men toward the end of their lives. Nonetheless, there remained a bond between them in their hearts. Shortly before his own death, Calvin wrote a short letter to his old brother in Christ, who was to survive him — in order to spare him a farewell jour-

10. Calvin was indignant when Farel had too easily readmitted Caroli to his circle of friends after the latter had apologized for the fact that he had accused Farel and Calvin of unorthodoxy. Calvin distrusted Caroli and felt that he had been maneuvered into an extremely awkward position. For that reason he heaped bitter reproach on his friend. See Wiley, "Calvin's Friendship with Guillaume Farel," pp. 200-201.

11. Oberman, "Calvin and Farel," in particular, points this out.

ney. "If it is God's will that you will live longer than I, ever remember our friendship, which was not only profitable for God's church, but also will bear its fruits in heaven." The letter did not stop Farel from paying a last visit to his dying friend. Their mutual love was that strong!

Quid volo, nisi ut ardeat ("what else do I wish for, but that it will burn") was Farel's motto. He was the instrument that caused the glow of the gospel that set Geneva on fire. But his great contribution, more than anything else, was to give this fire a more quiet and comforting glow by placing Calvin as the steady candle in Geneva. *Teram dum prosim* ("let me be consumed, as long as I am useful") was the motto Calvin lived by. The flame of this candle, which fully burned itself up in Geneva, spread its light throughout the world. And that was, at least in part, Farel's contribution.

PIERRE VIRET

The "Best Friend of All"

Pierre Viret, from Beza's *Icones*

Taking a Break Together

In the beautiful summer of 1550, Calvin was in urgent need of a short vacation. The person whose company he most desired, when he planned this little break, was one of his very best friends, Pierre Viret (1511-1571) of Lausanne. He wrote him a short letter cordially inviting him to come to Geneva on a given Saturday.[1] On the Sunday it would then be Viret's privilege to preach at the main service in the Church of Sainte Pierre, while Calvin himself would conduct a service in the Geneva suburb of Jussy. After Sunday dinner Pierre would join him in a visit to a mutual friend, the Lord of Falais, who lived near Lake Geneva. From there they would cross the lake and take a short break from the intense pastoral work in the Lord's vineyard in the home of some other friends in the countryside.

Calvin was enthusiastic about the plan. He evidently saw no problem leaving on a vacation immediately after the Sunday church service. His letter to Viret has fueled the legend that Calvin went sailing on Lake Geneva on the Lord's Day. But this boat trip on a Sunday afternoon was not just a pleasure trip: in Geneva the boat was a common means of transport to cross the lake. And the fact that this was Sunday posed no problem for either of them. As long as they had been to church, the remainder of the day was available for other activities, such as visiting friends. The Puritan approach to the Sabbath, practiced among their spiritual heirs in America, should not be attributed to these two Reformers.

Unfortunately, the plans could not be realized because Viret was not at home when the letter arrived. Considering the urgent tone of his letter ("again and again, I wish you well, until you come"), this must have been a major disappointment for Calvin. The fact that he had a fervent desire to spend a few free days with his colleague Viret is evidence that this friend and brother was his closest associate. This was also why Calvin often calls him "my very best friend" in his extensive correspondence with him, of which some four hundred letters survive.

1. *CO,* 13: 603-4.

Pierre Viret

A Witness of Calvin's Call

It may well be that the special bond between John and Pierre had everything to do with the most enthralling event in Calvin's life, the moment when Farel called him so compellingly to the ministry of the divine Word in Geneva. Calvin had met Viret before, in 1535, when he had withdrawn to Basel to write the *Institutes*. But the next time they met, Viret would, as the minister of Geneva, silently witness the momentous event in an inn in the city on the Rhone, when Calvin's tranquility would be disturbed once and for all by the appearance of the passionate Farel (which is told in the preceding chapter).

We do not know how Calvin felt after he had submitted to Farel's summons. Perhaps Farel had left immediately, with joy and gratitude that he had been able to recruit such a valuable worker for God's kingdom. But if Viret had stayed on at the inn a little longer, he could have told his new colleague that he had also been "arrested" by Farel a few years earlier in exactly the same way. Did this identical experience contribute to the special bond between these two contemporaries (Viret was only two years younger than Calvin)? Whether or not they shared their Farel moment at that time, they became very close friends for life.

The Son of a Tailor from Orbe

Pierre Viret came from Pays de Vaud, in the Francophone part of Switzerland.[2] Unlike Farel and Calvin, the two Frenchmen who, despite their lifelong service in Swiss cities, always remained "foreigners" in Switzerland to a degree, Viret was pure Swiss. In addition to his pleasant personality, his affinity with the Swiss mentality must have worked in his favor, which partly explains why he was more popular in Geneva than Calvin was.

---

2. On Viret, see D. Nauta, *Pierre Viret (1511-1571), Medestander van Calvijn* (Kampen, 1988). On his relationship with Calvin, see E. Doumergue, *Calvijn in het Strijdperk* (Kampen, 1986), pp. 151-81; Robert D. Linder, "Brothers in Christ, Pierre Viret and John Calvin as Soul-Mates and Co-Laborers in the Work of the Reformation," in *Calvin Studies Society Papers, 1995, 1997*, ed. David Foxgrover (Grand Rapids, 1998), pp. 134-58; W. Balke, "Jean Calvin und Pierre Viret," in *Calvin im Kontext der Schweizer Reformation*, ed. Peter Opitz (Zurich, 2003), pp. 57-92.

Viret was born in 1511 in the small town of Orbe. He did not come from a prestigious family, but his father's financial assets were such that it was no problem whatsoever to pay for his son's studies even in Paris. Pierre went there at the age of sixteen to get a thorough education at the same school, the Montaigu College, where John Calvin had matriculated just a few years before. We know little about this period of Viret's life, but it was a decisive time for him because he came into such close contact with Reformation influences that his heart was won for the gospel. When the persecutions against adherents of the new teachings erupted in Paris, he felt that it was sensible to return home. Though he had not yet completed an academic degree, he had gained sufficient knowledge to eventually become a fruitful instrument in the furtherance of the kingdom of Christ.

Orbe was in a peculiar situation: it was intermittently ruled by the Roman Catholic Freiburg and the Protestant Bern. This had caused few real problems up until 1531. Both the Roman Catholics and the followers of Luther enjoyed the freedom to express their religion as they wished. But when the situation became more confrontational, Bern sent a delegation to Orbe, and William Farel was a member of that delegation. This powerful preacher did not hesitate to deliver a passionate sermon about the gospel of free grace, even in the face of massive opposition. At first his preaching appeared to have little impact. After a week of continued preaching, while he was surrounded by hostility, verbal abuse, and even physical violence (with women, in particular, attacking him), Farel still had a small group of only ten listeners. One of them was Pierre Viret. Farel saw the twenty-year-old youth as a suitable instrument for the service of the Word. In his own inimitably convincing way, which we have already seen above, the fervent Farel was able to break through the timidity and shyness of the young Pierre. On May 6, 1531, Viret preached his first sermon. God blessed his ministry: one year after Farel had conducted a communion service for a handful of people, Viret would be distributing the sacrament at Easter to almost eighty believers, his parents among them.

Could Calvin Laugh?

Viret's personality differed from that of his two best friends, Farel and Calvin. In contrast to the intensity of Farel and the somewhat reserved character of Calvin, this third person in the Swiss Reformed trio exemplified a cordial warmth. Viret did not think very highly of himself; at least he believed that, in the domain of knowledge, he was no match for Calvin, whom he greatly admired. In a letter to Bullinger he expresses his hope that, though he does not see himself as a real scholar, he will be accepted by his friends "as a goose among the swans."[3] But Viret was certainly no brainless goose among the Swiss Reformers: his written legacy, which in quantity, content, and influence is second only to Calvin's among the Francophone Reformed, is proof to the contrary.

Viret was a peace-loving man. Beza portrays him as a man who, in contrast to his two better-known friends, possessed "the sweetness of honey." Nonetheless, his writing could be razor-sharp, and he used satire as few others were able to. The satirical style of writing has been described as "joking in earnest": it mercilessly unmasks follies and errors that appear to be serious — for the sake of truth. Calvin could laugh heartily when reading these humorous pieces, as he writes in his preface to Viret's *Christian Disputations*. He recognized his friend's magical skill in revealing "the superstitions of the poor world" in such a way that one could not help but laugh. In any event, we know that Calvin once said, "Nowhere has God forbidden us to laugh."[4]

Satire can sometimes have an unusually sharp edge, but that may be the very reason why it can coexist with a friendly and peaceable spirit. Apparently, this applied more to Viret than to Calvin. The story is told that Viret once saved the life of a Jesuit from the Reformed gallows, at the very last moment, by shouting that all retribution must be left to God.

Calvin was not always happy about what Viret wrote. With a satirical undertone of his own, he replied to Viret after the latter urged him to return from the quiet Strasbourg to Geneva: "This part of your letter, in which you express concern for my health, I could not read without

---

3. Doumergue, *Calvijn in het Strijdperk,* p. 161.
4. See Linder, "Brothers in Christ," p. 144.

The "Best Friend of All"

laughing. Should I go to Geneva to improve physically? Why not be crucified immediately? I would prefer to die just once, rather than to endure the pains of ever-repeated tortures. So, dear Viret, if you wish me well, then abandon your plan."[5] But Viret did not relent. He was the one who paved the way for Calvin's return to Geneva, but he was also the one who, throughout his friend's entire stay in this "crucial" city, did all he could with his support and friendship to make the experience bearable.

Crossroads in Geneva

As a youthful preacher of the Word — he had just turned twenty when he preached his first sermon in the town where he was born — Viret was employed by the city of Bern as well. That city, with its influential position in the entire region, also had a major say in the exciting developments surrounding the Reformation in Geneva. For a short period Viret replaced a Geneva minister who had been dismissed by the city council. This was his first experience in that city, where he would intermittently serve as pastor for short periods — and would often visit as Calvin's friend — for the remainder of his life. Viret complained to the authorities in Bern about the hostile attitude of the council in Geneva, and the Bernese, in turn, took measures to strengthen the Reformational influence there. When Froment, the minister who had been dismissed by the Geneva council, was allowed to return, Viret was free to go to Lausanne. But in 1534, he was once again called on to further the cause of the gospel in Geneva, along with the experienced Farel, in demanding the right of free proclamation.

During this exciting period at the beginning of the Reformation, it was also dangerous to be a pastor in Geneva. There was even an attempt to simultaneously kill Froment, Farel, and Viret by serving them poisoned spinach soup. Viret was the only one who ate some of the soup. He became deathly ill, but he survived the attempted assassination.

During these crucial years, though he was often to be found in Geneva, Viret was the designated pastor in Lausanne. This church did not want to see him leave for the Geneva church, which also wanted him

5. *CO*, 11: 35-37.

as their regular pastor. He was clearly popular in both places because of his pleasant character and the strong pastoral approach he showed in his preaching and interaction with the people. Even though Viret was not averse to moving to Geneva, he was led in a different direction. He continued to keep an eye on Geneva, and he cherished that church in his heart, but the other Swiss city — Lausanne — was to be the place where he would serve the major part of his life. And thus the trio of Swiss Reformers — Farel, Calvin, and Viret — would be forever linked to the three cities of Neuchâtel, Geneva, and Lausanne respectively.

Three Comrades in Arms

In 1538, Viret was in Geneva when Calvin began his ministry in that city, having come from Lausanne to provide some temporary assistance. Along with his senior colleague, Farel, Viret no doubt introduced the novice Calvin to the first elements of the ministry of the Word. After not more than three months, the three brethren traveled together to Lausanne to participate in a debate aimed at unmasking the theological errors of Rome.

The closeness of the bond between the three of them becomes clear in that preface to Calvin's commentary on Titus, where he refers to this friendship. He acknowledges that he became involved in Geneva as an "assistant" in the work that Farel and Viret had, with "great effort and danger," brought to the point of a breakthrough. Calvin regarded his friendship with Farel and Viret as something like a "holy bond," which should be a special testimony to his time and to later generations. "I do not think there ever was a group of friends who were so closely connected in their commonality of purpose in life, as we were in our service. I had the opportunity to serve with both of you in our pastoral office, but there never was a hint of jealousy. On the contrary, it was clear that we, you and I, were truly one. After some time we were separated from each other with regard to our places of work. For the church of Neuchâtel, which you delivered from papal tyranny to Christ, called you, Farel, to work for them. And, exercising the same right, the church of Lausanne has reserved you, Viret, for themselves. Whatever be the case, each of us looks after the place that had been entrusted to him with such care, that through our unity the children of God are gathered into the fold of Christ, where they are joined together as one body."[6]

However, Calvin notes that this unique friendship also evoked enmity, both outside and inside their own circle. But this hostility never succeeded in estranging the comrades in arms from each other. Here Calvin is apparently referring to the fact that all three of them — in their individual places of work — had to face the same problems with the authorities in their united plea for the liberty of the church to deal with disciplinary matters. This close trio succeeded in making something visible of the right of Reformed ecclesiastical life, as distinct from the so-called caesero-papism (the idea that the government has the final say in church matters) that Bern defended. That city refused to give full freedom in matters of doctrine and discipline to the churches within its sphere of authority, because this would reduce the power of the government in ecclesiastical matters. Eventually, this came to a breaking point for Viret, and he had to leave Lausanne in 1559, after many years of faithful service, to become a minister and colleague of Calvin in Geneva once again.

The Mediator of Geneva

It was Viret who prepared the way for the return of the exile in 1540, when Geneva once again urgently needed John Calvin. This was after the city fathers had first tried to bring Viret back to Geneva. But the latter felt that Calvin, with his enormous erudition and knowledge, was much better suited than he was to provide further depth to the Reformation in Geneva. However, he certainly was prepared to serve as guest preacher for a period of six months, the amount of time Calvin needed to move from Strasbourg to Geneva.

Once Calvin had settled into his new assignment, he did his utmost to keep Viret as his colleague. And Viret, in point of fact, was attracted to this idea, since his position in Lausanne was far from easy. But the final decision rested with Bern, and the Bernese authorities did not approve such a move. Viret had to return to his own church.

6. *CO,* 13: 477-78.

The fact that Calvin knew he could fully depend on Viret was not the only reason he wanted to keep Viret as his colleague. It was also true that the Geneva congregants liked the Swiss pastor better than the foreigner Calvin. Viret's lively style and exegesis made him far more popular as a preacher with the common people than was Calvin, the learned professor. The city showed its preference by providing Viret with a better parsonage and living conditions than they gave Calvin. At the later date, when he once again became a permanent preacher in the city, no effort was too great to look after his needs. Even when health issues forced him to go south for a significant period, the city council paid all his expenses.

In contrast to Calvin, Viret was more of a man from and for the people. He also was very generous when faced with communal and social injustice. He was far more critical about the state of the society than Calvin was. He would, at times, fulminate against the rich when they short-changed the poor. He once wrote to a friend how much he regretted the fact that he had no money to help a poor woman; fortunately, in that instance Calvin was able to provide some funds.

The relationship between Calvin and Viret was characterized by a great degree of trust, as is clear from the letters they exchanged. Calvin repeatedly told Viret how he had great difficulty in controlling his feelings of irritation. Viret, it seems, was the one who could show understanding toward Calvin, and he also had a beneficial, moderating influence on him. The fact that Calvin could react so forcefully in his letters to his friend may well have helped him restrain himself in his contacts with others. The goodwill Viret enjoyed in Geneva no doubt helped Calvin manage his depressions, especially during the years when the going was tough.

Of course, there were occasional irritations between the two friends. In one angry letter Calvin demanded to know why Viret had not returned from the south of France. Did he not belong in Geneva, where they could not live without him? Viret, in turn, voiced his anger at Calvin when the latter called Beza from Lausanne to Geneva. During the final period of his life — from 1561 until his death in 1571 — Viret served the cause of the Reformation in the southern part of Calvin's home country. Both men had become citizens of Geneva in 1559, but it is interesting that Calvin, a Frenchman, died in Switzerland, and the Swiss Viret died in France.

Pierre Viret is absent from the central section of the monument of the Reformation in Geneva, which is a regrettable omission. One of Viret's biographers maintains that he should have been included: his spot should have been close to Calvin, "touching his left shoulder."[7] Would that be because he was more "left-wing" in social matters than was his more conservative brother? No, the reason is that the heart beats on the left side of the chest, and Viret was a man after Calvin's heart. It is probably not overstating the case to say that Calvin was able to keep going in Geneva because of this friendship. In that sense, Viret was a central figure for the Reformation: he saved Calvin for the city where, in Calvin's own words, he feared to be "crucified" upon his return. His bond with Pierre Viret, his "very best friend," no doubt lightened the weight of that cross for Calvin.

7. Linder, "Brothers in Christ," p. 157.

MARTIN BUCER

A Fatherly Friend

Martin Bucer, from Beza's *Icones*

Was Calvin a Calvinist?

Did Calvin become a Calvinist through the influence of Martin Bucer (1491-1551)?[1] This would seem to be a somewhat strange question. Nonetheless, an expert on both Bucer and Calvin has pointed to the importance of the relationship between the Genevan Reformer and his older friend and colleague from Strasbourg for the development of Calvin's theology and praxis.[2] It was not for nothing that, exactly during the years between his first and second stays in Geneva, he was Bucer's neighbor. They lived next door to each other and could meet in their gardens for cordial personal conversations. We can justifiably say that the way Calvin shaped the ecclesiastical praxis in all its facets in Geneva cannot be explained without due recognition of Beza's influence. This three-year training in Strasbourg — a period Calvin thoroughly enjoyed after a turbulent time in Geneva — was of immeasurable significance for later Calvinism, the worldwide movement resulting from the work of the Geneva Reformer.

However, we should note that Calvin was not very keen on the term "Calvinist," which was considered a rather pejorative term in his time; in fact, he absolutely refused to be the leader of a confessional current that would be referred to as "Calvinism." In a 1563 letter to Frederick, the Elector of the Palz, Calvin expresses his strong displeasure with the way some of his opponents were trying to rebuff his doctrine of the Lord's Supper by applying the "Calvinist" label.[3] What was

1. On Bucer, see Martin Greschat, "Martin Bucer," in *Gestalten der Kirchengeschichte: Die Reformationszeit,* vol. 2, ed. Martin Greschat (Stuttgart, 1993), pp. 7-28; Martin Greschat, "Das Profil Martin Bucers," in C. Krieger and M. Lienhard, eds., *Martin Bucer and Sixteenth Century Europe,* Actes du Colloque de Strasbourg, 28-31 August (Leyden, 1993), 1: 9-17; David C. Steinmetz, "Martin Bucer (1491-1551): The Church and the Social Order," in *Reformers in the Wings,* ed. David C. Steinmetz (Oxford, 2001), pp. 85-92. On Bucer and Calvin, see Willem van 't Spijker, "Bucer und Calvin," in *Martin Bucer and Sixteenth Century Europe,* ed. C. Krieger and M. Lienhard, pp. 460-71; Willem van 't Spijker, "Calvin's Friendship with Martin Bucer: Did it Make Calvin a Calvinist?" in *Calvin Studies Society Papers,* 1995, 1997, ed. David Foxgrover (Grand Rapids, 1998), pp. 169-86; Andrea Wiedeburg, "Die Freundschaft zwischen Butzer und Calvin nach ihren Briefen," *Hist. Jahrbuch* 83 (1964): 69-83; Marijn de Kroon, *Martin Bucer en Johannes Calvijn* (Zoetermeer, 1991).

2. Van 't Spijker, "Calvin's Friendship with Martin Bucer."

3. *CO,* 20: 72-79.

Martin Bucer

at stake was not Calvin's own, particular opinion, but the proclamation of the kingdom of Christ!

In a 1548 letter to Bucer, Calvin mentions that attempts were being made to categorize the brethren in terms of "Calvinism" and "Bucerianism."[4] He does not appreciate that at all. The extent to which Bucer influenced later Calvinism would be an interesting study. But, as far as Calvin himself was concerned, one might say that, while his friendship with and closeness to Bucer did not make him a "Bucerian," it did increasingly make him the man he was. Calvin was a Reformer with his own independent method. What he learned from his teachers he incorporated into his method as valuable elements, but in such a way that these took on a final form that was ultimately his own. In this process Bucer was undeniably one of Calvin's most important tutors.

The Son of a Cooper from the Alsace

Martin Bucer was born on November 11, 1491, in a village in the Alsace, today known as Sélestat, in a region that is currently part of France but where the people speak German. This region is the gateway to Switzerland and thus a fitting birthplace for the Reformer who, like no other, worked for the unity of the church in Europe. From the Alsatian capital of Strasbourg, Bucer would, in the prime of his life, untiringly exert his pleasant and conciliatory influence. As a free imperial city that was close to Switzerland and France, and also connected with the German empire, Strasbourg was uniquely suited to serve as the home of a European Reformer.

Young Martin came from a culture of simple craftsmen. He grew up in the home of his grandfather because his parents were too busy building a private business — his father was a cooper — in Strasbourg to find sufficient time to care for the boy. Martin attended the Latin school in his town, which clearly exhibited a humanistic spirit. Inspired to a large extent by his grandfather, he opted for a life of complete dedication to spiritual matters: at the age of fifteen he became a novice in a Dominican monastery, and from there he was destined for an academic

4. *CO,* 12: 730.

career. This meant that in 1517 he was allowed to begin his studies in Heidelberg. There he met someone who would bring a radical change to his life: he attended Martin Luther's "Disputation" in Heidelberg, and after a personal encounter with the Wittenberg Reformer, Bucer was fully convinced of the teaching of free grace. Because this spiritual breakthrough made his position as monk untenable, he was successful in being released from his monastic vows; he left the Dominicans in 1521.

The village of Landstuhl was to be the parish where Bucer would begin his work as a priest. There he enjoyed the protection of Franz von Sickingen, a German knight and admirer of Luther. His new Reformational insights brought other surprising possibilities. In 1522, the evangelical priest married Elisabeth Silbereisen, a former nun. But the young couple was not destined to get much rest in those turbulent days. In fact, they had to flee Landstuhl after only a few months. They considered going to Wittenberg, but they ended up in Weiszenburg, near where Bucer was born. But when his protector was defeated, and the bishop decided to excommunicate him because of his preaching and his marriage, he saw no other choice but to make a nocturnal escape — like that of the apostle — which eventually brought him to Strasbourg.

Reformer in Strasbourg

Bucer started his ministry by giving free tutorials. The city council at first wondered what to do with this excommunicated priest. Nonetheless, they gave him the opportunity to preach, though he was not allowed to do so from the official pulpit. But when Strasbourg chose to fully accept the Reformation, the authorities entrusted the leadership to Bucer, along with Capito.

Although he came from a working-class background, Bucer's learning was far from basic, and his character showed a definite rigor and precision. Capito once called him "our farmer," which may have been inspired by the fact that Bucer received his citizenship in the city of Strasbourg as a member of the guild of gardeners. (Apparently, it was the custom to incorporate a pastor in a particular guild of craftsmen.) In fact, it was quite an evocative thought that Bucer belonged to those who cared for the magnificent vineyards of the Alsace, so that they might produce as much fruit as possible.

Bucer was an amiable man with a very modest nature. When necessary, he denied something for himself for the sake of the church, which he loved more than his own life. At home he was a dedicated husband and father, and his hospitality became proverbial. He embarrassed his second wife by the deep love and intimacy that he showed her. Wibrandis Rosenblat's life (1504-1564) is a story in its own right. She married Bucer after her husband, Bucer's inseparable colleague and friend Capito, died in the same epidemic to which Bucer had lost his beloved first wife. Bucer was Wibrandis's fourth husband: prior to her marriage to Capito, she had been married to two other scholars in Basel, Cellarius and the famous Oecolampadius. Thus she had been the wife of four different Reformers, and she bore them all children. Wibrandis had always shown great respect to her first three husbands, all of whom were much older than she, always addressing them with the formal "thou." But Bucer insisted that she use the informal "you" when speaking to him. He attached great value to the full equality between husband and wife in their matrimonial bond of love and loyalty. Bucer was a true family man, and he loved the children of his wife's previous husbands as if they were his own.

We get a touching picture of Bucer's family life in a personal account by Petrus Martyr Vermigli, a Reformer of Italian descent. He says that Bucer's home resembled an inn a great deal, albeit with great cordiality and order. His table was not extravagant, but sober. God's Word was read during the meal, and there was good conversation. "I have never seen an idle Bucer," Martyr says. If he was not preaching, he was involved in church business. He ensured that the other ministers led the people to the Word of God. He was also keen to lead by example, visiting schools and encouraging the authorities to practice benevolence. After a busy day, he would spend part of the night in study and prayer. "Seldom would I get up without finding him still awake. He would be preparing for the activities of the day or would plead with God for power to do his work." Such was the testimony of a guest in Bucer's home.[5]

5. E. Doumergue, *Calvijn in het Strijdperk* (Kampen, 1986), p. 278.

A Fatherly Friend

The "Bishop of Strasbourg"

In September 1534, an exile from France delivered a letter to Bucer's parsonage. The epistle had been sent by a young Frenchman from Noyon who had only recently experienced a "sudden turn around" toward an obedience to Scripture. The letter was addressed to "Lord Bucer, bishop of Strasbourg."[6] It begins on a remarkably solemn note: "The grace and peace of the Lord be with you, through the mercy of God and the victory of Christ." The sender signed it, "cordially yours, Calvinus." At the age of twenty-five, Calvin had the greatest respect for the Reformer in Strasbourg, who was seventeen years his senior. But this did not prevent him from appealing to Bucer — more or less on an equal basis — on behalf of the bearer of the letter, a poor friend whose identity remains unknown. Calvin asks Bucer to help this Christian brother, who had been forced to flee to Strasbourg and needed a credible recommendation because he had been accused of being an Anabaptist. Calvin's letter would seem to qualify as such, and that in itself is significant. It appears that Bucer had already heard about this promising young convert named Calvin.

It is also noteworthy that Strasbourg seems to have been regarded as a reasonably safe place for people suspected of Anabaptist sympathies, during a time when Anabaptists were rejected by both Roman Catholics and Protestants in every town and region. But they were not as fiercely persecuted in Strasbourg as they were in the Swiss cities. Bucer was totally opposed to Anabaptist teachings, but he tried to convince those adherents through the gospel. Some of them were actually won to the Reformation in Strasbourg. Later, Calvin himself was to marry the widow of a converted Anabaptist in Strasbourg. Bucer recognized that some of the Anabaptists' criticisms of the church were justified. His zeal for church discipline and for a holy life, as well as his attempts to organize small societies of true believers within the church at large (as a kind of "church within the church"), may well point to his recognition of some worthwhile elements in the Anabaptists' criticisms.

6. The date of this letter is still a matter of debate. Herminjard, 3: 201-4, puts the date at 1534. The most recent edition of Calvin's letters prefers 1536: Calvin, *Epistolae*, 1: 128-33.

A Man of the Middle

In January 1538, Calvin once again wrote Bucer a letter, this time from Geneva, where he and Farel had been battling for eighteen months to build the kingdom of Christ in the face of all the resistance it continued to experience.[7] A few months earlier Calvin had indirectly become involved with a synod in Bern, where Lutherans and Zwinglians had been diametrically opposed. The main issue was the doctrine of the Lord's Supper, the sacrament of communion around the body of Christ, which so sadly divided the Reformation. The Lutherans had won, at the expense of the Zwinglians, who had been forced to leave the city. Bucer played a key role, but he failed miserably to effect a reconciliation between the parties, which he passionately desired. In fact, the Zwinglians attributed most of the blame to the "Lutheran" Bucer and heaped bitter accusations on him.

It remains unclear to what extent Calvin was involved in this matter. But there is no doubt that Calvin held a very definite opinion about the way the key persons in this dangerous controversy within the Reformational camp played their role. With all the respect he continued to have for many of Luther's ideas, he was quite negative about Luther as a person. Luther's piety was beyond reproach, but Calvin had a strong dislike for his stubborn and arrogant attitude. However, Calvin also sharply criticized Bucer.

During his entire life Bucer tirelessly attempted to reconcile opposing views. But as a man of the middle he would always run the risk of being hit from both the left and the right. Many have called him an opportunist, a man who wanted to agree with everyone without ever taking a stand, arguing that the diplomat in him too often compromised the Reformer in him. That is an unfair picture, though it is probably true that Bucer remained too optimistic about the differences between Luther and the Swiss. Indeed, Calvin himself, who defended Bucer until the end as a sincere brother in Christ, regretted that Bucer considered the opposing views concerning the real presence of Christ in the emblems of the Eucharist too much as a mere battle of words; and he felt that Bucer gave in too much to Luther. Calvin believed that this was an

---

7. *Epistolae,* 1: 291-304.

important confessional matter that should not be reduced to a mere misunderstanding.

No Other Gospel

In his January 1538 letter to Bucer, Calvin does not hide his strong disagreement with his Strasbourg colleague. Despite the high regard he had for Bucer, and despite the age and experience difference between them, Calvin felt that he had to voice some serious objections. When dealing with controversial issues, he says, Bucer applied the Word of God in such a way as to irritate his readers as little as possible. Calvin had said this before to Bucer's face, but he now puts it in writing. In trying to make the gospel acceptable (plausible) to all, he was in danger of creating a "new gospel." This is a clear allusion to Paul's message to the Galatians, where the apostle condemns those who go down that path.

Calvin gives two examples to illustrate his objections, both of which he takes from earlier Bucer publications, which Calvin might have read while he was still in France. Calvin's sharp words in 1538 may very well be connected to some of his earlier objections to Bucer.[8] In 1534, Calvin changed from being a sympathizer with the evangelical movement in France to a committed Protestant who no longer wanted to live with compromise. Did Calvin detect in Bucer too much of an inclination to let unity take precedence over truth — because of all the suffering that following the truth might entail? Although Calvin never accused Bucer of unacceptable compromises, he paid much closer attention than Bucer did to the parameters of consistent Protestantism.

Via Strasbourg to Europe

It is proof of Bucer's magnanimity that, some months after he received Calvin's sharp reprimands, he decided wholeheartedly to call this critical colleague to Strasbourg — when Calvin was exiled from Geneva. As the pastor of that small church of French refugees in Strasbourg, Calvin

---

8. Cornelis Augustijn, "Bern en France," in *Ordentlich und Fruchtbar,* ed. Wilhelm H. Neuser and Herman J. Selderhuis (Leyden, 1997), pp. 155-69.

was to have the best years of his life. And it was there that Bucer evolved from a respected brother in the service of Christ's kingdom into his "fatherly friend."

From Strasbourg, Calvin also developed his contacts with Germany. The religious disputations that were held in the 1540-41 period were intended to restore the much-needed unity in a Europe that was threatened by Islam and internal confessional strife. Bucer had the key role in this, while Calvin, widely praised for his scholarship and intellectual rigor, served as his lieutenant. In Strasbourg, Calvin also absorbed the European perspective that so consistently inspired Bucer. The latter also helped develop *Calvinus oecumenicus,* the Calvin who wanted to gather the true church of Christ into one fold. We must note, however, that in that ecclesiastical debate Calvin was, from the very beginning, much more critical of Rome than Bucer was. Calvin's most important motivation in getting involved in German affairs was to aid the persecuted churches in France. He hoped that the relationship with the German churches and the political alliances with the king of France would have a favorable result for the Reformation in his own beloved homeland.

In the end, none of Bucer's attempts to promote reunification produced much fruit. The Wittenberg Concord in 1536 — the reconciliation between the Germans and the Swiss — seemed very promising, but Luther was not very impressed. And the attempts to reform the bishopric of Cologne with the help of the archbishop failed miserably. In 1548, as part of the German imperial policies, the reins of the old power tightened significantly. As a result of that tightening, Bucer had to flee to England, where he once again dedicated himself to the work of Christ's kingdom with the strength he had left. But he always felt homesick for Strasbourg, right up to the time of his death, in 1551.

No Calvin without Bucer

Without Bucer, Calvin would never have become the kind of person he was in Geneva. Bucer's observation that Calvin was the right man to lead out in the Reformation in France was correct. He also understood that Geneva, rather than Strasbourg, would be a much better basis from which to operate.[9] During the three years of his daily association with Bucer, Calvin had become so much attached to him that he only wanted to return to Geneva if Bucer would come with him.

Bucer's deepest desire, in his theology and praxis in the church, is expressed on the title page of a pamphlet he wrote in 1523, where he confesses "that man should not live for himself but for others." If Christ is king, we must live for him and for our neighbor. His Word must be first and last in every aspect of the church and society. The Holy Spirit then ensures that this becomes reality in a truly God-fearing life, in accordance with the discipline of the Word. Thus the kingdom of Christ, a central doctrine for Calvin and Bucer, takes on a concrete reality.

Bucer was a theologian of the Holy Spirit: his resulting views had a sound Christological foundation and a clear ecclesiological orientation. In those emphases Calvin could wholeheartedly recognize his own thinking. The way Scripture was to be interpreted, the doctrine of election, the concrete form of the praxis of the church, church discipline, the offices in the church, the emphasis on the *regnum Christi,* the reign of Christ — all these were characteristics of Calvin's Reformation in Geneva that Bucer continued to share. Van 't Spijker expresses this aptly: "Calvinism owes its most characteristic features to Bucer. But Bucer owes it to Calvin that his most essential ideas received the further elaboration, which he had never been able to provide himself."[10] Bucer eventually died as an exile in England, but Calvin was able to give the Reformation in Geneva the kind of concrete form that Bucer had wished for Strasbourg and all of Europe. From Geneva, Calvin's influence, as well as Bucer's, had a worldwide impact on church and society by way of what came to be called "Calvinism."

---

9. Ian Hazlett, "A Pilot Study of Martin Bucer's Relations with France, 1524-1548," in C. Krieger and M. Lienhard, eds., *Martin Bucer and Sixteenth Century Europe,* pp. 511-21.

10. W. van 't Spijker, "The Influence of Bucer on Calvin as Becomes Evident from the Institutes," in van 't Spijker, *John Calvin's Institutes, His Opus Magnum* (Potchefstroom, 1986), pp. 106-32.

PHILIP MELANCHTHON

A Lutheran Friend

Philip Melanchthon

A Lutheran Friend

True Friends?

Oh, Philip Melanchthon, I appeal to you, who is now living in God's bosom, awaiting us until we are gathered for that blessed rest. A hundred times, exhausted from labor and depressed by so many worries, you let your head rest on my breast, and you said, "I wished I could die lying against this breast." Ever since I have wished a thousand times that we would have had the opportunity to live together, for, surely, then you would have had more courage for the inevitable struggle, and you would have been stronger to detest jealousy and to count all accusations as nothing. And thus the animosity of many would have been curtailed. Your friendliness — which they referred to as weakness — encouraged them in their attacks.[1]

This touching outpouring came from Calvin's pen when, a few years after the death of his friend Melanchthon, he was engaged in a tense battle with fierce Lutherans, who were just as vehemently opposed to Calvin's doctrine of the Lord's Supper as were the Swiss Reformers.[2] A person who thus addressed a friend who was already delivered from the "fury of the theologians" into heavenly bliss must have enjoyed a very special bond with him during his earthly pilgrimage.[3] Nonetheless, some questions remain as to how deep this friendship between Calvin and Melanchthon really went.[4] Some have attributed the extreme friendli-

1. *CO* 9: 457.

2. The quotation is from the introduction of his pamphlet against the gnesio-Lutheran Tileman Hesshusen, published in 1561, entitled *Dilucida explicatio sanae doctrinae de vera participatione carnis et sanguinis Christi in sacra Coena, ad discutiendas Heshusii nebulas. CO,* 9: 457-517.

3. Melanchthon himself referred to his wish to die, so that he would at last be delivered from the "rabies theologorum."

4. Remarkably, little attention has been given to the personal relationship between Calvin and Melanchthon, in comparison to other relationships between Reformers. For studies on this theme, see Philipp Schaff, "Calvin and Melanchton," in *History of the Christian Church,* 8: 385-98; James T. Hickman, "The Friendship of Melanchthon and Calvin," *Westminster Theological Journal* 38: 152-65; Wilhelm H. Neuser, "De Versuche Bullingers, Calvin und der Strassburger, Melanchthon zum Fortgang von Wittenberg zu bewegen," in *Heinrich Bullinger 1504-1575, Gesammelte Auf-*

Philip Melanchthon

ness of the tone in their mutual correspondence mostly to the conventions of courtesy that Renaissance scholars were inclined to observe. They suggest that the positive tone should not lead us to think that they were truly kindred spirits: the theological differences were simply too great and the characters too diverse.[5] The only reason that they wished to remain on good terms with each other was the interests they shared as they were faced by common enemies. They were allies in the domain of church politics and could not afford to become estranged from each other. But were they truly friends?

Though it may be true that the two friends were not really "close buddies," the character and tone of their mutual correspondence give us ample reason to believe that their friendship was a sincere personal bond that endured against expectations. The fact that this bond stayed intact until Melanchthon's death, while neither man glossed over their differences and the relationship was often severely tested, offers sufficient cause to place Melanchthon — as probably the only Lutheran — within Calvin's circle of friends.

Luther's Second Man

In 1518 the University of Wittenberg welcomed a new professor of Greek, the twenty-one-year-old Philip Melanchthon.[6] He owed his surname to his great-uncle, the famous humanist Reuchlin, who may have

---

sätze zum 400. Todestag (Zürich, 1975), 2: 35-55; Daniëlle Fischer, "Calvin et la Confession d'Augsburg," in *Calvinus Ecclesiae Genevensis Custos* (Frankfurt am Main, 1984), pp. 245-71, esp. vol. 1: "Calvin et Mélanchthon: une légende à détruire?"; Randall C. Zachman, "Calvin and Melanchthon on the Office of the Evangelical Teacher," in *John Calvin as Teacher, Pastor, and Theologian* (Grand Rapids, 2006), pp. 29-53. For a survey, see also E. Doumergue, *Calvijn in het Strijdperk* (Kampen, 1986), in which the second chapter is entitled "Calvijn en Melanchton" (pp. 431-40); see also M. A. van den Berg, "Calvijn en Melanchton, een beproefde vriendschap," *Theologia Reformata* 41: 78-102, on which this chapter is partially based.

5. For that reason, Daniëlle Fischer calls the friendship between Calvin and Melanchthon "une légende à détruire" (a myth that should be unmasked).

6. On Melanchthon, see Heinz Scheible, *Melanchton: Eine Biographie* (Munich, 1997); Robert Stupperich, *Melanchton* (Berlin, 1960); W. J. Kooiman, *Philippus Melanchton* (Amsterdam, 1963).

felt that Melanchthon's original name, Schwarzerdt ("the black one"), did not befit such a brilliant boy. Already at an early age, Melanchthon showed a great interest in learning and an aptitude for the "modern science" of the new century, in which the languages of the sources of knowledge had become so significant.

Philip was born on February 16, 1497, in Bretten in the Paltz. This was the region of the "black, fertile soil" of his name's origin. His father was George Schwarzerdt, the officer of arms of Philip the Elector, after whom George named his oldest son. It must have been apparent from early on that the young Philip Schwarzerdt was a talented child. At the age of eleven he went to the Latin school of Pforzheim, and a year later he was registered at the University of Heidelberg. Later he moved to Tübingen, where he had earned the master's degree before his seventeenth birthday. His major was in the Greek language and the study of Greek literature and philosophy. Throughout his education the influence of his great-uncle had considerable significance. Unfortunately, Reuchlin did not follow his brilliant nephew in his subsequent choice in favor of the Reformation, and as a result, Melanchthon would not inherit Reuchlin's exquisite library.

In Wittenberg, the theology professor Martin Luther, thirteen years older than Melanchthon, soon perceived what kind of person he was. With a determination that was totally foreign to Melanchthon himself, the reformer put him to work: he asked the young humanist scholar not only to introduce his students to the treasures of the Greek sources, but also to apply his great gifts to the interpretation of Scripture. That Melanchthon was not a theologian posed no problem for Luther. Soon Melanchthon was granted the degree of candidate in theology, and that gave him the official status that allowed him to teach theology. Like Luther, he taught particularly in the area of New Testament theology.

The Reformational Right Hand of Luther

The young Professor Melanchthon, who remained connected with the University of Wittenberg for more than forty years — until his death — would not only become Luther's colleague but also the Reformer of Wittenberg's right-hand man. Luther was deeply impressed by the younger man's extensive knowledge, but he also realized that Philip's personality was better suited than his own for situations that required diplomatic finesse. This explains why Melanchthon was present at the Diet of Augsburg in 1530 to profess the newfound insights regarding the evangelical faith before the emperor and his princes. He was also the one who drafted that confession, which would henceforth be known as the *Confessio Augustana* and would be the foundation of the Lutheran Reformation for the future. During the 1539-1541 period, Melanchthon also served as the chief Lutheran negotiator at the religious disputations of Frankfurt, Worms, and Regensburg (where he encountered the young French theologian John Calvin).

Within the Lutheran camp, Melanchthon was the moderate theologian who did what he could to bridge the gaps between the Reformation camps. At times he would find himself painfully trapped between the sometimes impulsive Luther and other theologians who did not share his opinions. After Luther's death, Melanchthon became the successor who tried to safeguard the Lutheran heritage against the radicalization of Luther's followers, those who were opting for an increasingly uncompromising position against the Swiss Protestants, including Calvin. A year after Luther's death, when the evangelicals had suffered a heavy defeat from the side of the emperor, Melanchthon decided to stay in Wittenberg despite the fact that the Elector Maurice was now in charge. Maurice was regarded by all "real Lutherans" as the "Judas of Meiszen" because he had chosen to support the emperor. By making his choice to remain under Maurice, Melanchthon saw his position and authority undermined during his final years: both friend and foe showed little sympathy for his choice.

Philip Melanchthon's battles were finally over when he died peacefully in his home in Wittenberg on April 19, 1560, after a brief illness. A short letter, in which he listed a few reasons why he did not fear death, was the last thing he wrote: "When you die, you are freed from all sins and cares. At the same time you are liberated from the 'fury of theologians.' You enter into the light and will meet God, and see the Son, and learn wondrous mysteries, which you could not fathom in this life."[7]

7. Scheible, *Melanchton. Eine Biographie,* p. 263.

A Lutheran Friend

Kindred Spirits on the Battlefield

Calvin knew Melanchthon before he had the opportunity to meet him in the flesh, because the latter's name and fame had become well known among the supporters of the evangelical renewal of the church. Luther's spokesperson was often referred to as "Germany's teacher" because he was the source of new insights in the field of education in general, but also in the domain of theology.[8] Melanchthon's most important publication, *Loci Communes,* was a particularly important source of Reformational teachings of faith among the evangelicals. It is a textbook in which Melanchthon expresses the essence of the content of Scripture in a concise form. For all who were only familiar with theology in its scholastic form, this new "dogmatics" of the Reformation was a breath of fresh air and an inspiration, for it taught the people to speak about their faith on the basis of Scripture itself. When he was still in France, in the circle where he received his first impressions of the gospel, the young Calvin had already found himself on the track of Melanchthon's teachings, and he gratefully used them when writing his *Institutes.* Hence, in a sense, Melanchthon stood at the cradle of Calvin as a theologian.[9] It stands to reason that Calvin would have looked forward to an opportunity to personally meet this kindred spirit who was twelve years his senior.

That opportunity came up during the years that Calvin was banned from Geneva and lived in Strasbourg. He was part of Martin Bucer's entourage at the meeting in 1539 that was to prepare for the disputations to be held with a view toward possibly reunifying the divided Christendom in the German empire. In fact, Calvin wrote to Farel that the possibility of meeting Melanchthon was one of the reasons he had decided to accompany Bucer. The principal reason was that he wanted to do his utmost to ensure that the case of his persecuted brothers and sisters in France would be placed on the religio-political agenda. But his second — and no less important — incentive to travel to Frankfurt was the opportunity to discuss matters of faith and church with Melanchthon.[10]

Calvin stayed in Frankfurt only eight days, and he does not say

8. Praeceptor Germaniae.

9. See W. de Greef, *Johannes Calvijn, zijn Werk en Geschriften,* 2nd ed. (Kampen, 2006), p. 254, n. 7.

10. *CO,* 10: 329.

Philip Melanchthon

much about his actual meeting with Melanchthon, but it must have been more or less a matter of "love at first sight."[11] In later correspondence, Calvin regularly appeals to Melanchthon's love, and is sure, he writes, of the pleasures of friendship.[12] Apparently, the few moments of personal encounter were of such spontaneous congeniality that Calvin keeps referring to it throughout the years after 1541, even though the two never actually met again. The impression they made on each other seems to have been completely determined by this one personal contact, which they valued more than whatever extensive correspondence came after it. Calvin was delighted by the fact that Melanchthon wrote him from time to time, but Calvin would have preferred another personal meeting. On November 27, 1554, he writes to Farel: "If only he lived close by. A three-hour talk would exceed a hundred letters."[13] Calvin evidently believed that he would be able to make considerable progress in a personal talk with Melanchthon, and that he could overcome the latter's problem of "wavering" by means of personal encouragement.

Perhaps Calvin had reason to think this because his presence during the colloquium had been partly why Melanchthon had been more determined there than he usually was. In December 1540, during the disputations in Worms, Calvin once again wrote Farel, with whom he most frequently shared his thoughts about Melanchthon, and told him that the latter had been more courageous than ever: his opinion had not changed, but his courage had. "You would be overjoyed, if only you could hear him speak for half an hour," he assures Farel.[14] Without wishing to praise his own contribution to Melanchthon's tenacity, Calvin suggests between the lines that, via his cordial relationship with Melanchthon, he played an important role in his determination.[15]

---

11. The word "amor" regularly occurs in the correspondence, particularly in letters written by Calvin. He refers to his own love for his friend and gratefully assumes that Melanchthon's love endured, in spite of threatening tensions. See Calvin's letters, *CO,* 11: 515-17; *CO,* 14: 414-18; *CO* 15: 280-82; and *CO,* 17: 384-86. It remains uncertain whether this assumption of the reciprocation of his love was too high an expectation.

12. *CO,* 11: 515.

13. *CO,* 15: 321.

14. *CO,* 11: 139.

15. Cornelis Augustijn, "Bern and France," in *Ordenlich und fruchtbar,* ed. Wil-

Melanchthon experienced a second period of personal association with Calvin, in Worms, after he had gone through a deep personal crisis. He had been so embarrassed and worried by the enormous scandal of the bigamy of Philip of Hesse that it had literally made him sick.[16] His illness clearly had all the characteristics of a nervous breakdown.[17] Philip's highly questionable marriage had disastrous results for the Schmalkaldian League, and it turned one of the most important leaders of the evangelical camp into a lame duck: Philip of Hesse became like wax in the hands of the emperor. During those times of severe tension, it must have been a relief and encouragement for Melanchthon to meet a young and promising colleague with whom he hit it off immediately. Such personal and psychological factors are difficult to prove, but they may well have played a role in a relationship that was so cordial from the very first.

Theological Affinity

The question remains: What attracted these two men to each other? First, it probably was the mutual acknowledgment of two brilliant hu-

---

helm H. Neuser and Herman J. Selderhuis (Leyden, 1997), p. 170, believes that in his report of his first encounter with Melanchthon, Calvin considerably exaggerated his own role. It may indeed appear as an overestimation of his own contribution, when the young and as yet virtually unknown pastor from Geneva assigns himself such a central position in influencing the famous second man from Wittenberg. Nonetheless, I believe it is entirely possible that a rather insecure person like Melanchthon — happily surprised by the promising encounter with a new supporter, whom he estimated to be of great future value — felt himself greatly encouraged. And thus Calvin may have contributed to this more decisive way of acting than people had come to expect of Melanchthon. It would seem that Melanchthon had a character that was easily influenced by the fear that he might disappoint people for whom he felt sympathy in personal encounters. As a result he sometimes — unsuccesfully — tried to befriend people who were mutually incompatible. Usually he ended up in a squeeze between the two. Moreover, we cannot exclude the possibility that Calvin's influence on Melanchthon was a factor in his modification of the *Confessio Augustana* in the *Variata,* which made the text acceptable for those who were uneasy about Luther's doctrine of the Lord's Supper.

16. The Elector Philip of Hesse had married a second wife after consultation with Luther. This absolutely illegal bigamy caused him to lose all his credibility. As a result, he could hardly serve any longer as a valuable support for the Protestants.

17. See Kooiman, *Philippus Melanchton,* pp. 150-51.

manist scholars amidst a group of mediocre theologians of various persuasions. One might well speak of an *affinité théologique*.[18] As they dealt with the battle of opinions, they had a mutual understanding of their priorities: the appeal to the sources of Scripture, the respect for the church fathers, and the rejection of the scholastic approach. Calvin repeatedly expressed his great admiration for the simple and transparent character of Melanchthon's reasoning.

Calvin also saw Melanchthon as an exemplary exegete. He mentions his name first in his dedication to Grynaeus of his commentary on Romans. In Calvin's opinion, Melanchthon was an exegete who was able to expound the biblical teachings in a concise and clear manner — without attempting to be exhaustive in his treatment of all details. He did not want to unnecessarily exhaust his readers. Calvin's appreciation was based on his admiration of Melanchthon as biblical teacher and educator.

When Melanchthon finally published his commentary on the book of Daniel — Calvin, full of interest, had already asked him whence the delay[19] — the latter said that no recent book had provided him with more enjoyment.[20] Not only did he value Melanchthon's theological contribution, but the intense piety, along with his impressive erudition, strongly appealed to him. And Calvin not only appreciated Melanchthon's methodology, but also the content of his theology — despite their very real differences.[21] Melanchthon's book occupied a prominent place in the library of the Academy of Geneva.

In 1546, Calvin wrote an introduction to the French edition of Melanchthon's *Loci*.[22] Even though he is critical of certain sections, he

18. Alexandre Ganoczy, *La Bibliothèque de l'Académie de Calvin* (Geneva, 1969), p. 65.

19. *CO*, 11: 516.

20. *CO*, 11: 698.

21. Ganoczy, *La Bibliothèque de l'Académie de Calvin*, p. 65: The deep piety and the systematic thinking of the Wittenberg professor, his extensive erudition, his interest in pedagogy, his frequent use of the patristic tradition, his doctrine of imputative and effective justification, his idea of the "tertius usus legis" (third application of the law), along with his dynamic interpretation, and his view of free access to the Lord's Supper — all this was bound to please the author of the *Institutes*.

22. *CO*, 9: 847-50. It is not clear whether special significance should be attached

A Lutheran Friend

deems it desirable for the Francophone people to be able to get acquainted with Melanchthon's great scholarship. Calvin says that the writings of this author, who "is known and renowned as none other because of his extensive knowledge among scholars," should be available to a broader public.[23] Calvin praises Melanchthon for his "great simplicity," which is the highest virtue when dealing with the doctrine of Christ.

Did Melanchthon cherish a similar appreciation for Calvin's theological contribution? We know less about specifics, because his letters do not provide evidence of anything more than a general appreciation. It would seem that Ganoczy is correct in his assumption that there was a degree of disproportion, though this does not detract from their affinity.[24] Melanchthon says that it pleases him to hear how his younger colleague appreciates his "aspiration for simplicity."[25] And at times he expresses respect and appreciation for Calvin's theological skills. He read Calvin's publications with approval, including for example, the book in which the latter defends the doctrine of the Trinity against the views of Servetus. He differentiated between Calvin and those belligerents who only make inarticulate noise. He wanted to discuss these topics with Calvin: "I would like to speak with you, because I know you love the truth and do not have a spirit that is possessed of animosity or other foolish passions."[26] A few times in the correspondence Melanchton also mentions that he has full confidence in Calvin to come to an independent judgment in the Servetus controversy. But it remains an open question whether, in the matter of the conflict between Calvin and the Lutheran

---

to the fact that Calvin wrote this introduction to the translation of Melanchthon's *Loci* precisely in the year 1546. Calvin emphasizes the need for "nostre nation" to receive this instruction in the Christian teachings. The year 1546 is the year of Luther's death. Did Calvin see this translation as a possible "trait d'union" between Wittenberg and Geneva/France, which might become more feasible, through Melanchthon, after Luther's death? If so, the publication of the *Loci* may have had a significant political dimension. For, in Calvin's estimation, the line from Wittenberg — via Geneva — to France was of the highest importance.

23. *CO*, 9: 847.
24. *CO*, 9: 65.
25. *Corpus Reformatum*, 5: 107 (cited hereafter as *CR*).
26. *CR*, 8: 362.

Westphal about the Lord's Supper, this is courteous praise for Calvin or a clever ploy to avoid being forced to render his own opinion.[27]

A Ponderous Correspondence

Calvin and Melanchthon continued to write each other, but their correspondence was rather ponderous. Only a few letters survive, fourteen from Calvin and eight from Melanchthon (though we should note that it was sometimes difficult to find trustworthy couriers). This is a rather meager collection, especially in comparison with the number of letters Calvin exchanged with other correspondents. Moreover, it is clear that Calvin had a greater anticipation for letters from Melanchthon than the latter put a priority on writing his Genevan brother.

But both reformers were aware of the importance of staying in touch. During the disputation they had discovered that they both were lovers of peace and of the unity of the church: they knew that the more the brethren in the evangelical camp were driven apart, the worse it would be for the furthering of Christ's kingdom. This ecumenical love bound their hearts together. They did have distinct differences: Melanchthon did not share Calvin's view regarding the doctrine of election, and Calvin was worried that the former continued to place too much confidence in human "free will." Given that, it is all the more remarkable that he dedicated his pamphlet against Pighius, who defended the Roman Catholic view of the freedom of the will, to his friend Melanchthon.[28] It is a special way of "expressing criticism" toward a friend: you do not openly attack him because of his wrong opinion; instead, in a positive manner, you "suppose" that it cannot be true that he is of that opinion. Fearing that Melanchthon might deviate from Luther's course on free will, Calvin clearly wanted to remind him to remain a close follower of his great mentor.[29]

27. *CR*, 8: 482.

28. Defension sanae et orthodoxae doctrinae de servitude et liberatione humani arbitrii adversus calumnias Alberti Pighii Campensis, Geneva, 1543, *CO*, 6: 225-404.

29. This is W. Balke's opinion; see "Calvin and the Theological Trends of His Time," in *Calvinus Reformator: His Contribution to Theology, Church, and Society* (Potchefstroom, 1982), pp. 48-68, 60.

A Lutheran Friend

In his letters Calvin constantly tries to move Melanchthon toward a final choice; but he does not treat his diplomatic and somewhat evasive reactions as rejections. He believed that Melanchthon's silence could to some extent be regarded as assent, and that the latter was, in fact, closer to him than he wanted to admit openly. Of course, Melanchthon had his reasons for this. His position was far more difficult than was Calvin's. The Genevan Reformer did not work alongside Luther, who was so whimsical and so easily ignited that Melanchthon at times lost courage. Repeatedly, when, with extreme care and great difficulty, he had succeeded in bridging differences — particularly about the real presence of Christ in the emblems of the Lord's Supper — with theologians whom Luther did not trust, the latter would throw a wrench in the works. In Luther's final years, the quarrels between the two Wittenbergers reached such a level that Melanchthon seriously contemplated leaving. Calvin and the Genevans stood ready to receive him with open arms.[30]

A Precarious Position

Melanchthon did not leave Wittenberg, but it did not become any easier for him there after Luther's death. The die-hards among the Lutherans accused him of being a crypto-Calvinist. And amazingly, Calvin, in his most critical letter to his friend, dated June 19, 1550, expresses the same criticism that Melanchthon had to face from the most passionate anti-Calvinists: Calvin believed that Melanchthon could not credibly remain in Wittenberg while it was ruled by Maurice the Elector, who had betrayed the Schmalkaldian League of the evangelicals. Calvin came to the defense of the Lutherans who had left Wittenberg and continued to resist Maurice (we should note that these were precisely the people who were least sympathetic to Calvin).[31] Clearly, the Reformer of Geneva lived too far from Wittenberg to be able to appreciate the precariousness of Melanchthon's position.

30. See Wilhelm Neuser, "De Versuche Bullingers, Calvins und der Strassburger, Melanchton zum Fortgang von Wittenberg zu bewegen," in *Heinrich Bullinger 1504-1575, Gesammelte Aufsätze zum 400, Todestag*, vol. 2 (Zurich).
31. *CO*, 8: 596.

Philip Melanchthon

Nor did Melanchthon have the courage to act as courier for the only letter Calvin ever wrote to Luther (as far as we know). He feared that Luther would react so adversely that the relationship between them would become even more tense. This may have been a wise precaution on the part of Philip: he could remain in touch with Calvin without risking too many objections from Luther. But it is not clear that Calvin sufficiently understood this.

During the final years of their correspondence, the relationship became ever more tense because of the controversy regarding the Lord's Supper. We find only a few short, plaintive letters from Melanchthon, while Calvin continued his attempts to urge him to fully express his opinion on that subject. But the latter remained completely silent on the point. On October 8, 1558, he wrote his last letter to Calvin (as far as we know), after the attempts in Worms to bring reconciliation between the Wittenbergers and the Swiss had proved futile. Though Melanchthon praises the qualities of the men Calvin had sent to Worms, the letter does not hold out much hope for the future. The case for reconciliation seems to have failed, and thus the only option seemed to be to remain on the battlefield and to direct prayer to "the Son of God, that He may be our Arbitrator."[32]

Calvin's final letter to Melanchthon dates from November 19, 1558. The opening words transcend his irritation regarding Melanchthon's negligence in their correspondence with a quasi-ironic profession of amiable love. Calvin says that, even though Melanchthon would like to offer his negligence in letter-writing to his other friends as a gesture of his love, Calvin has nonetheless decided not to accept this friendly favor. Even though his sickness provides him with an ample excuse not to write, Calvin wants to lay on Melanchthon's breast what so heavily presses on him.[33] Apparently, they have remained brothers — born in distress and remaining in anxiety until the very end. Calvin comforts his friend, who now must experience how his friends, who are so much younger, fight him as their enemies and show no respect for his great merits. Calvin also suffers from their fanatical hostility. How-

32. *CR*, 9: 328-29.
33. *CO*, 17: 384.

A Lutheran Friend

ever, he says, "whatever happens, we will in all honesty maintain the brotherly love among one another, and no satanic guile will be able to break this bond."[34]

This completes the story of a friendship that was severely tested but — certainly from Calvin's side — withstood that test to the very last. The following words by Calvin may give us the ultimate summary of their friendship: "No separation through distance should take away from the fact that we are content with the bond which Christ consecrated through his blood and has enclosed in our hearts through his Spirit, as long as we live on earth, and from the fact that we remain firm in the hope, of which also your letter reminds us, that in the end we will live eternally together in heaven and will there for ever enjoy our love and friendship."[35]

34. *CO*, 17: 386.
35. *CO*, 11: 515.

Philip Melanchthon

IDELETTE VAN BUREN

A Loving Partner

Idelette van Buren

A Loving Partner

Among all friendships that people may have, there is one that has a unique character. It is the unqualified bond between two lives that have become one in body and soul: the partnership of marriage. Calvin had the privilege of experiencing the blessing and joy of marriage, even though it was only for the short period of nine years. The partner-friend whom he received from the hand of God was a widow from Strasbourg whose roots were in the Netherlands: Idelette van Buren.[1]

A Pastor Must Have a Wife

The question remains whether Calvin's wedding plans were primarily inspired by his own desires for a life partner. One cannot escape the impression that his friends and colleagues played a significant role in his plans for matrimony. He once wrote that they suspected he was an enemy of marriage. It was not quite like that, he said, but he was not sure whether he would ever get married. If he would ever take that step, it would be to dedicate himself fully, without any daily chores, to the service of the Lord.[2]

His friends were more than ready to help him take care of his health and to ensure rest and order in his home. And so they also assisted him in the search for a good and dedicated wife. For was it not Scripture that stipulated that it is not good for a man to be alone, and that it is good to have someone as a helper? This would apply in a special sense to a pastor, one who is so fully occupied with his ministry of the Word that the ordinary concerns of daily life should not distract him too much. A good wife would be of great service to him.

In a letter to his friend Farel, Calvin reports, with a degree of reservation, about the progress he has made regarding his plans for matrimony. After being exiled from Geneva, he has at last had some time to

---

1. On Idelette van Buren, see Jules Bonnet, "Idelette de Bure, femme de Calvin," *Bulletin de la Société de l'Histoire du Protestantisme Français* 4 (1856): 636-48; Christian Wolff, "Nouvelles Glanes sur la Famille de l'Idelette Calvin à Strasbourg," *Bulletin de la Société de l'Histoire du Protestantisme Français* (1991/92): 137-38; E. Doumergue, *Calvijn in het Strijdperk* (Kampen, 1986), pp. 364-98; Edna Gerstner, *Idelette* (Grand Rapids, 1963).

2. *CO,* 10/1: 228.

reflect on his personal future. For the first time this bachelor, who is now thirty-one years old, has apparently found the peace and quiet to think about starting a family. A certain candidate has been proposed to him, but Calvin does not, as yet, react as if he is really "in love." He does not give the impression that he is being propelled by passion when he confesses to a friend: "I do not belong to that foolish group of lovers, who are willing to cover even the shortcomings of a woman with kisses, as soon as they have fallen for her external appearance. The only beauty that charms me is that she is virtuous, obedient not arrogant, thrifty, and patient, and that I can expect her to care for my health."[3]

It is no coincidence that Calvin's wedding plans were realized in Strasbourg, and it seems reasonable to suspect that his older colleague and friend Martin Bucer played a key role in the matter. If there was anyone who was enthusiastic about marriage for a pastor, it was he![4] He had been one of the first "married priests," those who translated their newly discovered evangelical freedom into their abandonment of celibacy. He had married his first wife, Elisabeth Silbereisen, as early as 1522. Unlike Calvin, for whom marriage did not come to mind until he had found a measure of rest in his life, Bucer shared the turmoil of his early life as a refugee with his Elisabeth — the "married priest" together with the former nun! But as in the case of Martin Luther, his great examplar, who would also get married three years later, it was a testimony of obedience to God, who had created male and female with a view to the covenant of holy matrimony. In that sense, the marriage of a pastor was also a signal that the power of Rome was no longer to be feared. And it was much more pure than the immoral practices that had been rampant, as members of the clergy were seriously falling short of setting moral standards for the laity.

In addition, Bucer believed that a minister of the Word was hardly able, in his turbulent and often overworked existence, to function well without the help of a faithful companion. In short, Bucer may well be called the founder of the Protestant parsonage.

3. *CO*, 10/2: 348.
4. See H. J. Selderhuis, *Huwelijk en Echtscheiding bij Martin Bucer* (Leyden, 1994), esp. p. 160.

A Loving Partner

At Last, the Choice Is Idelette

The intended marriage of Calvin must have been a high priority on Bucer's agenda, but other friends were also involved. In 1539, during a meeting of Reformational ministers in Frankfurt regarding the upcoming religious disputations in the German empire, Melanchthon broached this sensitive issue during a meal these pastors were sharing. He wondered how the wedding plans of his young friend were progressing.[5] Apparently, even in the midst of all these serious religious matters, the subject of how this promising brother would acquire a life partner was deemed important enough to discuss.

At first, the plans did not seem to go very smoothly. Calvin kept his friend Farel closely informed about the developments.[6] Initially, the focus was on a young girl of noble descent; but Calvin felt uneasy because the dowry would be far beyond his humble state. Her brother was a dedicated follower of Calvin and was very keen on having the beloved preacher take his sister as his bride. But Calvin remained afraid that, in his modest situation, he would not be able to provide her with the kind of life that would befit her pedigree and education. Furthermore, the girl did not speak a word of French, and Calvin knew no German. Therefore, one of the conditions would be that she would learn the language of her future husband. There was some time for further reflection, but Calvin remained hesitant. He found it hard to respond with ingratitude to so much generosity from her family. But it had no future, he wrote Farel, even though he had already more or less invited Farel to the wedding because he very much wanted his beloved brother to conduct the wedding service.

In the meantime, however, he had another iron in the fire. He had asked his brother Antoine and a close friend to investigate whether a different woman might be prepared to become his fiancée. This second woman would not be able to bring much money to the marriage, Calvin writes, but if her reputation proved to be correct, she would bring her character as a "beautiful dowry." But that bridal recruitment also led to nothing.

5. *CO,* 11: 142-44.

6. A. L. Herminjard, *Correspondance des Réformateurs dans las Pays de Langue Française,* 9 vols. (Geneva/Basel/Lyon/Paris, 1878-97), 6: 846 (cited hereafter as Herminjard).

Idelette van Buren

It becomes evident that at that time marriage nearly always was primarily a business arrangement; "being in love" was a state that might develop once the people were married. Calvin's letters show his embarrassment with these matters. He had already invited Farel a few times in vain. At one point he tells his friend that it would be better to wait to come to Strasbourg until it is certain when Calvin will get married.[7] He even expresses his doubt about his own desire to continue the search for a wife. The second young woman did not, in the end, satisfy his expectations, and the family of the first young woman continued to urge him to take that candidate. This uncertainty is still present in a letter dated June 1540. But then we suddenly discover — in a letter dated August 17 of that same year, a letter addressed to Calvin from Fabri — that he is already married![8] It is not to one of the two aforementioned young women, but to Idelette van Buren, a widow whom no one had heard of up to that moment.

A Widow of the Congregation

We can only guess why Calvin decided the issue the way he did. A widow with two children, rather than a young woman, became his life partner. Had he run out of options? That may be a strange question, but it may well have been one that occurred to those who had tried to assist Calvin in handling his marriage proposals. At that time it was considered highly preferable for a man to marry a fairly young woman, even if the groom was not so young anymore. An identical situation came up a few years later, when Calvin got involved in finding a bride for his friend Pierre Viret. At that time, Calvin tried his utmost to convince a young woman from Geneva to become Viret's wife; but she did not want to leave her father. And since the pastor of Lausanne could not simply move to Geneva for the sake of his new wife, those plans for a possible marriage fell through. Viret was disappointed and indicated to Calvin that he would be willing to marry a widow, even though widows were not his preference. "But one does not always get what one would like to

7. Herminjard, p. 868.
8. Letter of Fabri to Calvin, August 17, 1540. *CO*, 11: 75-77.

receive," was his matter-of-fact conclusion. Nonetheless, Viret's marriage to his second wife, Sébastienne, became a happy relationship.

Calvin's choice of the widow Idelette proved to be a great blessing. He knew her because she and her husband and two children belonged to the small church in Strasbourg that he served. Idelette's first husband, Jean Stordeur, had been an Anabaptist from the region of Liège. On the basis of Calvin's preaching and his pastoral care, Stordeur had gladly exchanged his Anabaptist views for the Reformed teachings. This conversion must have led to a special relationship between this family and their pastor, a bond that was further intensified by the way Calvin provided spiritual support when Jean lay on his deathbed.

Did the kindhearted Bucer perhaps surmise that Calvin and Idelette may have had, without realizing it, a spiritual kinship that would in time prove to be such a blessing to their marriage? Could he have been the person who alerted John and Idelette to each other, but with intentions that went beyond merely pastoral concerns? We do not know, but it could well have been the case. In any case, it is clear that, after painfully deliberating for months about two young women whom he had probably not yet met, within a very short time he married a woman he knew well — Idelette.

A Woman from the Netherlands

Idelette van Buren's family was originally from the Netherlands: her surname may point to the town of Buren in the province of Gelderland. She may well have had her roots in that place, but she most likely came to Strasbourg from Liège, as did her first husband, Jean Stordeur. The surname "de Bure" (the French version of van Buren) was known in Liège: in 1533 a person named Lambert de Bure was forced to leave Liège because of his newfound faith. This man was, in all likelihood, the brother of Idelette, and he also would eventually come to live in Strasbourg. It may well be that Idelette and her husband, along with their children, joined their relatives when the persecutions flared up after the Munster debacle — they were in grave danger because of their Anabaptist leanings — and eventually made their way to the relatively tolerant city of Strasbourg.

Idelette van Buren

Jean Stordeur and his family may not have belonged to the extremists among the Anabaptists. In any case, in Strasbourg they became convinced, through the French church's young minister's preaching of the gospel, that the radical views of the Anabaptists were not supported by the Word of God. And thus they became loyal members of Calvin's congregation; he, in turn, must have considered it a blessing to have served as the divine tool to lead erring Anabaptists to the simplicity of the Reformational beliefs.

Jean's death was a heavy blow to Idelette on more than one level. As a skilled cabinet-maker, Jean probably earned enough to adequately provide for his family, though they would have been far from wealthy. Now his widow could expect a pitiful life, and the care for her two small children would be almost too heavy a burden if she would be unable to find a new husband. In a time when death at a young age was an ever-present reality, life was characterized by constant uncertainty, and it was almost a necessity for a widow to remarry. A woman found security in a good husband and a safe home, and this was especially true for a widow with children. Would Calvin be able to provide Idelette with this security?

Mistress of the House

Calvin married Idelette in August of 1540. Her character proved to be just what Calvin had wished for: she was not a woman who wanted to be in the spotlight; rather, her attraction was in her "gentleness and piety." But not only was her inner nature praiseworthy; she also must have been a physically attractive woman. The extroverted Farel expressed his astonishment that she was such a pretty woman! Though she was a couple of years older than Calvin, she had a youthful appearance. From the likenesses and portraits that have been handed down, it appears that she had a somewhat dark complexion. A true Wallonian beauty! As someone whose people came from the southern Netherlands, she would not be too different from Calvin, who was a Picardian from the north of France. In short, it was an alliance full of promise.

The house where she, as the new wife, was going to establish her domain was not a prestigious and spacious parsonage; rather, it was the overfull lodging of a poor preacher. Calvin earned but a meager salary in Strasbourg, and hence had to take in lodgers. In order to make room for Idelette and her two children, he had to send two of those lodgers elsewhere. Calvin and Idelette did not have much time for their honeymoon. About six weeks after their wedding, Calvin wrote to Farel — whom he could tell even the most intimate things — that the Lord had seen to it that he would not be totally absorbed in matrimonial bliss by placing all kinds of family concerns in the way.[9] A fierce argument between the housekeeper and his brother led to an outburst of Calvin's notorious anger, which, in turn, caused him to eat too much and become ill as a result. But whether that was the true reason for his illness remains an open question, for we note that his new wife was laid low by a fever as well. Today we would probably say that the Calvin household was suffering with a bout of the flu. But Calvin saw it as a sign from God's hand telling him to be more humble and restrained in his life, including in his enjoyment of his new married bliss.

Yet even this unburdening to Farel indicates that, from the beginning, Calvin clearly found marriage a special experience of joy. The marriage was more than simply a rational agreement; it became a true and solid bond of love and loyalty. The quiet and patient Idelette was an exceptionally suitable friend-in-marriage. God had given her to him in order to prevent such future outbursts of anger that were a result of the tensions that Calvin saw as obstructions to his calling as a minister of the gospel. It was a great blessing that she became in Strasbourg, during the short period they would continue to live there — and later in Geneva — the mistress of the parsonage.

The Joys and Cares of Married Life
Sharing life in love with another brings additional worries. This was Calvin's experience when he had to travel to Regensburg to attend a theological disputation. He could muster but little enthusiasm for this assignment because of his very limited expectations for it. But he was particularly troubled by the concerns for his new family when he was

9. *CO*, 11: 83-86.

Idelette van Buren

away from home. During his absence the plague hit Strasbourg. Some of his good friends, among them Claude Feray, a dear friend of the family, fell victim to this ever-recurring pestilence. Calvin was deeply worried about Idelette, who had found refuge outside of the city. "Day and night my wife is in my thoughts," he writes, "now that she is deprived of my counsel, and must do without her husband." He was a truly caring and loving husband who wanted to support his wife in these difficult circumstances, and he was thus grateful when he could go back home, which he did even before the debate had officially concluded.

However, this homecoming was an introduction to another move: a return to Geneva had been a possibility for some time, and now it became a fact. Calvin went first, followed soon after by Idelette and her daughter, Judith (the stepson remained in Strasbourg with relatives). In Geneva the living conditions improved considerably for the preacher's family. The city council had provided a beautiful parsonage on the Rue de Chanoines, in the higher part of the city, with a garden and a beautiful view over the lake toward the mountains surrounding Geneva.

A Pastor's Wife in Geneva

Idelette was the modest partner of the most prominent pastor in Geneva. She shared in the concerns and joys that her husband took home with him from his daily practice of ministry. Even though Calvin's position now differed from what it had been during his first tenure in Geneva, he still faced considerable opposition. Supporters from his earlier stay now became staunch opposers, at times ridiculing Calvin because of his strictness. This must have caused much pain to Idelette, who had great respect for her husband. The way she supported him was an important factor in his ability to persevere — despite all the resistance. It was not until about 1555, six years after her death, that the situation in Geneva calmed down: from that time forward, the supporters of Calvin were in the majority on the city council. Before that, Calvin continued to be an awkward stranger for many, a foreigner who was trying to reduce freedom in Geneva far too rigorously. Unfortunately, Idelette did not live to enjoy that later, less stressful period.

As a minister's wife, Idelette was herself actively involved in the pastoral care of the church. For example, while Calvin was visiting the deathbed of an old friend, Ami Porral, Geneva's former mayor, Idelette also came to say her farewell. The dying man sought to encourage her: he said that she had not come to Geneva in vain, but that the Lord had called her to serve the cause of the gospel in this way. Therefore, she ought to be of good courage, whatever might happen. The words of the dying man were a great comfort to his pastor's wife.[10]

Poor Health

Idelette did not enjoy robust health, nor did the children she had with Calvin. It is likely that Idelette and John had three children together. Sadly, two of them died just before or during birth, and the third child, a son named Jacques, lived only briefly. It was a great sorrow for John and Idelette that their love was not blessed with any children who survived birth or childhood. But when Calvin's enemies used this distress as a reason for unholy glee that he would not be survived by any offspring, he found enough courage — in the midst of all his and Idelette's sadness — to respond that he had tens of thousands of spiritual children.

In spite of the good care of her physician, Benoit Textor, to whom Calvin would later dedicate his commentary on 1 Thessalonians,[11] Idelette died on March 29, 1549, after having struggled with her health for years. In her impressive deathbed testimony she spoke of hope and perspective: "O glorious resurrection! God of Abraham and of all our fathers, never has any believer who put his hope on You been disappointed. I also will hope." When Calvin assured her that he would care for her children as a father, she replied that she had already commended them to the Lord.

Following the agony of losing his wife, Calvin was a broken man. Unlike friends such as Bucer and Viret, he never remarried. God's power enabled him to go on, but he would forever miss his wife. His testimony in a letter to Viret[12] is one of the most touching expressions of

10. *CO,* 11: 409.
11. *CO,* 13: 598
12. *CO,* 13: 230-31.

love Calvin has left us, words that will keep alive Idelette's great significance to her husband — and to the entire Reformation: "The best possible life companion has been taken away from me. If something bad would have happened to me, she would gladly have shared exile or poverty with me, and even death. As long as she lived she was my faithful co-laborer in my ministry. She never put the slightest obstacle in my way." What would Calvin's life have been without those nine happy years with a noble and pious wife, even though — humanly speaking — they were far too few?

BENOIT TEXTOR

A Medical Friend

Calvin at approximately fifty years old

Benoit Textor

For a man like Calvin, who suffered throughout the latter decades of his life from numerous serious physical problems, it was a special blessing to have a competent doctor among his friends. His name was Benoit Textor (ca. 1509-1560), and he was one of the two physicians in Geneva (that we know about), both of whom provided special care for the spiritual leader of the city. (After Textor's death, in about 1560, Sarazzin took his place in looking after this important patient with great skill and friendship.) Calvin called Textor his "brother and special friend."[1] And this was more than just a kind gesture, because Textor was one of the rare people to whom Calvin dedicated one of his publications. It was only sparingly that Calvin used that way of showing appreciation; as a rule, the dedications in his books were reserved for those in high places. He dedicated no more than ten to private persons, and those were mostly his teachers and most intimate friends. One of those dedications, however, was to his personal physician.[2]

Calvin dedicated his commentary on 2 Thessalonians to the "excellent man, Benedictus Textor, medicus."[3] This was a token of gratitude for the faithful service Textor provided him and his beloved Idelette during her years of sickness. Textor refused to accept any financial compensation for providing that medical care, says Calvin, which further explains the sentiment Calvin wanted to express — as a "sign of my love" — after the death of his wife.

Textor's concern for his health, Calvin further adds, was not just of a medical nature. In his meticulous medical care and loyalty, Textor was also mindful of the interests of the church. It was a matter of "dual care," Calvin says. It was not only his personal ambitions that prompted Textor to do whatever he could to foster the well-being of his friend, but also the great significance of Calvin's ministry: the proclamation of the gospel. That ministry meant more to Calvin "than [his] life." Apparently, that was also a motivation for his doctor, who was fully committed to the cause of the Reformation. Therefore, besides the professional relationship between doctor and patient, and the friendship between

1. *CO*, 11: 419.
2. Jean François Gilmont, *Jean Calvin et le Livre Imprimé* (Geneva, 1997), pp. 259-61.
3. *CO*, 13: 598.

two people who were fond of each other, it was the fact that they were "brothers" in the Lord's service that bound them together.[4]

A French Physician

We do not know how and where Calvin first met Benoit Textor (Tissier). There is little information available about him, but he must have been a contemporary of Calvin (he was born in 1509 and died in about 1560). He came from the town of Pont de Vaux, in a region in the south of France called La Bresse. It has been suggested that he was of noble birth, but nothing in the way he refers to himself in his correspondence or the way he is addressed by others would support this. The story that, as the personal physician of King Francis I, he had proven to be of great service after the defeat of the French in Pavia in 1524 is very unlikely. In that story the king was said to have heaped great riches and honor on him. But Textor writes in the preface to his first publication that in 1534 he had scarcely completed his studies. If he was twenty-five at that point, he would have had to excel as the royal physician at the age of fifteen. Therefore, that story would seem to be pure phantasy.

The young Benoit probably began his studies in Lyon or Macon, where Éloi de Verger, whom he mentions very respectfully a few times, was his teacher. He subsequently went to Paris to complete his medical studies, where he lived in the home of Jean Tagaut, a professor of medicine. The son of this Jean Tagaut, also named Jean, later fled to Switzerland because of his Reformational convictions. He found his way to Geneva, together with Viret, and he taught philosophy at the newly established Academy. This would give us reason to believe that Textor was part of the same milieu in which Calvin was also well known — the circle of the evangelically oriented humanists. He may have heard about Calvin while still in Paris; he may even have met him there, without having struck up an immediate friendship with him then.

Textor attended the lectures of the famous professor Jaques Dubois, who taught medical science at the College Royal. He must have

4. Alfred Cartier, *Arrêts du Conseil de Genève sut le Fait de l'Imprimerie et de la Librairie* (Geneva, 1893), pp. 121-42.

been a promising student, because he was encouraged by his teacher to prepare a publication on medicinal herbs. This pharmaceutical study was well received and was twice reprinted (in Cologne and Venice), and it was instrumental in gaining some recognition for the young doctor. We know of two other publications by him: a small book on the nature and treatment of cancer in 1550, and a study entitled *Prevention or Protection of the Human Body against the Plague* (1551).[5]

After he had completed his medical studies, Textor moved to Macon, where he started a medical practice. In 1536 he married Jeanne de Quincy, and of their resulting family, three sons deserve special mention. In 1558 his oldest son, Claude, would ask for Calvin's help: he asked the latter to try to convince his father that he should be allowed to complete his studies in mathematics. Father Benoit had demanded that Claude return to Geneva, where the Textor family then lived, to tutor his younger brothers. But Claude wished to continue his studies with professor Tagaut, the son of his father's former landlord in Paris. Father Textor allowed Calvin to persuade him to let the boy have his way.

As it happened, Claude did return home when Tagaut was forced to take refuge in Geneva because of the problems in the church of Lausanne. Subsequently, Claude was to become a famous mathematician in Paris. Vincent, another one of Benoit's sons, wrote a somewhat unusual study, entitled "Tractate about the Nature of Wine." Benoit Textor placed his third son, David, in the care of Nicolas des Gallars, Calvin's personal secretary. When Nicolas became a minister in London, he took David along with him. But young David was not able to settle in England and returned to the Continent to study literature in Paris, contrary to the wishes of his guardian.

We may perhaps conclude from this — particularly from the fact that the son appealed to Calvin to help make his father change his mind — that the senior Textor did not have a flexible personality. Calvin wrote to his friends that he knew that Textor's attitude was somewhat surly and that he was somewhat hard to deal with; but this in no way de-

---

5. Bernard Textor, *De la Manière de Preserver de la Pestilence & de Guérir, selons les bons* (Lyon, 1551).

A Medical Friend

tracted from Calvin's appreciation of and friendship with him. One simply had to put up with this trait in "this good man," since his extreme dedication to the care of his patients was beyond any doubt.[6]

A Dedicated Family Doctor of the Reformation

Textor must have had a rather restless life. He traveled a great deal, as he was called upon by various cities because of his medical expertise. He stayed for some time in Neuchâtel, found a home for a period in Lausanne, lived for a number of years in Geneva, and also returned from time to time to Macon. We are certain that he lived in Geneva in 1546, because the minutes of the Consistory tell us that his wife was called as a witness in a disciplinary trial.[7] It appears that he officially remained a citizen of Geneva, where he was valued highly as a physician, until his death. Calvin was a grateful recipient of his services, and the extraordinary way Textor assisted Idelette until her very last moments certainly intensified their friendship.

Textor was sometimes called to minister to patients outside of the city of Geneva. Among others, he treated Viret's wife, who, in spite of optimal medical care, would die in 1546. Further proof of the intensity of his dedication can be found in Calvin's letters: when a rumor swept through Geneva that it was Viret who had died instead of his wife, "Textor drove like a madman" to Orbe, where the misfortune was said to have taken place.[8] It was rumored that poison was involved, and Textor believed that, because of his considerable pharmaceutical knowledge, he might be able to administer an antidote. His dedication went beyond his care for a valued friend; he wanted to do all he could to save one of the Lord's instruments to build his church.

In one of his letters to Calvin, Textor mentions the fact that some of his opponents had accused him of false zeal in the care of his patients. His dedication supposedly resulted from love of money. *Coram Domino* ("before the Lord"), he absolutely rejects this accusation, and

6. *CO*, 12: 390-92.

7. R. M. Kingston and J. F. Bergier, eds., *Registres du Consistoire de Genève au temps de Calvin* (Geneva, 1962), 2 (1545-1546): 297.

8. *CO*, 12: 305-6.

Benoit Textor

Calvin likewise will not hear of it.[9] After Textor's death, Calvin wrote that his friend was so dedicated to his patients that sometimes he even neglected his own family, with the result that his children had to be satisfied with just a meager inheritance. "Alas, I wished the good man had listened to our advice," Calvin writes, and had paid more attention to himself and his family. Not only did the doctor worry about the pastor, but the reverse was also true.[10]

Written Consultation

Calvin was, particularly during the last twenty years of his active service, constantly battling a number of ailments. It is almost incredible that he could accomplish so much despite his poor health. The letter he wrote a few months before his death in 1564 to a few doctors in Montpellier is well known.[11] Without Calvin's knowledge, his physician Sarazzin had shared his grave concerns about his sick patient with his colleagues. Calvin wanted to know from his doctor why he had done this without telling him. Sarazzin replied that this had been at the express request of the physicians of Montpellier, who wished to do everything they could to contribute toward saving Calvin's life. The life of the pioneer of the Reformation was very dear to them.

Calvin was touched and very grateful. But in his letter he, in turn, asks them to take from his writings the spiritual medicine that he offers in them. Then he provides an extensive report of his many physical challenges. Twenty years earlier, some Parisian doctors had already helped him with their advice regarding his physical condition. But at that time he was not yet disturbed by his problems with gout. "I did not yet suffer from kidney stones and gravel. I was not yet encumbered by intestinal cramps or hemorrhoids, nor did I have to fear a sudden coughing up of blood. All these enemies have joined in a united attack, one after the other."

9. A. L. Herminjard, *Correspondance des Réformateurs dans las Pays de Langue Française,* 9 vols. (Geneva/Basel/Lyon/Paris, 1878-97), p. 1190 (cited hereafter as Herminjard).

10. Letter to Gallasius. *CO,* 18: 505.

11. *CO,* 20: 252-54.

This letter led Charles L. Cooke, an English physician, to attempt a professional diagnosis.[12] He concluded that Calvin suffered from gout, kidney stones, chronic lung tuberculosis, intestinal parasites, seriously inflamed hemorrhoids, spastic intestines, and migraines. It was a composite of illnesses that, among other things, were also related to his unhealthy lifestyle as a "workaholic." He was truly wasted away when he died in 1564, not yet fifty-five years old, probably from blood poisoning caused by infections, possibly combined with kidney failure. Dr. Cooke indicates that the fact that he died peacefully conforms to the way people who suffer from "septic shock" die.

There has been the question of why Calvin traveled so little during his final years (for example, he left all matters in France to his representatives). He never again visited the country of his birth, even when it might have been relatively safe. His only travels were occasional trips around Geneva, and, of course, the people of Geneva could not do without him. But it had also become physically impossible for him to travel because of his poor health. There had been a time when he could travel on horseback for several days. But how could he do that now, with painfully infected hemorrhoids and a terrible headache?

Twenty Years Earlier

However, it had been twenty years earlier when Textor wrote his introductory letter in 1542. At that time the army of ailments had not yet assaulted Calvin; rather, his concerns about his wife were what stimulated his search for the best doctors. We do not know whether Calvin approached Textor directly or whether others informed the doctor, but we can read in Textor's letter that he would gladly travel from Macon to Geneva to do whatever he could to improve Idelette's health. Yet he is perhaps overly apologetic when he adds that Calvin should not think that any danger or high travel expense would keep him from coming. He was aware that some might accuse him of not daring to go to Geneva because of the

---

12. Charles L. Cooke, "Calvin's Illnesses and Their Relation to Christian Vocation," in *John Calvin and the Church*, ed. Timothy George (Louisville: Westminster John Knox, 1990).

Benoit Textor

plague, which had just erupted in the city. But he strongly denies that he lacks the courage; if necessary, he says, he will risk his life. But he also has to think of his other responsibilities, for example, the care of his own wife and children, and there are so many more who need his help. And might there be still greater things waiting for the honor of God?

It is possible that Idelette's condition was not so critical that Textor needed to come hastily. Since he was an expert on the subject of the plague, he may also have thought that it was of little use to come from afar when the plague had broken out. In any case, Textor moved to Geneva not long after writing this letter. Even though he frequently returned to Macon — he sent Calvin letters from there in 1544 and 1546 — Geneva remained his home until his death, and he became the personal physician of the Calvin family. This explains why there are not many other letters between the doctor and the pastor, because the two had plenty of opportunity to speak face to face. Calvin was very content with his doctor and often recommended him to his friends.

A Mysterious Matter

After the death of Elisabeth Viret, there was a mysterious happening in Geneva involving Textor.[13] In 1551, the printer Jean Girard went to the magistrate requesting permission to print a small book written by "Hector" (a pseudonym frequently used by the doctor), entitled *The testament and the death of the wife of Pierre Viret.* But the printer was unable to get the necessary approval to print the booklet: the authorities deemed it devoid of any religious relevance. Any further motivation for that denial of approval — as well as the contents of the book — remain unknown. But when the printer disobeyed the authorities and insisted on printing the book, he was immediately arrested. (He was freed within twenty-four hours, after Calvin personally contacted the council to plead for him.) The widower, Pierre Viret, did not get involved in the matter; he had to make it clear that he had nothing to do with the disobedience of the printer. But nothing was said about the author, Textor.

13. Alfred Cartier, *Arrêts du Conseil de Genève sur le fait de l'imprimerie et de la librairie* (Geneva, 1893), pp. 126-32.

A Medical Friend

Was this no more than an attempt on the part of the authorities to harass Calvin's friends? In the years prior to the change of power in 1555, the majority of council members were quite hostile toward Calvin and his circle. Apparently, they considered it unnecessary to spread the blessed deathbed testimony of the wife of Calvin's best friend throughout Geneva, and thus they denied the request to print the book. Calvin's involvement can be seen in his successfully securing from the council the release of the printer. But the matter remains mysterious: it seems very unlikely that the book was defamatory and that Viret would thus have sought to prevent its publication in Geneva.[14] Textor was such a close friend of Calvin and his wife that it is most likely that Viret and Calvin would have fully supported Textor in circulating his spiritual report of Mrs. Viret's death.

A Spiritual Physician

This portrayal of Textor has shown that he was not just interested in writing about physical ailments. He was a positive example of what Calvin expected of his doctors: that they would partake as students of the "spiritual medication" of the Word of God. And Textor himself was also known as the author of spiritual writings, for example, a little book on the Christian faith that he had printed in 1551. And even his medical publications contained a spiritual emphasis. One can clearly recognize him as a follower of Calvin in the dedication (to Jean de Tyard, the lord of Byssi) at the beginning of his study of the plague. Textor wishes to emphasize that the plague is, among all other evils, a clear sign of divine wrath. It is a righteous judgment on the sins and injustices that cause havoc in the entire world. "Therefore, this sickness, together with famine, war and other tokens of divine wrath, are the temporal reward for man's self-centeredness and his denial and rejection of God and his Word."[15] There

14. As Robert D. Linden, unjustifiably, proposes in his *The Political Ideas of Pierre Viret* (Geneva, 1964), p. 132.

15. "Donques ceste maladie, comme assi famine, guerre et autres vengeances de Dieu, est un salaire temporel du contennement, du reitettement & du renoncement de Dieu et sa Parole." Precaution A, preface by Bernard Textor, *De la Manière de Préserver de la Pestilence.*

follows an extensive list of all kinds of sins that evoke God's righteous wrath. Textor opposes a purely natural explanation for the plague. God's hand is visible in this ever-recurring pestilence, because nothing happens by chance. It is not "Madame Fortune" who decides who will be affected and who will not.

God's children are not always spared from this plague. But when those children are killed by the plague, we may say that God has delivered his own out of this life to his glory. This approach reminds us of what Calvin once wrote to Madam de Coligny: "Illnesses serve us as medicine, to purify us from the desires of this world and to cut away what is superfluous in us. They are messengers of death and they can teach us to free our feet so that we can depart from this life, whenever it pleases God."[16]

Yet Textor remains enough of a physician to write an entire book on what people can do to defend themselves against the plague. Should we then not simply submit to God's providential ways and let the plague do what it wants? No, says Textor, because it would be tempting God not to use the means he has put at our disposal to use for our good. We may seek protection and healing by humbling ourselves before God, confessing our sins, and using the means he has provided to us, as a loving God, who not only guides and directs the sickness but also works through the medicines. Here we can clearly perceive the student of Calvin coming through.

16. *CO*, 20: 129-30.

ANTOINE CAUVIN

A Brother and Friend

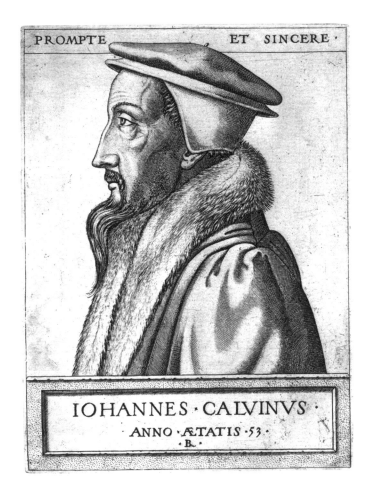

PROMPTE   ET SINCERE ·

IOHANNES · CALVINVS ·
ANNO · ÆTATIS · 53 ·
· B ·

Calvin at age fifty-three

Antoine Cauvin

Calvin lived the greatest part of his life in a foreign country. Far from his Noyon birthplace and the environment where he felt at home, his home became a Swiss border city where he would remain a foreigner — not being granted Geneva citizenship — until five years before his death. His departure from France was somewhat like that of Abraham from Ur of the Chaldees: he did not know where he would eventually go. His plan was certainly not to seek out Geneva as his permanent place of residence, but that was the place to which God directed him.

But, like Abraham, Calvin would not be without relatives. His younger brother Antoine (ca. 1511-1573) was his inseparable companion during the entire period of his "exile." Everywhere John set up a household we also find Antoine serving him as his right-hand man. A blood tie is not in itself, of course, a guarantee of kinship of spirit; but a very close friendship developed between these two brothers. With reason, Doumergue called Antoine Cauvin "Calvin's most intimate friend."[1]

A Family from Noyon

The continued presence in his life of his brother Antoine was a constant reminder for Calvin of his French family name, Cauvin, which he, like all academics of those days, had Latinized to Calvinus. Though he was driven from hearth and home, Calvin still had someone with whom he could share the experiences of his childhood years throughout his whole life. Those memories were warm but also must have been filled with sadness about the early loss of their beloved mother. Calvin was only six years old when his mother died, but the impression of that huge loss undoubtedly remained with him for life. His brother Antoine, younger than John by a couple years, probably had but scant recollections of their mother, if any.

Charles (?-1537), the oldest son of Gérard Cauvin and Jeanne Le Franc, stayed in Noyon his whole life and became the priest of Roupy. After serious problems with the church authorities, however, he was excommunicated. He may well have had something of the same flammable nature that at times afflicted Calvin, but he was apparently less able

1. E. Doumergue, *Calvijn en Genève* (Kampen, 1986), p. 421.

to control himself. The story is told that he once hit a clerk in the face. There must have been more to it than that, however, because he was also suspected of heresy: he had caused "annoyance" while speaking of the sacraments. Whether he acted out of a genuine Reformational conviction remains unclear. Unlike Antoine, he did not follow his brother John into exile. But when he died in 1537, he refused the sacrament of the dying, so he was buried in a dishonorable manner, "under the gallows."

In addition to these two brothers and François, who died early, Calvin had two half sisters from his father's second marriage. We know the name of one of them, Marie; other than that, we only know that, like Antoine, she accompanied her brother into exile. But not even that is completely certain.[2] The only time we find her mentioned in the sources is in a letter Calvin wrote in 1532 to his friend François Daniel in Orléans: he ends that letter with the request that Daniel share this letter with his "sister Marie Paludanae." She must have been living near Orléans at that point and was married to a certain Paludanus. We do not know her husband's occupation, but Paludanus was not an uncommon name. We know of artists with that name in the southern Netherlands and in the north of France. A famous dictionary that was circulating in many cities at that time (including Strasbourg and Geneva) was commonly referred to as the "Paludanus," after its author. In addition, a family of sixteenth-century Dutch ministers bore this name.[3] But we can only guess whether these Paludani from the Low Countries were relatives of Calvin's sister.

A Critical Family

Gérard Cauvin's sons did not get their critical attitude toward ecclesiastical authorities from any stranger. Their father was an assertive citizen, a man of the law with a commendable civil and ecclesiastical career. He had more difficulty dealing with the latter category than with the former. As the solicitor of the chapter of the cathedral of Noyon, he got into

2. Calvin, *Epistolae*, 6. 1: 56, n. 4.
3. Since Reformation times, the second minister in the Dutch city of Zoetermeer (near The Hague) has this title.

Antoine Cauvin

such controversies with his ecclesiastical bosses that he was placed under a ban. One cannot escape the conclusion that Gérard had a strong sense of justice that made it impossible for him to assent to dishonest practices.

Having a critical attitude toward church authorities was not without risk, because, besides the citizens' spiritual dependence on the church, there was also a social and financial aspect. By losing the favor of his church employers, Gérard could well play havoc with the future of his sons. From early on, they were dependent on pastoral positions, slots that they were granted because of the corruption in the system. The Cauvin family fully availed themselves of this dubious system to use spiritual appointments as a source of income. For instance, John Calvin himself had already received a position as priest at the age of twelve — a position that he was never actually to assume. This functioned as something like a study stipend: he was only concerned about the revenue and never showed the least bit of interest in actually serving as a priest. He allowed his brother Antoine to take his place as a chaplain. This was apparently the way things were done in the Cauvin family until the light of the Reformation broke through.

Gérard Cauvin died on May 26, 1531. Since the reason he had been "banned" was largely financial, his oldest son, Charles, was able to make a settlement to ensure that father could be buried in consecrated earth. He was thus able to arrange for his father what would not be possible for himself six years later. On February 14, 1532, the brothers Jean and Antoine Cauvin were in Paris; Jean (John) was now a law graduate and Antoine might be listed as a member of the clergy. They visited an attorney to arrange for the authorization that would enable their brother Charles to finalize matters regarding the family inheritance in Noyon. Did the two brothers simply agree to meet in central Paris for this occasion to deal with their business matters, or was Antoine already John's constant companion who had by now left Orléans to continue his studies in Paris? In any case, this occasion points to a cordial fraternal relationship. Antoine, no doubt, had respect for Calvin's legal expertise; without any problems they together entrusted the matter to Charles, their older brother. It is clear that Cauvin's sons got on well together, and they shared the inheritance harmoniously.

A Brother and Friend

The Exile

Four years later, after many wanderings, the two brothers once again met in Paris. This time their meeting was not about the distribution of their patrimony, their father's inheritance, but about their preparations to leave the *patria* — the fatherland — for good. In the spring of 1536, Calvin was suddenly forced to end his stay at the court of Ferrara because of the persecutions against the sympathizers of the Reformation there. He now understood that it would be impossible for anyone who openly supported the principles of the Reformation to stay in France. Since it had become clear to him that his calling in life would henceforth be to serve the gospel, he decided that he would have to leave his beloved France. He hoped to be able find a place in Basel or Strasbourg where he could study and write; and he hoped that he could serve the church in France from his Swiss exile.

Did Calvin find it difficult to leave his home country? Many years later, in 1561, he begins a letter to his persecuted compatriots in France, which was published as a preface to his lectures on Daniel, with these words: "Even though I have now been absent, without any remorse, from my land of birth, which I have in common with you, and which has such an attractive climate that it attracts many foreigners from the farthest corners of the earth, it does in no way seem pleasant or desirable to live in a region where the truth of God, the pure religion and the teaching of eternal salvation have been banned, and the kingdom of Christ has been struck down! For that reason I have no desire to return."[4] The question — which Calvin himself could no longer answer — was whether, deep in his heart, he continued to miss his native country. There is no doubt that, even as he continued to live in a foreign country, Calvin remained a real Frenchman.

Taking advantage of a temporal relaxation of the stringent measures against the reform-minded, Calvin did visit France only once more. We do not know whether he went to Noyon, but official documents show that he was in Paris to make some arrangements regarding his earthly possessions. But more important than money was the fact that he succeeded in convincing the members of his family — and

4. *CO,* 18: 615.

Antoine Cauvin

possibly Marie (with her husband?) — to join him on the uncertain path of exile.

An Unexpected Place of Exile

It had never been Calvin's intention to go to Geneva, but the most direct route to Strasbourg was too dangerous due to the war situation. Therefore, a detour via Geneva was necessary, and that is when and where Calvin was "arrested" by Farel for the cause of the gospel. This also meant that Antoine was to stay in a city that had never entered *his* mind. From the very first, it was clear what his older brother would do: he would teach from Scripture in order to foster the Reformation that was still in its infancy. Antoine later reported that he found the calling for his life in quite a different arena. Among other things, he became a book publisher, and he also kept busy with various orders and commissions that often came from his increasingly important brother, but at times also from the city.

One wonders why Antoine did not also become a minister of the gospel, for he was a priest when he left France. It would be safe to assume that he had embraced a wholehearted choice for the Reformation, which had led him to decide to join his brother. If so, would it not have been natural for Antoine to continue to serve the church as a converted priest? Especially since there was a serious shortage of preachers at that time. Yet there is no indication whatsoever that his thoughts or aspirations ever went in that direction. The only church office Antoine was to accept in later years was that of deacon.

During John Calvin's first period in Geneva, his brother Antoine stayed with him and assisted him with his daily tasks. When Calvin was banned from Geneva after two tumultuous years, Antoine remained there for a while — more or less as his brother's representative. This we learn from a letter Calvin sent to Thomas Grynaeus, in which he urgently demands a chest containing personal possessions that he needed on a daily basis.[5] (Apparently, Antoine had first sent it to a friend in Bern, with the request to forward it to Basel.) As soon as

5. *Epistolae*, 1: 415-16.

A Brother and Friend

Calvin had found a permanent abode in Strasbourg, Antoine joined him again.

The Parsonage of Strasbourg

Upon Calvin's marriage to Idelette van Buren in 1540, Antoine remained part of the household — indeed, an integral part of the family — as he had been before. During Calvin's extended periods of absence, it put him at ease that Antoine, together with another family friend, Clause Ferray, looked after his wife and the running of the home. Antoine was also a good substitute for his brother in the pastoral care of sick people, who were rather numerous in the city because of the recurrent epidemics.

A strange incident in the Strasbourg parsonage, which Calvin tells Farel about in a letter, reveals how Antoine's personality differed sharply from John's.[6] In the early days of his marriage, Calvin's parsonage was rather overpopulated because financial constraints had forced him to take in several lodgers. The result was not much private family life. Among the people who lived under his roof were a French woman and her son. This woman was not able to control her temper or her tongue, and she would often blow her top at other inhabitants of a house that was far too small. At one point, yet another instance of this person's verbal abuse was too much for Antoine. He did not react to the abuse in person; he simply left the house without giving any notice. When his brother asked for the reason for his departure, he was adamant that he would not return as long as this woman remained in the house. This was an intolerable thought to Calvin: he absolutely did not want his brother to disappear from his house. He apparently made that clear to the French woman, who then drew her own conclusion and left the house. But her son stayed, and Calvin did his utmost not to show his irritation toward the boy. But this is where his personality differed from Antoine's: John could not hide his irritation and anger. He had become so enraged that he ate more during the meals than his weak stomach could endure, and the result was that he was sick the next day. So why

6. *CO,* 11: 238.

Antoine Cauvin

did Calvin overeat? It was his effort not to show the son how much his mother had angered him; that would have been obvious had he stayed away from the meal. His attempt to control himself thus had a reverse effect. The impression remains that Antoine did indeed have a greater equilibrium of personality.

Back to Geneva Together

Calvin was called back to Geneva in 1541. He came back alone, with his family to follow later. Antoine proved once again to be the loyal family aide. After a few months he moved Idelette, along with her daughter, Judith, and their meager possessions, from Strasbourg back to Geneva. This time Calvin had received a good and spacious house from the city authorities, who were happy to have their minister back from his exile. So there was space for Antoine to continue living with his brother. Somewhat later, when he started his own family, he moved into the house next door to his brother's.

What would Antoine do in Geneva? The French fugitives were involved in the economy of the city in all kinds of ways. Some noblemen became craftsmen and went into business. Antoine became a publisher and bookseller of, among other publications, his brother's books. But he was also involved in other lines of commerce. At times, for example, the city fathers sent him to Germany to buy wheat. Yet, in spite of all the things he did to earn a living, he remained first and foremost his brother's alter ego. He not only assisted Calvin as his personal secretary; he also represented Calvin in the trial of Servetus. He remained ever the faithful brother whose continued presence must have meant a great deal of support to Calvin — more than the historical sources seem to reveal.

The city council understood how important Antoine was to his brother. He was declared a citizen of the city in 1546, much sooner than other French refugees were. And unlike others, he did not have to pay for it, because "Monsieur Jehan Calvin, minister in Geneva, greatly exerts himself for the furtherance of the Word of God in the city and for maintaining the city's honor."[7] Antoine was thus rewarded for the es-

---

7. Doumergue, *Calvijn en Genève*, p. 422.

teem in which his brother was held. Calvin himself would not receive his own citizenship in the city in which he lived for more than half of his life until 1559. The occasional suggestion that for a long time the city council did not want to offer Calvin citizenship is based on a misunderstanding. Prior to the Reformation, it was not the custom to extend citizenship to members of the clergy because they belonged, in final analysis, to a different *civitas.* Could it be that the continued influence of this pre-Reformational mode of thinking was the reason it took so many years for Calvin, the minister of the city, to receive citizenship? Or had it been offered to Calvin at some earlier date, and he had declined to become a citizen until the year his most important spiritual child was born? That was the Academy of Geneva, the institute where servants of the Word who would advance the kingdom of Christ in France were to be trained.

Antoine had served the church and the city in various capacities. As one of the deacons, he was responsible for the so-called Bourse Française, a fund established by the diaconate to assist poor refugees from France.[8] Toward the end of his life he also held a few civil positions: he was a member of the council of two hundred, as well as of the council of sixty. Therefore, he was in all respects well integrated into Geneva.

A Tragic Marriage

Unfortunately, the last aspect of Antoine's life that needs to be mentioned is the tragic history of his marriage.[9] Antoine married the daughter of a businessman from the southern region of the Netherlands who had sought refuge in Geneva. Her name was Anne le Fert, and she brought much reproach on the family of the Reformer by her adulterous conduct. Although she never admitted that she actually committed adultery — not even when the thumbscrews were used on her — the indications of her licentious behavior were so numerous that a second ac-

8. Jeannine E. Olson, *Calvin and Social Welfare: Deacons and the Bourse Française* (London/Toronto, 1989), p. 64.

9. Robert M. Kingdon, *Adultery and Divorce in Calvin's Geneva* (Cambridge, MA / London, 1995), pp. 71-97.

cusation was followed by an official divorce. She was said to have misbe-
haved with a young citizen of Geneva, who, it was reported, visited her
bedroom in the middle of the night. The latter confessed to the assigna-
tion but said that Anne had definitely refused to let things go as far as
full-fledged adultery. Her unfaithfulness was forgiven. Nine years later,
however, Anne was reported to have committed adultery with a certain
Daguet, an unreliable servant of Calvin known as "the Humpback." The
fact that Anne was so keen on other men that she even got involved with
a misshapen servant made the charge even more serious. This time
there was no more clemency, and there is reason to believe that it was
now Calvin himself who did everything he could to effect the divorce.
The unfaithful Anne was sent into exile; but she was immediately
joined by a young man from Geneva, who accompanied her into exile.
In other words, she was a real femme fatale, and she differed radically
from Antoine in temperament. After her departure, Antoine was able to
remarry — this time to the widow of a pastor.

This marriage tragedy had its consequences for even the sons of
Antoine and Anne, Samuel and David, who received only a small portion of the inheritance in the last wills of their Uncle John and their father, Antoine — because they appear not to have followed in the path of
godliness.[10] This pathway may have been caused, at least in part, by the
trauma of their parents' broken marriage.

Thus the extended family in Calvin's house was not only a cause
for joy; sometimes there was the other side, the side of worry and sadness, which had a major impact on Calvin. (When his stepdaughter, Judith, also proved unfaithful in her marriage, Calvin was so distressed
that he withdrew for some days to his brother's cottage.) But Antoine, in
his modesty and gentleness, in being the family member who was always there, must have been invaluable — more than the historical
sources are able to tell us — not only as Calvin's brother but also as his
most intimate friend.

10. Olson, *Calvin and Social Welfare*, p. 242.

A Brother and Friend

LAURENT DE NORMANDIE

A Friend from the Same Birthplace

Laurent de Normandie

On July 10, 1550, as a rare honor, Calvin dedicated one of his publications, the *Treatise on Scandals,* to a good friend.[1] The date is noteworthy because it is his own birthday, his forty-first. Rather than receiving a gift, the one who is celebrating his birthday gave something to his "truly beloved brother," Laurent de Normandie (1510-1569).

It appears as though Calvin consciously chose this date to dedicate his book, for Laurent also came from Noyon (he had arrived a few years earlier), and, like Calvin, he had come to Geneva as a refugee. Was the presence of a friend from his own birthplace so special to Calvin that he chose his own birthday as the date for this dedication? May it have been his way of telling de Normandie how much he was a living gift — not because he was just any friend, but a friend from the same hometown?

Refugees from Noyon

In the years of the fiercest persecutions of the Reformation, the arrival in Geneva of refugees from France must have been an almost daily spectacle. Yet the group that entered the city gates on a certain day in August 1548, after a long and dangerous journey, must have captured Calvin's immediate attention. For these people were not just any French refugees: they had fled from Noyon, his hometown. The mayor himself, Laurent de Normandie, with his family and friends, had finally decided they could no longer endure the situation in France, despite their high and influential position in Noyon. He placed greater value on the freedom to live in good conscience in conformity with the gospel than on the honor and glory that could have been his in his own country had he simply submitted to the demands of the authorities.

Calvin felt a close involvement with his friend, whom he had known from his early youth. And there was a good reason why he dedicated his *Treatise on Scandals* to Laurent.[2] This polemic is a passionate defense against all the accusations that had been advanced against the

1. John Calvin, *Des Scandales,* ed. Olivier Fatio (Geneva, 1984).
2. W. de Greef, *Johannes Calvijn, zijn Werk en Geschriften,* 2nd ed. (Kampen, 2006), pp. 184-85.

A Friend from the Same Birthplace

155

evangelical Reformation, both by the humanists and by those from Roman Catholic circles. Calvin intended it to provide believers who were in the midst of the fiery furnace of the persecutions with arguments to defend themselves against the libel that was showered on them, accusations that the gospel of Christ would lead to unrest and disorder. The treatise also reflects the situation in which Laurent had found himself before he eventually had to flee to Geneva.

Calvin's dedication served as a "refugee mirror": what so many had to experience becomes visible in the fate of de Normandie. Laurent's father had died four months after the escape from Noyon to Geneva, and Calvin remembers how he himself had been charged to bear this sad news to the family. Then Laurent was even scolded as the "murderer" of his own father. Calvin comforts him by saying that his situation is like Abraham's: he was also reviled for having caused the death of his father by bringing him along from Ur. And Calvin says that Laurent should regard the privilege of sharing in the insults directed at Abraham as a God-given honor.

More Than Conquerors

But the death of his father did not prove to be the highest price de Normandie had to pay for his flight from Noyon. Not long after his arrival in Geneva, his wife, Anne de la Vacquerie, and their little daughter died, taken from him in the prime of their lives. In his dedication, Calvin has not forgotten how dejected his friend felt and what temptation this might mean for him. For was this the price one had to pay if one wanted to be obedient to the gospel? Nonetheless, the death of Laurent's dear Anne was to be — for Laurent as well as for his friend John — the opposite of discouragement. They experienced it as proof that, in the midst of all trial and tribulation, they could be "more than conquerors" in Christ. Anne's testimony on her deathbed was the undeniable evidence that their faith decision to prefer the life of a refugee over the miserable certainty of the home country had been the correct one to make.

Calvin ministered to her as she lay dying, and he later remembered how she took his hand and thanked God for having brought her

Laurent de Normandie

to a place where she could die in peace. The story of her deathbed is a touching testimony to the assurance of faith. Calvin wrote to Madame de Cany, a noblewoman from Noyon, to tell her how Anne, until the very last moment — even when she could no longer speak — was able to praise God. This could be reported to her father as a comfort. How grateful she was that, in spite of her weak health, she had been able to endure the difficult journey to Geneva to die there, free from the "Babylonian exile" in which she found herself in Noyon. Here in Geneva she was able, she said, to glorify God in all freedom. But she also gave thanks that she could, during her final months, through Calvin's preaching and pastoral care, be assured of her salvation. Reading the report of this deathbed testimony, one looks directly into Calvin's heart and gets to know him as a very compassionate pastor and dear friend.[3]

A "Most Special" Friend

Calvin placed special value on this friendship. The small book that he dedicated to his friend was, for those who know him, a clear proof of Calvin's deep affection for de Normandie. The attachment between them, so Calvin writes, surpasses every other kind of bond, even that of blood relationship. It seems as though he is almost shocked by what he writes. What will his brother Antoine think when he reads this? Yet Calvin is not afraid that his blood brother will have any difficulties with the way he describes his friendship with Laurent. On the contrary, Antoine himself shared in this friendship and would echo his brother's words with respect to Laurent. For years he closely cooperated with de Normandie in publishing books. In short, these three friends from Noyon were linked by more than friendship and familial ties. Coming from the same town — two from a middle-class family of a clerk and one from a noble family — they were, in their new home, more than friends who shared the same place of birth. Above all, they were brothers from the heavenly New Jerusalem.

3. John Calvin, *Writings on Pastoral Piety,* ed. E. A. McKee (New York, 2001), pp. 301-5.

A High Position

Laurent de Normandie was born in Noyon in 1510, and he belonged to the nobility of that city. We do not know whether Calvin and he knew each other when they were children, but it is certain that they met when they were students. In the early 1530s, Laurent was, like Calvin, part of the "Picardic nation" (as they were called because they were all from the same region), a group of students in Orléans who had formed a debating society in the faculty of law. They all sat together in the lecture halls to prepare for a legal career in the service of the government. It is likely that this is not only where Calvin and Laurent met but where they were also touched by the evangelical wind that blew through the world of academia. They went their separate ways after their studies ended, but it would appear that the bond between them remained, though there is no correspondence to prove it.

Laurent de Normandie was bound for a promising and distinguished career, and the young lawyer soon found his way into the highest circles. In 1545 he was even appointed personal secretary to the crown prince of France, who two years later was to succeed his famous father, Francis I, as King Henri II. De Normandie was also appointed lieutenant of the king in Picardy and mayor of Noyon. In addition, he had ties with the court of Navarre, where he enjoyed the confidence of the "charming and gracious Marguerite d' Angoulême," who was attracted to those of the evangelical persuasion.[4] Evidently, his reformist conviction did not prevent him from reaching these high government positions. He had friends among the well-known evangelical companions of Calvin. Jean Crespin, the author of a popular martyrology, was a good friend, and Laurent wrote Calvin that Crespin had found a place of refuge in Noyon. In his letters to Calvin, Crespin refers to their mutual friend Laurent in very laudatory terms. Both de Normandie and Crespin were witnesses at Beza's secret marriage celebration in Paris.

It may well be that, from Geneva, Calvin considered de Normandie an important pawn in the delicate political scheme to further the Reformation in France — through the authorities and even the monarchy. If there was any correspondence between the two, it has not survived —

---

4. Abel Lefranc, *La Jeunesse de Calvin* (Paris, 1888), p. 130.

Laurent de Normandie

possibly because Laurent immediately destroyed Calvin's letters upon receiving them. The two correspondents certainly perceived how dangerous it would be if it were to become common knowledge that they were in contact; and it would have done no good for the work of the Reformation in France. But Calvin was surely aware of the situation in Noyon. Under the leadership of Mayor de Normandie, the young Reformed church experienced a degree of freedom that resulted in growth, and it looked as though Noyon might become the Reformed capital of Picardy. But the success of freedom was reversed when the Roman Catholic powers flexed their muscles to turn the tide.

Noyon against Geneva

The fact that Noyon was the city where the "heretic" Calvin had been born did not go unnoticed, and its relationship with Geneva was more than suspect. There were regular contacts — letters and books from Geneva — that betrayed the Reformational influence. Under the guise of making a pilgrimage, citizens from Calvin's birthplace would visit Geneva, the city where he had become such a prominent minister of the Word. It was just a matter of time before the tensions in Noyon between the reformists and the Roman Catholics would turn into open conflict.

That moment came when a crucifix was desecrated, an act that caused a great disturbance. The authorities opened an inquiry, and they made a connection between this act of vandalism and propaganda from Geneva. Even though the perpetrators remained unknown, the result was that those in Noyon who were known to be friends of Calvin understood that the time had come to leave. It must have been quite a shock when the mayor himself, de Normandie, headed the group of "Calvinists" that chose to go into exile. Because they had a few days to make preparations, their departure was not an unorganized flight. However, it did mean a great loss for the city, since those who left Noyon were mostly influential and affluent citizens.

It remains a question whether de Normandie could have stayed in Noyon. The results of the inquiry into the crucifix incident did not place the blame on him; in fact, the outcome was so vague that the Roman Catholic party could not claim a victory. At the same time, it was clear that those who were known to be connected to Calvin would not have much freedom to push for the Reformation of the church. It may well be that de Normandie and his friends decided to leave Noyon in order that other believers might find it easier to quietly exert their influence. He may have seen his departure as a way to divert the attention of the enemies of the gospel.

But calm did not return to Noyon. All kinds of solemn ceremonies were organized to offset the desecration of the holy cross, to purge Noyon of all Calvinists. All of this ceremonious piety, however, did not keep the unknown iconoclasts from repeating their actions several times. When a cross was vandalized yet again in 1552, the parliament in Paris decided to act. On September 7, 1552, Laurent de Normandie and several citizens of Noyon were formally charged with heresy.[5] They were found guilty of blasphemy and condemned to being burned at the stake. This judgment was to be publicly announced in Noyon, and the possessions of the condemned were to be confiscated.

Since the condemned had long since departed for Geneva, their place of refuge, they were burned in effigy, meaning that a picture of de Normandie and his whole household was burned at the stake in Noyon. But this was not the last fire to burn in Noyon. A few months later, a big fire swept through the town, devouring the public notice board that had announced the condemnation of de Normandie. Significantly, the house in which Calvin was born remained unscathed. For Calvin and his friend — and not just for them, but for all their companions of kindred spirit in Noyon — this must have been a token of divine justice in the midst of all the sadness over the distressing developments in the town of their birth.

The situation in which their mutual friend in the nobility, Madame de Cany, found herself became so untenable that she also considered fleeing to Geneva. But her husband was so opposed to the new faith that he more or less kept her a prisoner. Calvin urged her to do everything in her power to escape this hostile environment. But in the end that proved to be unnecessary: surprisingly — and providentially — her husband became a Protestant and turned into as zealous a Huguenot as he had once been an intolerant Catholic. And thus she was able to stay.

5. Lefranc, *La Jeunesse de Calvin,* pp. 213-15.

Laurent de Normandie

Resident of Geneva

Six months after arriving as a refugee in Geneva, de Normandie acquired the status of legal resident of Geneva. This was not the equivalent of citizenship, which he received six years later and which would also allow him to be elected to membership on the city council. The Geneva authorities tended to be quite careful about these matters of residency and citizenship; but that did not mean that de Normandie was not welcome from the very beginning. The city council appreciated the fact that persons of name and means were choosing Geneva as their place of exile. And it may well be that the council expected these French refugees to be able to give a boost to the city economy.

Laurent de Normandie took up life in Geneva in a house on the cathedral square, not far from Calvin's home. The latter must have liked the idea of having his good friend living so nearby. On September 14, 1550, he conducted the ceremony of Laurent's second marriage — to Anne Colladon. This marriage was blessed with two sons and a daughter, and there were also two sons from his first marriage.

But what would a lawyer of noble birth and illustrious public service in France do for a living in Geneva? Although he would later be allowed to exercise his legal profession once again, he changed his career. De Normandie became a bookseller, specializing in the publishing and distribution of reformist books in France. As a wholesaler he supplied vendors at markets with these kinds of books and thus greatly stimulated the spread of reformist literature throughout France, and his business survived even after his death. This provides a good insight into the extensive network of publishers and booksellers in the service of the kingdom of Christ.[6] The printing of evangelical literature had been totally prohibited from 1542 onward. This made Geneva the center of illicit books that played an invaluable role in the furtherance of the Reformation in France. Titles by Calvin, in particular, were part of de Normandie's publisher's list: at the time of his death, more than 10,000 books by Calvin were counted in his stock of 35,000 books.

6. See H. L. Schlaepfer, "Laurent de Normandie," in *Aspects de la Propagande Religieuse* (Geneva, 1957), pp. 176-230.

A Friend from the Same Birthplace

Despite the fact that his possessions in Noyon were confiscated when he was condemned, de Normandie must have been quite wealthy, for he had the means to finance a business in the risky area of book publishing. In all his modesty — he did not reveal his own name in his business projects — he was the most important person behind the religious propaganda in France. In his heart and soul, he felt very close to all those simple folks who plied their trade of selling evangelical literature in towns and villages everywhere — under the guise of some other occupation. Their work was so important and so feared by the authorities that it would, if they were caught, result in very severe punishments. De Normandie was intensely concerned about the fate of the scores of people who, because of this work, were killed by the sword, by means of strangling, or burned at the stake. Many were willing to sacrifice their lives for this work! De Normandie made sure that the families of these martyrs would not be left without sufficient means.

From time to time de Normandie was brave enough to act in person in defense of such martyrs. In 1552 he even traveled to Lyon in an attempt to secure the freedom of five young Lausanne ministers who had been taken prisoner en route to their new churches in France. However, his endeavors were unsuccessful, and the young men died martyrs' deaths. It does indicate to what extent de Normandie felt a personal responsibility for the people — often young men — who ventured into the fiery furnace of the French persecution.[7]

De Normandie often used ministers who had received their training in Geneva and other Swiss cities for the service for Christ in France as channels for book distribution. There are indications that he also recruited people to help him with the illegal export of books through the Bourse Française, the diaconal organization for poor refugees from France.[8]

7. E. Doumergue, *Calvijn en Genève* (Kampen, 1986), pp. 465-66.
8. Jeannine E. Olson, *Calvin and Social Welfare: Deacons and the Bourse Française* (London/Toronto, 1989), pp. 50ff.

Laurent de Normandie

Back to France

Laurent de Normandie lived in Geneva until his death; he survived his friend Calvin by five years, but succumbed to the plague in 1569. In the end, the fact that he had been condemned to death in absentia did not deter him from visiting his native country, which he did frequently during the final years of his life. One reason for his visits was that he wanted to try to recover his confiscated possessions. One wonders whether such visits to his country of birth were not very dangerous. In point of fact, some twelve years after he had been symbolically burned at the stake, he was basically left alone — not threatened in any way. It may well be that his former contacts in high circles provided him with a degree of safe-conduct; and there were new possibilities in the 1560s that had not existed ten years earlier, which de Normandie exploited as much as possible. In March 1562 he could be found in Picardy; and in April of that year he visited the duchess of Ferrara, Renée de France, in her castle of Montargis, before he returned to Geneva.

In summary, we might call Laurent de Normandie Calvin's "lieutenant" as he served to promote the empire of Christ the King. One can see in his physical portrait a man of distinguished appearance but with a somewhat melancholy look. The promising lawyer, destined for a glorious career in the service of the king of France, became a wholesale bookseller in Geneva and a most trusted friend of Calvin, a man who was of greater service to the cause of the Reformation than he could have ever imagined. This friend from Calvin's birthplace remains known as a person who was determined to stay in the background in order to distribute the literary fruit of Geneva's Reformer throughout all of France and Europe.

AMI PERRIN

A Friend Who Turned into an Enemy

IOANNES CALVINVS, ÆTATIS SVÆ XLVIII.

Calvin at age forty-eight

Ami Perrin

There are no worse enemies than those who were once friends. That is certainly true of Ami Perrin (?-1561), who changed from a passionate supporter of Farel and Calvin to a bitter opponent.

In the early 1530s, Ami Perrin was one of the leaders of the so-called "Guillermins," the followers of Farel (they derived their nickname from his first name, Guillaume). At a time when Geneva was changing over to the Reformation, he was a courageous man who showed hospitality to those who preached the doctrine of free grace and who, along with other respectable citizens of Geneva, exchanged the yoke of Rome for the freedom of the gospel. Fifteen years later, however, he became the leader of those in Geneva who fiercely opposed the authority of the ministers and the consistory. His followers were referred to as "Perrinists"; but Calvin called them "Libertines," because he regarded their resistance as a sign that they wanted to have nothing to do with the beneficial discipline of God's Word. They preferred the name "Children of Geneva" themselves, which referred to the role of their party during the early period of the struggle for freedom. A white cross on their jackets underscored their view that they should be distinguished from other inhabitants of Geneva; they saw themselves as the only true patriots.

It appears that the growing hostility between Calvin and his supporters, on the one hand, and the Perrinists, on the other hand, was closely linked to the issue of Geneva's original inhabitants versus the foreign influx. The Geneva-born citizens were rather worried that their city was gradually being taken over by the growing number of French newcomers. This was not what they had envisioned when, in the 1530s, they had succeeded in gaining their freedom from the Duke of Savoy.

Genevan Friends

It is remarkable how most of Calvin's friends whom we have met so far came from outside the city of Geneva. The circle of intimate associates around the Reformer, even in Geneva itself, retained its largely French character. The many refugees from France who had chosen Geneva as their place of exile continued to cherish their own French identity, and they mingled only to a limited extent with the original citizens. This is clear from the marriage patterns: most of the French-born exiles married men or women from within their own community.

One might well ask whether Calvin, in fact, had any truly Genevan friends — that is, ones who had been born and raised in that city. There were undoubtedly many Genevans who treated the Reformer with great respect and appreciation. But the fact that he was also at times fiercely attacked by Genevans has naturally remained better known than the appreciation of those who quietly accepted the service of this exceptional servant of the Word. It is not easy to actually list names of people who were born and grew up in Geneva and who Calvin could count as belonging to his circle of personal friends. Perhaps one such person was Ami Porral, a mayor of Geneva who had great authority. Both Calvin and his wife, Idelette, visited Porral on his deathbed, and he indicated that he had considered it a blessing when the Lord had returned them to Geneva after their three-year absence. But this friend did not live to see how his namesake and colleague, Mayor Ami Perrin, despite his name ("ami" means friend), turned into one of Calvin's bitterest opponents.

Perhaps Calvin remained too much of a Frenchman to cherish real Genevan friendships. In any event, he did make some enemies, especially — in the years before 1555 — among those who had been the traditional rulers of the city. One of them was Ami Perrin, who once had been a fellow fighter for the cause of the gospel.

A True Citizen of Geneva

Perrin was the only child of a well-to-do family.[1] His father traded in wooden casks and in cloth, and his mother was the daughter of a chemist from Piemont. It has been suggested that Ami, being an only child, was rather spoiled by his parents — a circumstance not favorable to the development of one's character, and perhaps part of the cause of his later megalomania, which eventually became his downfall. He considered himself the most important person in the city: not only did he succeed in becoming the mayor, but he also had himself appointed the captain-general of Geneva. His inflated sense of importance must have

---

1. Bernard Cottret, *Calvin* (Paris, 1995), pp. 201-10.

Ami Perrin

been somewhat comical: when the controversy reached its nadir, Calvin derisively referred to him as our "comedy caesar."[2] The fact that Calvin calls him a "caesar" (or emperor) indicates that he saw Perrin as someone who wanted to link all power in Geneva to his own person. Perrin put himself forward as the leader of a group of prominent Genevan families, but he failed to convince people that he really was the authoritative leader. One thing is clear: the dynamics between the former allies changed dramatically, and the partisans in the fight for freedom had become the fiercest opponents.

Farel's Supporters

In the early 1530s things had looked so promising! When Farel arrived in Geneva to preach the gospel, Ami Perrin was among those who were most prominent in providing their enthusiastic support. And the debates could be extremely intense. On New Year's Eve, 1532, Perrin and a few friends went to the home of a Catholic priest for such a debate.[3] They put down their swords and laid them on a bed; they ordered wine and sat down for a solid discussion, demanding that the priest explain why he thought that the preaching of Farel was not in accordance with the Word of God. The priest did not just base his arguments on Scripture; he built his defense partially on the ideas of Nicolas of Lyra. When the audience of Farel's followers was dissatisfied with this defense and protested strongly, a group of priests suddenly dashed into the room with drawn swords. Perrin and his comrades also seized their weapons, which led to a very intimidating situation. The mayors had to intervene, with their official insignia of power, to prevent bloodshed. As a consequence of this incident, the city council decided that the ministers would not be allowed to proclaim anything in the churches of Geneva but the Word of God.

It is clear that Perrin was still fully in the camp of the Reformers at that time: he was a member of the Guillermins and, with his friends, wholeheartedly in support of Farel. And when Calvin was recruited by

2. *Caesar comicus. CO,* 14: 657.
3. Hugh Y. Reyburn, *John Calvin: His Life, Letters, and Work* (London, 1914), p. 49.

Farel in 1536 as a member of the elite corps of the Reformation, it almost goes without saying that Perrin would also develop a close relationship with this young Frenchman. How deep a friendship this was we do not know; but from the only (extant) letter Calvin wrote to Perrin we may conclude that there was a period during which they had a close relationship. Why else would Calvin refer to himself as "your affectionate and true brother," as he did at the end of that letter?

Parties in the City

The breakthrough of the Reformation did not automatically bring unity in Geneva. The city had always been notorious for its multitude of factions, and this would not change in the next couple of decades.[4] This was, to some extent, a result of the unique geographical location of the city. Because it was situated on the border of France, and as a Swiss city along the route to Italy, many of the surrounding rulers had their eye on Geneva and were keen to bring the city within their sphere of influence. Consequently, there were numerous factions in the city. When the party that supported the rule of the duke of Savoy and the prince-bishop had to face the final demise of their influence, the Children of Geneva, who wanted a free Geneva within an alliance of Swiss cities, were victorious.

Perrin was the most important leader in the Children of Geneva party. He and his fellow patriots were not at all interested in now being ruled by the city of Bern. Even though they needed the protection from that most powerful Swiss city, they refused to become its satellite. Another party in Geneva, which went by the name Articulants, or "Artichokes," was in favor of close ties with Bern; but the Guillermins successfully resisted it. The Articulants lost, and Geneva retained its independence.

The problems Farel and Calvin had to face in their attempts to put the life of the church in order via city structure were linked to the political tensions between Geneva and Bern. Eventually, it seemed that the ideas of the Bern party led to the exile of both Reformers in 1538: the

---

4. An illuminating study on this subject is William G. Naphy, *Calvin and the Genevan Reformation* (Manchester, 1994).

Ami Perrin

Bern sympathizers were adamant that the ecclesiastical discipline should be detached from the city authorities. Later, in the 1540s, Perrin and his group would become totally estranged from Calvin because of the way they themselves became the subjects of that church-state discipline. But in 1541 it was precisely Perrin who brought Calvin back from Strasbourg. Evidently, in the 1536-1538 period, he did not yet perceive this to be a problem that would create distance between him and Calvin. On the contrary, the fact that it suited Bern's intentions for Calvin to leave Geneva at that time most likely was the reason Perrin continued to support the Frenchman. But that was to change dramatically.

Calvin Is Brought Back

In 1540, Geneva faced both a political and an ecclesiastical crisis. The banishment of the two most important ministers had left the church without real leadership. Cardinal Sadolet made some shrewd attempts to use the occasion to return Geneva to the safety of the Roman Catholic camp. There were also political tensions, which resulted in the ignominious death of those who had been most responsible for the exile of Farel and Calvin.[5] Subsequently, when two additional ministers decided to leave the city of their own free will, the council was so discouraged that it decided to do everything possible to bring Calvin back. This decision was probably inspired and applauded by the party of the Guillermins; their leader, Ami Perrin, was appointed to implement this decision. He traveled to Strasbourg at the head of a delegation to kindly request the exiled preacher to return.

Calvin was not at home when the committee from Geneva arrived, but its mission did result in his eventual return to his former parish in 1541. His position had been, of course, greatly reinforced by all that had happened. Apart from whether or not the Geneva authorities liked him, they truly needed him. The city, which found itself in such a precarious position, could not be without him. We may interpret the fact that

5. Two mayors who supported Bern were killed: one was executed after being condemned for a murder, while the other died during an attempted escape (T. H. L. Parker, *John Calvin* [Tring/Batavia/Sydney, 1975], p. 95).

Perrin was the man given the personal responsibility to bring Calvin back to Geneva as a sign of the close ties between the two. The relationship was good. And Calvin, upon his return, worked with Perrin to introduce the urgently needed church order.

Order Established

After 1541, Calvin used every opportunity to promote order in the kingdom of Christ. He had two main concerns: to bring together a competent and dedicated group of ministers, and particularly to establish a consistory that would be essential for giving a concrete form to the discipline that was so necessary for the well-being of Christ's church. However, these plans also contained the seeds of new conflict. For the city authorities, and especially the "real" citizens of Geneva, deplored the fact that Calvin's church was gaining increasing independence from the other institutions of power. Furthermore, they increasingly regarded these new institutions as an encroachment on the old Genevan traditions that went far beyond what was acceptable. That this strange Frenchman went so far as bringing self-conscious Geneva citizens before a church tribunal to pass judgment on them — that was going too far.

Indeed, it might happen that a respected citizen of Geneva would bring his child for baptism and tell the minister that his son was to be named Claude, but then, to his utter dismay, hear the minister say, "Abraham, I baptize you." Giving children the names of a saint was prohibited! Such incidents naturally caused great resentment in many, and over time that resentment toward the new spiritual regime increased, particularly among the original residents of Geneva. Such members of old Genevan families as the Favres, Bertheliers, Vandels, and Septs felt more and more irritated by the new measures. Sometimes they would cough and sneeze dramatically during Calvin's sermons, to the extent that the minister lodged a complaint with the city council.

The relatives and friends of Perrin were among those who were least enthusiastic about all the new — and French — regulations. And Perrin himself? He may have hoped to underscore his own importance in Geneva via his close relationship with Calvin. If that was the case,

Ami Perrin

---

however, he would quickly have discovered that it did not work with the Reformer. In fact, the opposite occurred. Something happened that made Perrin a fierce opponent of Calvin once and for all.

Discipline Is Maintained

In April 1546, the Geneva Consistory had to deal with an awkward problem. There had been a wedding where no attention had been paid to the prohibition of dancing, a prohibition that was in force in Geneva. Members of some prestigious families had been guilty of persisting in that old tradition. Even some of the most prominent people were accused, including Perrin and Mayor Corne, who happened to be the head of the consistory. Calvin wrote extensively to his friend Farel about what happened next.[6] Perrin's wife (whom Calvin jokingly refers to as "Penthesilea," the queen of the Amazones) reacted fiercely. Her father, a Favre, had earlier been condemned because of lewdness, and she snarled at Calvin that his only goal was to get at her family. Calvin remained unperturbed and replied that, if she wished to continue living in sin, she should build a city for herself and her family. But in Geneva, he said, people who refused to live under the yoke of Christ would not be tolerated. Every resident of Geneva, high or low, had to bow before the Word of God.

When that particular consistory meeting took place, Perrin was not in town. He happened to be on a trip to Lyon, and he thought he might escape the disciplinary measures. His colleague Corne, unlike him, showed deep remorse. As the chairman of the consistory that had to condemn him, he humbly accepted the punishment, which was a temporary suspension from his office. But Perrin did not escape his penalty. He pleaded adamantly with the council on behalf of his wife and father-in-law, but to no avail. He, too, had to submit to the spiritual tribunal.

In an attempt to lovingly bring him to this point, Calvin wrote a letter that clearly indicates that he continued to see Perrin as his friend and brother, a person he wholeheartedly wanted to guide in the right

6. *CO*, 12: 333-37.

path. His tone is serious but cordial. Calvin basically says, You know who I am. There is nothing that can deter me from maintaining, in good conscience, the justice of the heavenly inheritance. He adds that he believes that Perrin does, in fact, have the very same desire. Calvin knows that threats toward him have been uttered in Perrin's home; and he realizes that he must be careful not to experience the same fate that he did seven years before (the exile of 1538). But he leaves this for what it is worth. His concern is the well-being and future of the church and the state. He does not consider departing quietly. Calvin believes that it is not Perrin himself who initiates these threats, but his malicious wife. It is in Perrin's best interest to submit to the discipline, which will enhance his position and reputation. In closing, Calvin remarks that the punishments from a true friend are to be preferred over insincere flatteries from others. He ends with: "Sincerely and cordially yours. Your brother J.C."

Irreconcilable Enmity

At first it seemed as though Calvin's sincere and friendly words did have a positive effect: Perrin accepted the verdict of the consistory in all humility. Yet the seeds of hatred were slowly germinating in his heart. Things were never the same again between the two fellow pioneer-combatants. Perrin faced new problems in 1547, when, as a deputy from Geneva, he attended the coronation of Henri II of France. Upon his return he was accused of scheming with the French — to the detriment of Geneva. He was imprisoned and lost his prestigious office of captain-general. He was accused by a certain Meigret, who was considered to be in Calvin's camp. That would have had the effect, no doubt, of muddying the mutual relationship even more.

In spite of all his setbacks, Perrin returned to the center of power in 1553. And when he did become the mayor, he did everything he could to cause problems for Calvin and the French. He even tried to introduce legislation that would require residents from outside of Geneva to wait twenty-five years before they could apply for citizenship, an absurd rule that caused much chagrin. Geneva badly needed the immigrants — and the financial "contribution" they made to acquire citizenship. The is-

Ami Perrin

sues with Perrin became so hot that Calvin fully expected to be fired once again.[7] But it did not come to that. Eventually, after a great deal of difficulty and controversy, the right of the consistory to refuse obdurate sinners access to the Lord's Supper was confirmed. Calvin was allowed to stay.

Inevitably, however, the power struggle was to escalate further, and it reached its peak in 1555. Perrin's elitist party gradually lost more and more of its popularity with others, and that is how matters would run their course. The elections of that year brought a huge defeat for the Perrinists, and Calvin's supporters once again gained the upper hand. Perrin and his people could not stomach their defeat, and on May 16 they drunkenly took to the streets with the intention of teaching all these Frenchmen in Geneva a lesson. There was a brawl, during which the former mayor, Perrin, tried to seize the mayoral staff from the current mayor. This act was seen as no less than a coup d'état, and it spelled the end of the power of Perrin and his supporters. They had to flee immediately to the region of Bern, where, having been sentenced to death in Geneva, they could live out the rest of their days full of spite. Some of the Children of Geneva were indeed arrested and executed. Calvin and Geneva were at long last delivered from those who did all they could to keep the new citizens from France from receiving their rights. One of the insurgents in the May riots, François Daniel Berthelier — the son of a martyr of 1519 — mockingly expressed the bitter frustration of the Children of Geneva before he was executed: "Farewell, Geneva, the time will come when even the king of France will be a citizen of Geneva."[8]

The year 1555 was a turning point in the relationship between Calvin and the city, the beginning of a period during which the citizens of Geneva would be much more accepting of the foreigners from France. That brought a blessing to the church and prosperity to the city, despite the bitter hatred of Calvin's former friend, Ami Perrin.

---

7. He wrote about this to Bullinger on November 6, 1553. *CO,* 14: 656-57.
8. Naphy, *Calvin and the Genevan Reformation,* p. 139.

A Friend Who Turned into an Enemy

NICOLAS DES GALLARS

A Trusted Friend

Calvin, as drawn by an unknown student during a lecture

Friendship is a matter of quality rather than quantity. A circle of friends does not have to be large if those who belong to it truly deserve the qualification "friends." It appears that Calvin had more enemies than friends in Geneva, especially in the difficult years. He experienced a good deal of resistance to his forceful efforts to give concrete form to the kingdom of Christ in a city of sinners. However, there is no doubt that he was also respected by many of the citizens as a servant of the divine Word, though he never made himself dependent on their favors. However, he trusted his friends; he knew he could rely on them, and he gratefully used their services.

Some of his trusted friends became co-workers who tried to lighten the burden of his many responsibilities by giving him daily assistance.[1] Some helped him in the preparation of his publications: there were those who were able to record Calvin's sermons and lectures via stenography, and those could then be published after a final check by Calvin. We owe it to their distinct contributions that Calvin's ideas were disseminated and that we have so much sermon material from Calvin even today. Had it not been for them, those sermons would never have appeared in print, because Calvin himself lacked the time to edit them.

The names of Charles de Jonvilliers and Denis Raguenier deserve special mention in this regard. In addition, François Bourgoing, Jean Cousin, and Jean Budé should be listed as faithful co-laborers in the service of the gospel. When we speak of Calvin's immense capacity for work, despite his chronically poor health, we should not forget those who sometimes sat at his sickbed to record the words that came from his mouth. Calvin would not have been able to function without these helpers in the service of the gospel.

Calvin's *Famulus*

One of these men, perhaps the most trusted among them, was Nicolas des Gallars (ca. 1520-1581).[2] Viret called him Calvin's *famulus,* a term

1. Doumergue devotes an entire chapter to Calvin's secretaries, in *Calvijn en Genève* (Kampen, 1986), pp. 442-61.

2. Hans J. Hillerbrand, *The Oxford Encyclopedia of the Reformation* (New York, Oxford, 1996), 3: 154.

often used for a servant who is inseparably connected to his master. As secretary he may not have been the most accurate one: at one point Calvin had to call on someone else to correct a publication that Nicolas apparently had not handled with sufficient precision. But as a confidant he was, in a very special way, Calvin's right-hand man. Calvin could totally rely on him, and he used him as his envoy without any concern that this representative would put him to shame. Nicolas's relationship with Calvin was much like that between Paul and Timothy.[3] Though the difference in age between them was but little more than ten years, Nicolas regularly refers to Calvin in his letters as "my father," and to himself as "your more than ever dedicated son."[4]

A Nobleman from Paris

Sometime around 1544 a young nobleman from Paris arrived in Geneva. He was one of those exiles who preferred the freedom of serving God in accordance with his Word to a promising future that they could in all likelihood expect in Paris. He was called "Lord of Saules," indicating that he was of noble birth and came from the region of the French capital. We know only a little about his background.[5] His father was Richard des Gallars and his mother, Ysabeau; he had two sisters, Jehanne and Marie. He would later have to travel back from Geneva to France in order to deal with the family inheritance. Being exiled to Geneva evidently did not mean that he had no further concern for business interests in his home country. Calvinists knew that they had to make every sacrifice to be able to worship God in freedom, but this obviously did not mean that they should no longer defend their rights in their home country.

Nicolas's date of birth is unknown, but he must have been born in about the year 1520. At the age of twenty-four, he arrived in Geneva with the clear intention of sitting as a pupil at the feet of Calvin. He had probably received a good education in Paris, though it is unknown in

3. Hugh Y. Reyburn, *John Calvin: His Life, Letters and Work* (London, 1914), p. 280.
4. *CO,* 18: 145.
5. Jeannine E. Olson, "The Family, Second Marriage, and Death of Nicolas des Gallars within the Context of His Life and Work: Evidence from the Notarial Records in Paris and in Pau," *Bibliothèque d'Humanisme et Renaissance* 63 (2001): 73-79.

what subjects he majored. But his desire to become a minister of the Word brought him to the best training school he could have imagined.

It is remarkable how quickly the relationship between Calvin and des Gallars developed into an intimate bond of trust. Very soon — as early as August 4, 1544 — Nicolas became one of Geneva's ministers. In part through his own experience during his first period in Geneva, Calvin knew how essential was the unity among the ministers of the Word if they were to deal effectively with all the problems and opposition the Reformation had to face. Even though the appointment of ministers was not Calvin's official prerogative, but that of the city council, he would certainly have ensured that his new colleagues would support his views with regard to the reform of the church. Together the ministers of Geneva nominated the candidates, but the council made the decision. In Nicolas's case it must have been "trust at first sight," because from the very beginning Calvin accepted him as his personal right hand. We do not know whether Calvin had met him, or any of his relatives, earlier in Paris. But we may suspect that it was not without someone's favorable introduction that Nicolas became part of the circle of Calvin's confidants.

Calvin's Colleague and Secretary in Geneva

Nicolas soon felt at home in Geneva. Just before he entered the ministry, he married Gabrielle Morones, and their marriage was blessed by a considerable number of children. This "treasure" provided Calvin with an excuse to joke (in a letter to Viret) about the Roman Catholic accusation against the Reformed pastors of Geneva, that the ministers were financially enriching themselves in their service of the Word. Was it really true that they were getting rich? Yes, says Calvin, just look at how rich des Gallars is — "when one counts his children."[6]

Several times des Gallars served as Calvin's envoy on special missions. In 1545, Calvin wrote to Viret repeatedly about the precarious situation of the Waldenses.[7] Des Gallars visited them along with Calvin, and he served as an eyewitness when he reported on their terrible plight

6. *CO*, 13: 376-77.
7. *CO*, 12: 82-83; *CO*, 12: 87-88.

to those who might be able to offer help. Through him, Calvin tried to persuade the Swiss to plead with the king of France in favor of these fellow believers who faced so much persecution. For that reason he sent Nicolas as his personal envoy to Bern.

In 1551, Calvin sent des Gallars on a mission to England. He was to present a copy of Calvin's commentary on the book of Isaiah to the young English king, Edward VI, who had expressed openness to the ideas of the Reformation. Nicolas himself had been responsible for recording the lectures Calvin had given on Isaiah and had edited them into book form. (It appears that Calvin was not entirely satisfied with his secretary's work on that commentary: in 1559 he would review the entire work and republish the commentary as fully his own work.)[8] Des Gallars also translated a few of Calvin's writings from French into Latin. When translating, and thereby making available the characteristic French of Calvin in the scientific Latin of the scholarly world, des Gallars repeatedly says that he was not able to fully convey the depth of Calvin's writings through his Latin. Nicolas apparently shared Calvin's preference for his mother tongue.

A Pseudonymous Publication

In 1545, des Gallars was involved in a remarkable publication in which Calvin defended himself and his friends Viret and Farel against Caroli's allegation that they deviated from the faith of the church of the ages. Caroli was a theologian who had gone back and forth between Rome and the Reformation. He believed that the ideas of Calvin and his friends were tainted by Arianism, the refusal to accept the full godhead of Christ. Such a serious accusation demanded a response. With a stock of paper, Calvin and des Gallars withdrew for a few days to Antoine's cottage to formulate a reaction on paper.

The trip to this retreat had some obstacles, Calvin says in a letter to Viret. First of all, Calvin had misplaced a few documents that Farel had sent him and that he needed in composing his defense. He got

8. W. de Greef, *Johannes Calvijn, zijn Werk en Geschriften* (Kampen, 2006), pp. 125-28.

himself into a rage because he immediately thought that foul play was involved — that someone had stolen these documents rather than that it was the result of his own carelessness. While they were en route without those documents, Calvin could not sleep in the inn because of the fleas. When, in their misery, they decided to continue their journey at about three o'clock in the morning, the rain made further travel impossible and they had to "rest" a few hours in the chilly night under a shelter. When they finally arrived at Antoine's cottage, they succeeded in completing the defense in a minimum of time.

But who was the author of this book? Calvin put des Gallars down as the author, even though Calvin himself was responsible for the content. The reason is not that he didn't want his name connected with it: anyone who read it at the time — or reads it today — can tell that it is Calvin rather than des Gallars who so convincingly responds to Caroli. Did Calvin simply want to grant his co-worker the honor of having something he wrote himself? Or was there another motive behind this pseudonymous publication? Viret criticized Calvin for the way the book had only praise for the trio of Farel, Viret, and Calvin, while it had only blame for Caroli. Calvin replied that he opted for this strange method of publication because he wanted to preclude any idea that he was praising himself too much in this book. Whether he fully succeeded remains an open question. But it is clear that Calvin believed that a certain amount of "self-glorification" was permissible when the defense of the truth of the gospel was at stake.[9]

9. Calvin writes: "I admit that the laudatory words in this publication, that glorify us, and me in particular, will cause, as you already suspect, a negative reaction from those who are angry at us and are hostile towards us. But I feel they only put themselves up for ridicule, if they begrudge us this honor. For do I not write the name of our dearest Des Gallars above this work, rather than my own? Of course, they may think that he wrote it with my assistance and that but little of it is from him. But now I have through his mouth so spoken about myself that I can, by referring to this glorification, laughingly dispose of all those who point at me as the author. It enables me to say that people would do me an injustice if they were to think that I would be foolish enough to glorify myself. And yet, what, in fact, but a certain fame of name is attributed to me? If reference is made to the three of us, it is because we are praised as pious men, and we deserve this because of the church. I would not be ashamed to also apply this second round of glory to myself." CO, 12: 107-8.

Separation

Though Calvin did not want to do without his valuable secretary for anything in the world, there was to be a period during which they would no longer be in close proximity. Des Gallars worked as pastor in Geneva from 1544 until 1557. He did make an occasional trip to France, and once even traveled to England, but he always returned to the city where he had found refuge. During that period in Geneva, however, there were two years of greater distance. In the minutes of the Company of Pastors in the year 1553, we read of an outcry over the decision of the city council to move des Gallars to a region outside of Geneva.[10] He was ordered to serve the church of Jussy, while his colleague Bourgoing would return and take his place in Geneva. The reason for this exchange remains unclear; the only reason that comes to mind is that they took this action to directly hurt Calvin by removing his personal assistant from him. We should note that this was at a time when the relationship between the government and the church was at its lowest ebb, and the ministers' protest was not successful. Here is yet another proof that the suggestion that Calvin had so much authority that he could manipulate everything is unjustified. During most of his ministry in Geneva he simply had to submit to what the council decided, even in matters that were clearly in the church's domain.

While serving his new congregation, des Gallars still met with the ministers of Geneva, but because of the geographical distance he was no longer in daily contact with Calvin. But as soon as the situation changed (in 1555) and Calvin's opponents had once and for all departed from the political scene, the council decided that des Gallars could return to the city.[11]

However, it would not be long before another city would call on his services. In August 1557 the minutes tell us that, a month earlier, one of the most prominent elders from the church in Paris had come to Geneva with due credentials, charged with bringing one of the ministers of Geneva with him when he returned.[12] The council decided — ap-

10. R. M. Kingdon and J. F. Bergier, eds., *Registres de la Compagnie des Pasteurs de Genève* (Geneva, 1962), 2: 1.
    11. *Registres de la Compagnie,* 2: 64.
    12. *Registres de la Compagnie,* 2: 78.

Nicolas des Gallars

parently with Calvin's approval — that des Gallars would be the most suitable person for this assignment: he was to go with the elder "to assist the brethren there." The choice may have had something to do with his Parisian background. The elder from Paris was to leave with his new pastor on August 16. It is likely that the assignment was for a limited time period, and that des Gallars remained connected with Geneva, but it did mean that he had to say goodbye to his friends and his family, who remained in Geneva.

The journey to Paris took a dramatic turn. The elder, Nicolas du Rousseau, fell into the hands of pursuers, was arrested, and taken to Dyon. He had been harshly warned not to carry any letters or reformist books with him while traveling, but he had been unable to resist the temptation. He apparently loved the writings he was able to acquire in Geneva so much that he was willing to risk his life. He died a martyr's death in prison, and his body was publicly burned. But he had accomplished his mission. Miraculously, des Gallars was able to escape and make it to Paris, where he began his work.[13]

Paris

His stay in the French capital would be brief. Hardly had he arrived when, on September 4, the "Affaire of the Rue St. Jaques" took place. A meeting of the Reformed church of Paris in a large house was rudely disturbed by an angry mob. A few hundred church members, women and children among them, were beaten and scattered. This resulted in a great many arrests and trials. The cruel persecution of the Reformed was rekindled in Paris, and many died martyrs' deaths.

Des Gallars was not very keen on working under such dangerous conditions. He reported what happened to his colleagues in Geneva, and he thanked God that he was spared. Although he was not among those directly involved in the "affair," he more or less requested a return to Geneva. Calvin responded on behalf of the ministers and asked him to stay for the time being, saying that he should not discourage the

13. *Histoire Ecclesiastique des Églises Réformées au Royaume de France,* new ed. (Paris, 1883), pp. 161-62.

A Trusted Friend

flock of his sheep by departing. Calvin mentions that he has had a visit from des Gallars's wife because she was naturally terribly concerned about her husband. But, Calvin says, he had never had greater admiration for her than at this moment, for "she puts the interests of the church and the honor of Christ above your life."[14] You know, he adds, how much I value you, but the salvation of so many souls means even more to me.

But that very same day Calvin also wrote to the church in Paris, preparing them for the fact that they would not have their new pastor for very long. He says: "It may be better that this shepherd leaves, so as not to incite the anger against the sheep too much."[15] He thought that a less prominent minister might be a better idea. That was what was arranged: a few months later, Macar became the pastor of the Paris church, and des Gallars returned to Geneva.

To England

His return after the dangerous interlude in Paris did not, however, prove to be the beginning of a long and quiet period of service in Geneva. A little more than two years later, des Gallars left for London to lead the congregation of Francophone refugees there. Calvin found it hard once again to let go of his faithful assistant. He wrote that it was "not without bitter grief" that he saw des Gallars depart. But the fact that des Gallars was chosen as the pastor of the French-speaking church in England indicates that there probably was no one who was better suited than he to lead the Reformed church in exile in the spirit of Calvin. In theological and ecclesiological matters he kept this refugee church on the track of Calvin and protected it against deviating tendencies.[16]

One should not underestimate the kinds of personal sacrifices such a mission entailed. Des Gallars's wife and his large family stayed

14. *CO,* 16: 627-28.
15. *CO,* 16: 629-32.
16. P. Denis, "Un combat aux frontières de l'orthodoxie: la controverse entre Acontius et Des Gallars sur la question du fondement et des circonstances de l'èglise," *Bibliothèque d'Humanisme et Renaissance* 38 (1976): 55-72.

behind in Geneva. It would be a long time before their husband and father was able to have them join him in his new church. In the meantime, the city council of Geneva decided that they were to vacate the parsonage because Beza would need to live there. Even though Calvin assured his colleague that his family was well taken care of, we can imagine that des Gallars in faraway London and his wife in Geneva must have had great concerns about each other.

At one point des Gallars dropped a hint that he might want to return to Geneva, but this cautious suggestion was not well received. In a letter Calvin reminds des Gallars that his task now lies in England and that the vacancy he left in Geneva has been filled. He suspects, he says, that the complaints of his wife were at least partly the reason Nicolas was longing for home. But des Gallars responds that that was not the case. Eventually, he was able to move his wife and children, but it would be the beginning of a family tragedy. The chilly climate in England proved fatal for Gabrielle and some of the children. By 1563, des Gallars himself was forced to return to Geneva, because his own health was in danger, as Bishop Grindal wrote to Calvin.

Calvin's Alter Ego in France

The return of des Gallars to Geneva did not mean that he simply could take up his place once again among the other ministers of the city. After he had served for a brief period, in 1561 he was again sent to France as the English representative at the important Colloquy of Poissy. This was to be the last — and ultimately unsuccessful — attempt to find an agreement between the Roman Catholic and the Reformed within the context of the church in France.

Calvin sent him to Orléans, the city he personally knew so well from his younger years, a city where the Reformed movement was showing significant growth. In the midst of all the anxieties created by the religious wars in France, des Gallars's enthusiastic letters must have been a great encouragement and comfort to Calvin, who was in the final phase of his earthly sojourn. After the death of his "spiritual father," Calvin's trusty servant increasingly occupied a key position in the young church of the Reformation, which was becoming increasingly characterized by order and unity. He presided over the national synod of 1565 in Paris, and he was the secretary of the synod of 1570 in La Rochelle.

This international envoy of the Reformation found his final place of ministry at the court of the queen of Navarre, Jeanne d'Albret, whom he had met in La Rochelle and who had urged him to come and assist her in fostering the Reformation in her realm.[17] After Pierre Viret's death, des Gallars was the most prominent minister and theologian of the Huguenot churches in Béarn. He accompanied the queen during her political missions to the French court and was the pastor at her side as she lay on her deathbed. Toward the end of his life he received an appointment as a professor at the academy of Lescar.

This servant of the kingdom of Christ had, in the shadow of his spiritual father and role model, an enormous significance for the preservation of Calvin's spiritual heritage for the church in France. That was far more than he, in his modesty, must have expected.

17. S. Amanda Eurich, "The Death of Nicolas des Gallars: Evidence from the Notarial Records of the archives départmentales des pyrenées-atlantiques," *Bibliothèque d'Humanisme at Renaissance* 60 (1998): 739-40.

LORD AND LADY DE FALAIS

A Dutch Couple

Title page of *L'Excuse*,
with the coat of arms of the De Falais family

Calvin had a special place in his heart for the Dutch. In a letter to Bullinger he refers to himself as a "Belgian," the Latin name for someone from the region of the Seventeen Provinces, that is, the Low Countries near the sea. Bullinger had given a young Dutchman the responsibility of carrying an important letter to Calvin, but the mailman was not very punctual with the delivery. It took him five days after he arrived in Geneva before the epistle reached Calvin, and Bullinger became impatient. He concluded from a letter that he received from Calvin that his correspondent had not yet seen the letter in question, and he may well have worried that this confidential letter had fallen into the wrong hands.

Fortunately, Calvin could put him at ease. With his mild irony, he criticizes the "excellent young man" who had been so slow in fulfilling his task, but, he says, "I am used to the 'barbarity' of this neighboring people." Since he came originally from the north of France, Calvin was well aware of the national character of the "Belgians" (the Dutch). He adds in Latin: *Sum enim Belga ipse quoque* ("I am a Dutchman myself").[1] He meant this with a degree of humor, of course, but at the same time the remark reveals that Calvin always felt a degree of affinity with those close northerly neighbors.[2] Idelette, his wife, was naturally the Dutch person dearest to him, but other Dutch people also belonged to his circle of friends. Of those, Lord and Lady De Falais were among the most important.

Dutch Nobility

Lord and Lady De Falais derived their name from one of the properties they had in the Netherlands. Their original names were Jacques de Bourgogne and Yolande van Brederode.[3] Both had prestigious pedi-

---

1. *CO,* 18: 204-8.

2. E. M. Braekman, "Sum enim Belga ipse quoque, Calvin et les ressortisants des Pays-Bas," in Millet, *Calvin et ses contemporains,* pp. 83-96.

3. For De Falais and his family, see F. L. Rutgers, *Calvijns Invloed op de Reformatie in de Nederlanden voor zoveel die door hemzelven is uitgeoefend* (Leyden, 1899), pp. 10-12, 21, 85-92. See also P. Denis, "Jacques de Bourgogne, seigneur de Falais," in André Seguenny, ed., *Bibliotheca Dissentium: Répertoire de non-conformistes religieux des*

grees. Jacques's grandfather was an acknowledged bastard-son of Duke Philip the Good of Burgundy. That made the grandson a distant cousin of Emperor Charles V. Because he was a member of the family, the latter granted him a high position at the court. He was probably born in about 1520, and until his departure to the Netherlands he served as a personal aide-de-camp to the emperor. On his father's death, he received custody of the feudal estates of Falais (southern Brabant) and Bredam (Zeeland).

Yolande was born into an old family of high Dutch nobility, the Brederodes. She was born in 1525, a daughter of Walraven II van Brederode; she was an aunt of the well-known Hendrik van Brederode, who, on behalf of the noblemen, signed the famous Petition of the Nobility that was presented to Governess Margaretha. This event gave him and his allies the designation of "geuzen" (beggars), which eventually became a name of honor.

It is remarkable how early Calvin's name and fame must have circulated through the Netherlands; thus those who were reform-minded sought contact with the Reformer of Geneva as early as during his second period in Geneva, when the Reformation there began to take on a more concrete form.[4] Those who asked for advice or support were often members of the nobility. It was not just Jacques, but also his brothers, sisters, and other relatives from the Netherlands, who would stay in touch with Calvin over the years. And Geneva became the preferred city of refuge for many who, because of their faith, sought a new home country.

Calvin corresponded extensively with Lord and Lady De Falais until their friendship ended unhappily in 1552. Their letters to Calvin have not survived; it is possible that he disposed of them when the friendship ended. But Calvin's letters to them have, miraculously, been preserved. They were discovered two centuries after they were written, and they were published in the Netherlands.[5] These letters bear witness to a very intimate friendship that must have meant much to Calvin. One gets the impression that Calvin felt honored to have the important nobleman, who was so close to the emperor, as a good friend.

seizième et dix-septième siècles (1984), 4: 9-52; Jean Calvin, Lettres à Monsieur et Madame de Falais, ed. Françoise Bonali-Fiquet (Geneva, 1991), pp. 7-34.

4. The title of Rutgers's book points in that direction (p. 10).

5. In Amsterdam, by J. Wettstein, in 1744.

Exile

The first contact of this couple with Calvin dates from 1543, which was even before they had acted on their decision to leave the Netherlands. It would appear that they had not been married for very long. When introducing himself to them, Calvin uses his "noble" pseudonym, Charles d'Espeville, and signs off as "your servant, humble brother and genuine friend," in his first personal letter to both on October 14, 1543.[6] He also gives his addressees pseudonyms: Jacques and Katerine le Franc.

In the beginning of this letter Calvin admits that it may seem a bit preposterous to address them right off in such a confidential manner. Yet he takes this liberty because he has heard from one of his friends how welcome his counsel is to them — though he would have preferred a personal encounter. They would need at least a half a day to discuss the serious matter of their approaching exile. But because they do not have this occasion, Calvin is content to have this dialogue via the letters. He is grateful that their obedience to Christ carries so much weight that Jacques and Yolande can no longer remain in an environment where Christ is not welcome. Calvin understands how difficult it is to leave everything behind. De Falais will not only abandon his rights and privileges, he will also leave his family and the country that is dear to him behind. But as soon as the tide turns, Calvin says, he will be able to return. At present, however, peace with God and a good conscience should prevail. Calvin points to Abraham's pilgrimage: we should not go against our conscience if we cannot live to the honor of God.

Remarkably enough, Calvin does not address husband and wife in the same letter; both of them receive their own letters from him on the same day, indicating that Yolande had her own independent role in the friendship and association with Calvin. We come to realize that she preceded her husband in her religious commitment, but she supported him in a special way when he decided to leave the Netherlands. She did not merely follow him without hesitation; she even took the lead.

Thus inspired and encouraged from Geneva, Lord and Lady De Falais departed for Cologne. Bishop Hermann von Wied resided in this imperial city and, together with Bucer, made plans for a Reformation of

6. Calvin, *Lettres à Monsieur et Madame de Falais,* p. 40.

Lord and Lady De Falais

his bishopric. Unfortunately, nothing materialized. The couple found a cordial welcome in the home of an uncle of Yolande, Duke Wilhelm von Neuenahr, and they remained in contact with Calvin, who made sure that they would have their own minister. As a result, the first French Reformed church in Cologne was established in their home. However, this congregation, which Calvin admired with gratitude, was to be short-lived. When the emperor came to Cologne, Jacques and Yolande felt the situation had become too dangerous. They fled to Strasbourg, where they received a warm welcome, which the council showed them in the form of a gift barrel of wine. They joined the Wallonian colony. It was not until they were in Strasbourg, sometime during 1545, that the first personal meeting between Calvin and his new Dutch friends took place.

Accountable to the Emperor

Emperor Charles V was not going to accept the departure of his aide-de-camp without raising any objections. In a letter dated March 15, 1545, he summons De Falais to give account of his decision. Why did he go to Cologne without asking for approval? And why did he not report to his lord and master when that was required? De Falais responds that he had not been able to report to the emperor because he was ill. And he had not fled from the jurisdiction of Charles, since Cologne was part of that jurisdiction. He also does not want to leave any doubt that he still adheres to the "ancient and Catholic faith," that the emperor would be wrong if he were to think that he had become a heretic. He had left his home, he says, because his uncle, the Duke of Neuenahr, had expressly asked him to visit. Due to his weak health, he says, he has not yet been able to return, and the doctors have advised him to go to a health resort.

Even after reassuring the emperor in this exchange of letters, however, Jacques de Bourgogne did not dare remain in the sphere of Charles V's authority. When the emperor passed through Cologne on his way to the Diet of Worms, Lord and Lady De Falais were already gone. On May 6 they arrived in Strasbourg, and from there Jacques responded once again to a summons from the emperor — but without obeying it.

Calvin kept in frequent contact with the couple. After his arrival in

Strasbourg, Jaques played with the idea of asking for a safe-conduct in order to visit the emperor during the Diet of Worms, where he would be able to give account of his religious choice. But Calvin strongly advised him against this. It was far too dangerous, he said, to continue to trust the good will of the emperor.[7] The refusal to give account of his choice to the emperor eventually resulted in the confiscation of all possessions of the noble "heretical fugitive." A charge of June 10, 1546, declared that Jacques De Falais had been deprived of "all his goods, lands and manors."[8] A plea to the emperor by the delegates from Strasbourg who were present at the Diet on behalf of their guest was not successful.

An Apologia from the Noble Lord

Calvin did his utmost in his letters to comfort and encourage his friends, who were now experiencing how suffering for the sake of one's faith becomes a reality. Driven from hearth and home, they had to bear a cross for the sake of the gospel. But submitting to that cross did not mean that they no longer had the right to protest the false accusations that were raining down on them. The supporters of the Reformation were not sectarians or agitators. Therefore, they could in all dignity defend themselves against the false portrayals being painted of them. For that reason Calvin composed a public apologia for De Falais to present against his accusers.

The question was, so Calvin writes, whether or not the matter of possessions should be included in this document. Would it not be wasted energy to claim restitution of the confiscated goods before De Falais had been restored to grace? Calvin was also worried about De Falais's Christian brothers. Might it not have an adverse effect if the matter of possessions would be so bluntly addressed in this defense? In addition, he said, one should avoid the suggestion that the loss of earthly possessions would be the worst pain one could suffer. It would be a powerful testimony if De Falais could be seen to endure the loss of his possessions steadfastly for the sake of God's honor. When consider-

7. Calvin, *Lettres à Monsieur et Madame de Falais,* pp. 58-59.
8. Denis, "Jacques de Bourgogne, seigneur de Falais," p. 16.

ing the inestimable value of Jesus Christ and all that he possesses, should not all other things be seen as having the value of dirt?[9]

After a personal dialogue between Jacques and Calvin, this apologia led to the publication of a pamphlet in 1547 entitled *Excuse of the noble lord Jacques de Bourgogne, the lord of Falais and Bredam: to purge himself before his imperial majesty of the accusation lodged against him with regard to his faith, about which he has made his confession.*[10] Even though Calvin wrote it in Geneva, the pamphlet does not mention the author or place of publication. They thought that it would have an unfavorable effect if it became known that Calvin wrote the pamphlet. The word "excuse" should not be misinterpreted, as if to mean that De Falais is making apologies in it. On the contrary, he freely testifies to his faith, and he is convinced that Charles V will be assured of the genuineness of his faith if he makes an effort to be informed about it. He says that filthy lies have been spread about him: he is said to have squandered his goods, he is rumored to be an Anabaptist and an enemy of the Catholic faith. None of this is true! He fails to understand why the faith that he confesses would be condemned by theologians, since it is nothing but that of the prophets, apostles, and martyrs. De Falais assumes (via the words of Calvin) that the emperor must have been falsely informed and wrongly advised to take such severe measures against his servant, who always so consistently enjoyed his favor.

It is hard to tell whether Calvin and De Falais really expected Charles V to give the case an honest review. One gets the impression that, based on his experiences during the religious disputations between 1538 and 1541, Calvin did not harbor merely negative feelings about the emperor. This would also appear from what he wrote in 1543, when he pleaded with Charles to look with favor on the Reformation of

---

9. Calvin, *Lettres à Monsieur et Madame de Falais,* p. 89.

10. *Excuse de noble seigneur Iaques de Bourgoigne. S. De Fallez & Bredam: pour se purger vers la M. Imperiale, des calomnies à luy imposées en matière de sa Foy, dont il rend confession* (Geneva, 1547). Eight hundred copies of this document were printed, originally in French. The name of the Rihel printshop in Strasbourg is on the title page, which caused some commotion in Strasbourg. The copies that were still available for sale had to be altered so that the connection with Strasbourg would disappear. Denis, "Jacques de Bourgogne, seigneur de Falais," p. 37.

A Dutch Couple

the church. A fascinating question remains about whether the interest Calvin seems to have received from a number of Dutch noblemen was based on what may have been a personal encounter between Calvin and Charles V during one of the religious disputations. Many of the Dutch nobility were, of course, part of Charles's entourage. We can only speculate, but could it have been possible that the young De Falais, as the aide-de-camp of the emperor, had seen from a distance how Calvin operated? Or that his noble kin in the Netherlands had informed him about the great importance of the young Reformer in Geneva for the cause of the gospel? We do not know, but this could explain why so many of the Dutch noblemen were strongly oriented toward Geneva.

In Geneva at Last

During the years of regular correspondence between Calvin and the De Falais couple, their friendship deepened to the extent that they developed a mutual desire to live closer to each other. Due to the political situation, Lord and Lady De Falais moved from Strasbourg to Basel in early 1547, and from there they made plans to make Geneva their permanent place of residence. Like an accomplished realtor, Calvin did all he could to find a suitable house for the family: at the very least, it had to be a house with a large garden. Such a place was impossible to find within the city limits. After much deliberation, which even involved Mayor Ami Perrin, they finally settled on a small castle located in Veigy. This was not far from the city but it did, in fact, fall under the jurisdiction of Bern. Jacques and Yolande moved there in 1548, and from then onward Calvin and these friends — who had also become well acquainted with his family — had ample opportunity to meet face to face and enjoy each other's company. The mansion in Veigy became a place to which Calvin could withdraw from time to time, be in good company, and temporarily forget his heavy responsibilities.

John and Jacques shared their joys and concerns with one another. It is noteworthy how often their letters refer to concerns about each other's health: both men were ill rather frequently. Neither Jacques nor Yolande lived to be old: he died in 1556, after having lost his wife a few years earlier. After her death, he married Ysabeau van

Reimerswaal, who came from the Dutch province of Zeeland. But along with the illness and death, Calvin was also able to find joy in the family of his friends. We get a glimpse of a side of Calvin that we would perhaps never suspect existed when we read what he wrote to them in 1547, after the birth of their child: "I am sorry that I cannot at least spend half a day there with you [they were still living in Basel] to laugh together with you, trying to make the little child also laugh, at the risk of having to experience how it would start to weep or cry." Who would have imagined the venerable Reformer of Geneva, with the stern face that we have seen in portraits, spending half a day above a baby's crib — trying to make the child laugh? Yet this was a side of Calvin, and it came out among friends with whom he felt at ease.

A Dramatic Rift

Nevertheless, after the De Falaises moved to Geneva, the friendship with Calvin lasted less than four years; in 1551, a dramatic rift developed between Calvin and the De Falaises. It was caused by the conflict surrounding Jerome Bolsec, a physician who became so critically involved in the debate over the issue of double predestination that he was imprisoned and later banned from Geneva. Unfortunately, Bolsec was the family doctor of the De Falais family. In this conflict of loyalties, Jacques De Falais sided with his doctor unreservedly. And this meant an abrupt and radical end to his friendship with Calvin.

In his last letter to De Falais, Calvin enumerates the arguments for ending the relationship with his dear friends. Brief and businesslike, he rejects all further rapprochements: someone who is a friend of a deadly enemy of the truth, he says, must himself be an enemy. In this letter Calvin quotes a statement that originated among the friends of Bolsec, who had established their base of operations in the De Falais family home in Veigy: "Calvin's God is a hypocrite, a liar, who is not to be trusted, is unjust, a God who commits and cherishes shameful acts, and is worse than the devil."[11]

It must have been unbearable for Calvin to know that such dread-

11. Calvin, *Lettres à Monsieur et Madame de Falais,* p. 206.

ful notions were coming from the very same home where he had spent so many pleasant moments with his friends. And even though the words in question were not from the mouth of De Falais himself, it meant that further communication would henceforth be impossible. The friendship had suffered a fatal blow, and Calvin could no longer hear anything positive about his friend. This was more than a personal hurt: it concerned the heart of the doctrine of salvation, which he believed Bolsec and his followers had totally destroyed. De Falais was no longer worthy to be remembered as one who had been befriended by Calvin.

An uncharacteristic act of Calvin shows how much pain he experienced when his friendship with his Dutch friend Jacques de Bourgogne ended. In 1556 he even went as far as withdrawing the honorable dedication to De Falais that he had written at the beginning of his commentary on the First Epistle to the Corinthians (1546). In the letter by which he changed this dedication, he complains: "If only the man whose name I am now eradicating had been unknown to me when I wrote this commentary, or if only I had at least known him well."[12] Calvin tries to explain that in that case he would not have been forced to do what he now felt compelled to do with so much pain: to remove the name of the person he had esteemed as a friend, but who had now turned into a complete stranger. He does not want to get into any further detail, but the pain of the lost friendship is still palpable. De Falais's attitude in the affair of Bolsec, when, in spite of their friendship, he chose the camp of the opponent, had wounded Calvin deeply. He had thought he had a close friend, but when the doctrine of salvation was at stake, Calvin had to conclude that De Falais had become an enemy of the truth.

In view of the deeply unhappy end to this friendship, the question remains whether De Falais, despite his personal friendship with Calvin, had ever fully accepted the latter's teachings. Did Calvin's "love" for this friend from the high nobility possibly blind him to some of De Falais's less than orthodox convictions? The basis for this doubt may be found in one of Calvin's letters to Farel, in which he tries to put his older brother at ease about De Falais. After a meeting with Calvin's fellow re-

12. *CO,* 13: 35-36.

former, De Falais was under the impression — so he told Calvin — that Farel did not fully trust his faith. Farel had asked De Falais for his confession, because he apparently had his doubts. Calvin tells Farel in a letter of August 27, 1548, that these doubts were not justified. In retrospect, however, one wonders whether Farel's suspicions may have been closer to the truth than was Calvin's assessment.

GALEAZZO CARACCIOLO

An Italian Friend

Galeazzo Caracciolo, portrayed on a medallion (1556)

Galeazzo Caracciolo

Replacing a Lost Friend

In 1556, when Calvin withdrew Lord De Falais's name from the dedication of his 1 Corinthians commentary, whose name could he substitute and now feature in the dedication to this important book of the Bible? It is the person of whom Calvin says, "Had I known you ten years ago, there would have been no need for me to change this dedication."[1] Once again it is an important man of noble birth, this time from regions south of Switzerland. Originally from the kingdom of Naples, Galeazzo Caracciolo (1517-1586) was an Italian nobleman who, as a new friend of Calvin, replaced his former confidant.

It is noteworthy that the same Bolsec affair that cost Calvin a friend also brought him a new brother in Christ. Caracciolo had only just arrived in Geneva when he presented himself as a faithful follower of Calvin, particularly during the troubles swirling around Doctor Bolsec, who was ravaging the very heart of Calvin's doctrine of election.[2] Thus the reason De Falais severed his ties with Calvin was precisely the reason Caracciolo allied himself with Calvin. And this was probably why Calvin so quickly embraced this new nobleman brother: in essence, it shows that the common bond of a precious faith rather than personal feelings of empathy determined Calvin's friendships. Furthermore, the new dedication of his commentary to his new Italian friend was very fitting: whether or not Calvin realized it when he wrote this new dedication, Caracciolo had been converted in his native country through the influence of his countryman Petrus Martyr Vermigli's exegesis of Paul's Corinthian letters. The First Epistle to the Corinthians would also acquire, in his later life, a very special significance for his marriage, as we shall see in due course.

The Marquis of Vico

On June 15, 1551, Calvin wrote to his friend William Farel that the number of inhabitants of the city was growing daily because of the constant

---

1. *CO*, 16: 11-14.
2. Caracciolo was the witness *à charge* against Bolsec, representing the camp of Calvin.

flow into Geneva of fugitives seeking refuge because of their faith. One of the newcomers he mentions by name is the Marquis of Vico, and he was not just anybody. Even though he was accompanied by just a few servants when he arrived in Geneva from Naples, he belonged to the highest circles of Italian society. He had connections with the pope and the emperor. But he had left the great riches and a glorious future behind for the sake of his faith, and he had decided that he would live the life of an exile in the city of Calvin from that time forward.

Galeazzo Caracciolo was born in Naples in 1517, the son of Colantonio Caracciolo, the Marquis of Vico.[3] From his birth onward, all the ingredients seemed in place to assure a future of wealth and influence. His mother was a niece of Pierro Carafa, an influential cardinal who had introduced the Inquisition in Rome in an endeavor to halt the growing influence of Protestantism. In 1555, Galeazzo's great-uncle, Pierro, was to become Pope Paul IV. By that time, Galeazzo had already been living in Geneva for some years, and the fact that this nephew of the pope was held in high esteem in the city of Geneva must have caused great consternation in Rome.

Because of the Caracciolo family's Spanish connections, there was also a close tie between them and Emperor Charles V. This is why the fifteen-year-old Galeazzo was sent to the court in Brussels in 1532 to serve as a page of the emperor, an honorable position that would lead to a promising future. Is it possible that at the imperial court the young Italian nobleman met Jacques de Bourgogne, the friend whom he would replace in Calvin's heart after 1551? Lord De Falais had been an aide-de-camp of the emperor, so that does not seem too far-fetched.

At the age of twenty, Galeazzo married Vittoria Carafa, the daughter of the Duke of Noecera, an extremely wealthy family that would further ensure his affluence. Their relationship was characterized by genuine

3. As early as 1587, just a year after his death, the first biography of Caracciolo appeared in Geneva, written by Nicolao Balbani, a close friend and pastor of the Italian church in Geneva, and translated into several languages. See E. Doumergue, *Calvijn en Genève* (Kampen, 1986), pp. 470-75, who uses this as his source; see also Benedetto Croce's biography, entitled "Il Marchese di Vico, Galeazzo Caracciolo," in *Vite di aventure di fede et di passione* (Bari, 1936), translated into French as *Galéas Caracciolo, Marquis de Vico* (Geneva, 1965).

love and affection and was thus more than a marriage of convenience, as was so often the case in the circles of nobility. This would make their subsequent divorce — due to their religious choices — even more painful. Galeazzo lived in great opulence with Vittoria and their four sons and two daughters: the luxury of Renaissance palaces was their daily fare, and a glorious future of carefree wealth seemed to lie ahead of them. And yet the moment came when Galeazzo would give up all of that worry-free opulence to follow his heart, a heart that had been won for the gospel of free grace.

Galeazzo's Conversion

Even in Italy, so close to Rome, the influence of the Reformation was felt and the works of Martin Luther were known. A circle of aristocrats and intellectuals in Naples had begun to worry greatly about the spiritual and moral decay in the Roman Catholic Church, which they could witness from a nearby perspective. The Spanish mystic Juan de Valdés had a great impact on them through his preaching of justification without the works of the law. However, though the spirit of reform was very palpable, they did not want to break with the Church of Rome; rather, they wanted to try to reform the church from within. The passionate preacher Bernardino Ochino was active during that same period, and he even held the position of confessor of Pope Paul III at one point. So it stands to reason that initially there was hope among some people around Rome that the new sound of the gospel would have a wholesome effect — that it might even reach the heart of the pope!

But things turned out quite differently. The Inquisition tightened its grip on Rome, and all reform-minded preachers eventually had to leave for safer places. In 1542, Ochino became the first minister of the Italian church in Geneva. Later developments brought estrangement between him and Calvin, but at first Ochino and Valdés were the spiritual fathers of the Reformational movement in Italy. In addition, there was Vermigli, the Augustinian monk from Toscane whose preaching from 1 and 2 Corinthians brought about Galeazzo Caracciolo's experience of an intense conversion. A good friend, Gian Francesco Alois, introduced Galeazzo to the circle of Valdés, who also took him along to listen to Vermigli's sermons. These were to be a great blessing to Galeazzo, and in 1541 the twenty-four-year-old nobleman was drawn, through God's grace and Vermigli's preaching, from darkness into God's glorious light.

Exile

The ten years between Galeazzo's conversion and his final departure from Naples were a period in which he found it increasingly difficult to live according to his Reformational convictions. And it was his great-uncle, the cardinal, who wanted to exterminate every trace of those ideas that deviated from Rome. Those who openly declared their allegiance to the new doctrines could not stay, including Vermigli, the new convert's spiritual father, who fled to the north to find a place of refuge. He developed into a reputable biblical scholar who worked in Strasbourg, Oxford, and Zurich, and became a faithful ally and friend of Bucer, Calvin, and Bullinger. Galeazzo visited him in Strasbourg, but he returned to Naples after that trip.

Years of inner turmoil followed, but his firm belief in free grace did not diminish; but the difficulties to live according to that conviction only increased. His friend Alois was his support and shield. But when Alois gained too much of a reputation of being one who wanted to reform the church, he was arrested by the Inquisition and executed. Caracciolo knew that the time had come for him to leave his beloved city.

Caracciolo left Naples on March 21, 1551, without notifying his family of his decision. Since he had a close relationship with his father and experienced tender love in his married and family life, he must have taken this step with great pain in his heart. How much he had to give up in order to live in freedom in accordance with the Word of God, to follow the convictions of his heart!

He did not go directly to Geneva, but first sought the familiar setting of the imperial court in Augsburg. It may have been a diversion, that is, not yet allowing his family to think that he had left them for good. He may have hoped to meet people at the court who would be sympathetic toward his religious choice. And as long as he remained at the court of Charles V, the door to Naples remained open. But it did not take long for him to discover that Augsburg was closer to Rome than he had thought. It was clear that there was no other option but to look for a place where he would be able to live according to the prescripts of God's Word, and thus he walked through the gates of Geneva on June 8, 1551.

A Place of Honor

At first Geneva citizens regarded this refugee of noble birth with a degree of suspicion: they found it hard to believe that this courtier of Emperor Charles V was prepared to surrender his high position to henceforth live as a private citizen in Geneva. Could Caracciolo be a spy serving the interests of the emperor in this city that was so strategically located on the border with France, the country Charles had been waging war against for so long? Authorities decided to carefully monitor whatever contacts he had with people and whoever came to visit him in the hotel where he was staying.

But soon Caracciolo's sincerity was beyond doubt. His devotion to Calvin, with whom he soon had a close relationship, must have been an important factor in removing all possible misgivings. Before long, Caracciolo was one of the most respected residents of the city. The council and citizens of Geneva felt honored that such an important nobleman, who had moved in the circle of pope and emperor, had chosen their city as a place of refuge. He was known by all as "the lord marquis," though Galeazzo never really used that title himself.[4] When important guests visited Geneva, they were usually introduced to Caracciolo, and he would then be invited to the state banquets as well. The council assigned him a special bench in the church of St. Pierre, and in 1555 he became a citizen; he was appointed a member of the council of two hundred, and subsequently of the council of sixty. His presence was regarded as such an honor that the city minted a coin bearing his portrait in 1556 with this inscription: "Galeazzo Caracciolo, son of the Marquis of Vico."

4. He was said to have received this title when his father died, but when he fled, the emperor removed this future honor. His son, rather than he, would later be allowed to use the title "Marquis of Vico." Nonetheless, the Genevans respectfully used this appellation for him.

What counted for Calvin was not primarily his prestigious pedigree but the singular spiritual nobility of this Italian exile, which he valued gratefully. It was the invigorating power of the gospel that he found manifested in Caracciolo, rather than the honor he brought to Geneva, that led Calvin to focus attention on him by dedicating his commentary on 1 Corinthians to him. Here he praises the grace that he has seen in abundance in the steadfastness of this new friend and brother. Calvin writes that everyone should realize what a miracle it is that a man of such high nobility, rich with honor and possessions, a father of numerous children, with a happy and harmonious family life, has left everything of his own free will to come over to the camp of Christ. Calvin personally admits that the choice Caracciolo made for his faith had meant a lot to him as well. "I have noticed," he writes, "how your example has strengthened my faith and piety."[5] In Caracciolo, Calvin truly found a trusted friend who never disappointed him. For Calvin believed that denying oneself and steadfastly following Christ were the marks of a genuine Christian life.

This was, however, a life "under the cross." In 1556, Caracciolo had already been living in his new home for five years, and Calvin knew how his friend had faced the constant temptation to return to his former security. That much is clear from what he writes about him, but it makes the miracle of his endurance the more remarkable.[6]

Steadfast in Spite of Temptations

Caracciolo had left his family, relatives, and native country in order to live in Geneva in freedom and in conformity to the Word of God. But his relatives did not simply let him go. His sudden and definitive departure was undoubtedly a severe blow to them, the more so since there was an intimate bond of love and trust. Galeazzo had a good relationship with his father, whom he highly respected. And his marriage was truly a covenant of genuine love and faithfulness. But Galeazzo had understood

5. *CO*, 16: 12.

6. Caracciolo was sometimes pictured as a "second Moses," because Moses had left the wealth of Egypt behind and was willing to share in the sufferings of the people of God.

Galeazzo Caracciolo

what Christ meant when he had said that anyone who loves father or mother or wife or children more than him cannot have a part in the kingdom. The realization of obedience did not, of course, lessen the pain he felt in Geneva, particularly because he knew how much sadness he had inflicted on his loved ones by leaving them because of his faith.

The people in Naples were not yet prepared to accept that Galeazzo had left and would not return. Of course, his flight had also caused embarrassment to the family. But his father and other family members enjoyed so much respect that they did not suffer from the shame that could taint an entire family when someone had been condemned as a heretic. Colantonio remained in his high position at the court of the emperor, and Galeazzo's son was to inherit the position his father had forfeited. The family could have distanced itself completely from the apostate Galeazzo, but they did not do that. Their love for him prompted them to make several attempts to win him back.

First they sent a cousin who had always been like a brother to Galeazzo to Geneva to talk with him. But his attempt did not have the desired result. With tears in their eyes they said goodbye when the cousin left. They agreed that Galeazzo would meet with his father somewhere on Italian soil — someplace where he would not run too great a risk. This led to two cordial meetings between father and son during which they spent much time together. They even visited the court of Ferrara together, where Galeazzo delivered a letter from Calvin to Renée de France. In the end, however, the son returned to Geneva, and the father went back to Naples, unable to convince him to return to the fold of Rome. Furthermore, Galeazzo was unable to persuade his wife and children to join him. He even suggested that he could find a place to live in neutral territory in Switzerland, where his wife, Vittoria, would be allowed to practice her Roman Catholic faith, while her husband would remain Reformed. Ultimately, however, his wife and children refused to leave their city and their church.

The most dramatic encounter took place when Galeazzo could no longer wait for his family on a small island off the Dalmatian coast, and he decided to cross the water in person to visit his father's castle in Vico. In doing so he was putting his life in danger, for he was entering the jurisdiction of Naples, where he had been condemned as a heretic.

His father, wife, and children thought that at long last he had come to his senses and returned, and their initial joy was great. But the pain was even greater when it became clear that, for the sake of his faith, Galeazzo was unable to stay — despite his great love for them all. His father lost patience and cursed his son. His dear wife embraced him and pleaded with him not to abandon her. A little daughter of twelve cried and clung to his legs. But Galeazzo tore himself away, with great difficulty, from their embraces. He fled from the castle and hastened back to Geneva.

We can imagine how Calvin and the other people in Geneva held their breath concerning all these travels of "the lord marquis." But each time, when he returned, they saw in his steadfastness a confirmation of the truth of the Reformed faith.

A New Marriage

When Caracciolo understood that all his attempts to bring his wife to him in Geneva had failed, he wished to have the marriage dissolved so that he would be free to remarry.[7] During that last visit to his wife he had been told that, according to her confessor, she would not be allowed to live with him as his wife, even if he would return to her, as long as he was a heretic. He now knew that she would never come to Geneva, and hence he asked his friend Calvin and the city council whether he could under these circumstances obtain a legal divorce.

This request was problematic and was not simply endorsed without further discussion. Even though Caracciolo appealed to 1 Corinthians 7:15 (once again, the Corinthian correspondence that was so important to him), Calvin feared that the camp of Rome would conclude that the Reformed, by simply granting a divorce, were no longer paying attention to the divine laws and institutions. He asked his friend discreetly whether he might not be able to live without a wife. When Galeazzo indicated that that was not what he wanted, Calvin reluctantly gave him his support. But they proceeded with caution: they asked for

---

7. Robert N. Kingdon, "The Galeazzo Caracciolo Case: Divorce for Religious Desertion," in Kingdon, *Adultery and Divorce* (Cambridge, MA, 1995), pp. 143-56.

Galeazzo Caracciolo

the counsel of other authorities from elsewhere, and those authorities advised positively.

In the end, on behalf of the council, Calvin wrote Vittoria once more, giving her a two-month deadline for rejoining her husband, as the Bible prescribes. When this demand remained fruitless, Caracciolo's marriage was declared null and void. Not long after that, he married a wealthy widow, Anna Framéry, to whom he was to be happily married for twenty-seven years, until death separated them in 1586. During the entire period of that marriage, Caracciolo lived as an honorable citizen of Geneva and as an elder of the Italian church there. He lived near Calvin's home and remained a trusted ally and warm friend until Calvin's death.[8]

Reformed believers do not recognize saints, as is common in the Roman Catholic Church. Nevertheless, in Calvin's Geneva — and in the later Reformed tradition — Galeazzo Caracciolo was almost elevated to such a status, even though it was always clear that his admirable steadfastness was the fruit of grace alone.[9]

8. Caracciolo was Calvin's trusted pillar of support in the Italian community in Geneva, where heterodox opinions were regularly part of the landscape. We repeatedly see his name on the list of those to whom Calvin sends greetings in letters. This indicates that he belonged to the select circle of friends with whom Calvin was in daily contact.

9. A year after Caracciolo's death, Nicolao Balbani, the minister of the Italian church in Geneva, wrote a biography in which he holds up the steadfast faith and courage of that Italian nobleman as an example for all to follow. The book was translated into several languages, and others also related the life story of Caracciolo. Well into the nineteenth century, the story of this faithful witness remained popular reading. Christian Gottlieb Barth (1799-1862), a Pietist minister from the German city of Möttlingen, wrote an essay about Caracciolo that was used by J. F. Schimsheimer, a representative of the Reveil, when he wrote his brochure *Galeazzo Caracciolo, Geschetst als Mensen als Christen* (Amsterdam, 1844). The publisher, H. Höveker, officially presented this modest publication to the city fathers of Amsterdam, as is evident from the copy that is kept in the Royal Library in The Hague.

An Italian Friend

THE BUDÉ FAMILY

A French Family as Friends

Guillaume Budé, from Beza's *Icones*

The Reformation in Geneva may be characterized as the "Reformation of the Refugee," which is the characterization that church historian Heiko Oberman has proclaimed with great insistence.[1] Calvin's theology and his work in Geneva were strongly impacted by the mentality of the refugee community, which Geneva increasingly became during his years of service, when many exiles from France found a safe haven in this free border city.

This "refugee motif" has been of determining significance for the heart of Calvin's theology. His so-called doctrine of election is thus not primarily a chapter in a systematic theology but a concrete and powerful confession of comfort. Driven into exile, the refugees may well have thought that the cause of Christ's kingdom did not look very promising. Yet their faith in God's gracious election encouraged them in the face of the triumphant dominance of the enemy. For it was through small numbers that God chose to establish the kingdom of his Son on earth.

Calvin had to leave the country of his birth in order to live in freedom according to his faith, and he never was able to return. But his heart and his interest were constantly focused on France. Geneva was not just a place of refuge; it was also a base of operation. From this city many young men who had been trained by Calvin were sent to France, especially in the latter phase of his life, where they were to serve the cause of the gospel.[2] After 1555, when the resistance to Calvin had been broken in Geneva, there was an unprecedented increase of Reformed churches in his native country. Geneva was not just a goal in itself, but it was a training ground for a much larger "project": the reform of one of the most important nations of Europe — France. That's why the French connections were of such importance to Calvin, and why he remained constantly focused on France.

Calvin's best friends, those who lived in close proximity to him in Geneva, and whose names are mentioned in the greetings of numer-

1. Oberman's work that defends this thesis, *The Reformation of the Refugees,* is to be published posthumously by Droz in Geneva and is forthcoming.
2. Robert M. Kingdon, *Geneva and the Coming Wars of Religion in France, 1555-1563* (Geneva, 1956); Kingdon, "Calvin's Last Years," in *Calvinus Paeceptor Ecclesiae,* ed. Herman J. Selderhuis (Geneva, 2004), pp. 179-87.

A French Family as Friends

ous letters, were fellow believers from France almost without exception. The neighborhood in Geneva where Calvin lived was like a "little France": old friendships were constantly being renewed with the arrival of French people whom Calvin had known in his youth. Thus he must have been happy to see the widow of one of his early teachers, Guillaume Budé, when she arrived in the city in 1549 along with her family.

A Teacher Who Did Not Want to Follow

The learned nobleman Guillaume Budé (1468-1540) was one of the leading figures of French humanism, a friend of both Erasmus and Thomas More. He was renowned throughout France as a legal scholar. In the early 1530s, when Calvin was back in Paris for study, he became acquainted with Budé and his family. The young lawyer, with his great predilection for literature, must have regarded it as a singular privilege that he had the opportunity to move in the intimate circle of this prominent scholar who was in the forefront of a scientific revival. With his passionate plea for knowledge of the classical languages, Budé proved to be of great influence for Calvin's further development, first as a humanist and later as a servant of the divine Word.

Guillaume Budé had a cordial relationship with King Francis I, and probably had something to do with the latter's favorable attitude toward humanists. His influence was such that he succeeded in establishing a separate Parisian college, where science would be based on knowledge of the three classical languages. In March 1530, the Collège Royal, which was later to become the famous Collège de France, was founded with the approval and support of the king.

The old conservative current of the Sorbonne University did not share in the enthusiasm of many young students for this new spirit of scholarship. They believed that this new approach to the Bible, which was based on close study of the original languages, sounded too much like "Lutheranism." But the people of the Sorbonne failed in their attempts to secure a prohibition of the reading and study of the Bible in the original languages. The "alliance between the Crown and the humanist," for which Budé had been personally responsible as a servant

The Budé Family

of the king, prevented the opponents from wiping the Collège Royal off the face of the earth.[3]

Although Calvin was initially an eager student of Budé, his teacher never followed him in drawing out the full ramifications of this new understanding of Scripture. In 1535 a rupture took place in the relationship between teacher and student, and the stimulant was the so-called Affair of the Placards. Protesters were putting up posters all over France that condemned the Roman Catholic mass as idolatry in the light of Holy Scripture. The shock caused by this spiritual earthquake in France also brought about splits in the circle of evangelical humanists. King Francis I was deeply disturbed when he found a pamphlet on his bedroom door that referred to the holy sacrament as blasphemy. Guillaume Budé vehemently opposed these protests and attacks. In a book he wrote in 1535, he presented a picture of a gradual shift from Greek thought toward Christianity, and he pleaded for a dialogue between the Catholic and the reform-minded spirits. At the same time, however, he spoke with disdain about the Protestant Reformation, which he considered too great a break with tradition and far too populist. As a reaction to that, he proposed a large conciliatory procession that would be held in Paris, a service of the worship of the body of Christ in the Eucharist.

The Affair of the Placards may have driven Budé to be far more Catholic than he wanted to be deep in his heart; it prompted Calvin, on the other hand, to leave France for the sake of his faith. The question remains whether Budé was as solidly in the Roman Catholic camp as he appeared to be. Could it also have been the frustration of a man who saw his life's work endangered because a campaign in the name of the rebellious Reformation had gotten out of hand? The French king was certainly driven back into the conservative camp by what had happened.[4]

---

3. Cottret, *Calvin* (Paris, 1995), pp. 66-68, 98-99.

4. Calvin defends himself in his "Letter to King Francis I," which serves as an introduction to his *Institutes,* against those who want to view the Reformation as a rebellious movement. Even though he does not spell it out, he turns against moderate spirits such as Sadolet and Budé, who were among those who influenced King Francis I to regard the Reformation as a popular uprising. Against Budé, Calvin tries to convince the king of the legitimacy of the Reformation. See J. Bohatec, *Budé and Calvin* (Graz, 1950), pp. 128-29.

A French Family as Friends

Did Budé see his hopes shattered? Did he see that a gradual increase in the knowledge of the Bible would inevitably result in a reformation of the church? Whatever the case may have been, after 1535 teacher and student were on opposite sides of the divide between Roman Catholic and Reformed. Calvin left for Basel, and Budé stayed in Paris. This makes it even more noteworthy that, after everything was said and done, Budé's widow, along with some of her children, eventually joined Calvin in Geneva in 1549.

Encouraging Immigration

On June 28, 1549, Calvin wrote to Bucer, who lived in England at the time, about his worries regarding Geneva, where he found little true piety and godliness.[5] It was only three months since Calvin had lost his wife, and the fact that he was still mourning the loss of his beloved partner may to some extent have stimulated his sense of loneliness and gloom. How much Calvin must have longed for the communion of the saints, bonded in the fear of God, that enables a person to live and die happily!

But even as he writes this, he immediately corrects himself. Not everything is negative. On the contrary, as long as he sees devout people from all sides flocking to Geneva to rally around the gospel banner, his hope that the Lord will be the patron of Geneva remains alive. In this connection he adds: "The widow of Budé has arrived with her children. Other members of this family have also voluntarily accepted exile, so as to serve God in peace together with us. Oh, that our Pharaoh [referring to the king of France] would at last come back to his senses, so that he would not inflict so much damage on himself and others." This last lamentation indicates how much the arrival in Geneva of the family of France's most famous humanist must have meant to Calvin. It must have given the French food for thought that a rigid opposition against this religious movement had led to such a loss of prominent citizens to Geneva. On the other side, Calvin and his city regarded it as an encouraging confirmation of a righteous cause.

5. *CO*, 20: 393-95.

The move to Geneva in the year 1549 was certainly not a decision that the Budé family made lightly.[6] The mother's name was Roberte le Lieur, and she had been married to Guillaume for thirty-five years at the time of his death in 1540. Together they had raised a large family of seven sons and four daughters. It is certain that at least four sons and one daughter joined the Reformation, because we meet them later in Geneva. A few of the children accompanied their mother, who had already become quite old when she moved to Geneva. Unfortunately, she was not destined to enjoy her new place of residence for very long, for she was called to her eternal dwelling place in 1551.

Already in the years prior to their departure, there had been regular contact between the Budé family and Calvin. Jean Budé visited Geneva in 1547, and Calvin used him to deliver a letter to the Lord De Falais in Basel. Calvin recommends him in the letter, telling his friend that young Budé deserves respect, not just because he is the son of a famous father, but also because he does not belong to "those people who have such an inflated ego." Calvin writes that his modesty gives him even greater value, and he also expresses his concern about the travel his friend is about to embark on. It is unwise to put oneself in danger unnecessarily.[7]

A Letter to a Widow

What prompted Budé's widow to reach such a momentous decision — to go into exile — some nine years after her husband's death and at such an advanced age herself? We have one of Calvin's letters, probably dating from the end of 1546, that is addressed to an unnamed widow in France (it is assumed that it was Budé's widow).[8] In this letter Calvin responds at considerable length to a message he had received from her (it may well be that this letter was carried to her by her son Jean after his visit to Geneva).

6. For more about the friendship between this family and Calvin, see Jeannine E. Olson, "Les amis de Jean Calvin: La famille Budé," in *Calvin et Ses Contemporaines;* see also Olson, "The Friends of John Calvin," in David Foxgrover, ed., *Calvin Studies Society Papers,* 1995, 1997 (Grand Rapids, 1998), pp. 159-68.

7. *CO,* 12: 535-36.

8. *CO,* 12: 452-55.

A French Family as Friends

The letter is a touching example of the intensely pastoral manner with which Calvin dealt with the dilemma that many kindred spirits were facing in France: How could they, with a clear conscience, live according to God's Word as long as they were still expected to participate daily in the rites of the Church of Rome? Calvin has no doubt that Madame Budé passionately longs to be delivered from this misery, and he knows that she will be filled with concern and sadness as long as she is in the midst of this. But is true peace to be found in Geneva? Calvin gives an honest answer: No, not even Geneva can offer eternal rest. For as long as we are in this world, we are like a bird perched on a branch. This is God's will and this is for our good. But now that this "little corner of the earth [i.e., Geneva] is offered to you, where you may either end your days in the service of God or, if it pleases him, will make further progress and gain further strength in his Word, so that you may even endure persecutions, if that would be God's will, you have no reason to refuse this offer."

Calvin is pressing her hard in this letter. He says, in effect, I know how difficult it is to leave your own country, especially for a woman at such an advanced age and of such high pedigree. But these hesitations must be overcome by a better consideration. There is no place more suitable for us to live in our older years than where we can live in God's church, where he peacefully sits on his throne. Calvin's powerful plea to come to Geneva did not mean that he was not aware of the major consequences such a step would entail for the entire family. But he insists in his letter that she should, with peace in her heart, commit this to the providence of God. Nor should her concern for a favorable marriage for her daughter keep her away from Geneva. God is also able, Calvin assures her, to provide a husband with whom she may serve God. Indeed, this turned out to be true: Roberte Budé's daughter Marguerite, who arrived in Geneva along with her mother, soon married Guillaume de Trie, Lord of Varennes, a nobleman who was a personal friend of Calvin.

A New Place of Residence
A few years after receiving the above letter from Calvin, Roberte Budé did take the decisive step. Nine years after her husband had died, she

left France for good. It may well be that the death in 1547 of King Francis I, with whom her husband had enjoyed such a close connection, contributed to her decision. The new king, Henri II, was a much fiercer persecutor of the Reformed than his father had ever been.

Not all of her children came with her at that time. All of them were already adults, and some remained loyal to the Roman Catholic Church and thus had no reason to leave France. Others followed her to Geneva at a later time. She arrived in the city with her sons Jean and Louis and her daughter Marguerite, and they found a house on Calvin's street. François joined the family five years later, in 1554, but by that time his mother had already died (probably in 1551). The family apparently had not left France without some means, and they were able to buy some estates and other possessions to assure their sustenance.

The Budé children soon found their way in their new city. Louis Budé followed in his father's footsteps by using his gifts as a linguistic scholar in his new environment. He was appointed professor of Hebrew and Old Testament. He prepared a French translation of the book of Psalms, which appeared in 1551 and was highly recommended by Calvin, as is shown by the latter's preface to it. But Geneva was not to enjoy Louis's gifts for a long time: he died on May 25, 1551, leaving a considerable sum of money to the Bourse Française in support of poor French refugees.

Jean Budé, Sieuer de Vérace

Upon the death of his mother and brother Louis, Jean (1515-1587) became the head of the Budé family in Geneva. He was totally dedicated to Calvin, and the latter, in turn, regarded Jean as one of his most intimate friends, a friend he trusted implicitly. As a result, Calvin frequently sent Jean on missions as his personal envoy to other Reformers and royalty in support of the persecuted Huguenots. In addition to the information conveyed in the letters, Calvin usually indicated that the oral information from his messenger Jean — which was too confidential to put down on paper — would further clarify the urgency of the matter.

In a letter to the ministers in Zurich, Calvin refers to him as an "excellent and, above all, courageous man, my deeply beloved Lord Jean

A French Family as Friends

Budé," who braved the difficulties of the awful season in his travels for the sake of the church.[9] In a letter to Renée de France, he asks her to give an oral account of the news from Montargis, for he is "one of my most trusted friends, a man who is so reliable that he may be believed even concerning the smallest details."[10]

But this friend was not so far above reproach that he did not have faults: toward the end of his life he had some problems in Geneva. In 1580 he was called on the carpet for his lack of care in dealing with the custody of funds owned by his two nieces. In the end, this affair fizzled out; but the city of Geneva decided to cut some of the funds for Jean's travels and his pension. He apparently had some difficulties with financial matters. But Jean knew what genuine remorse meant. He confesses in his last will and testament, dated March 9, 1587, that as "a poor and miserable creature," who discovers in himself only "reasons for death and doom," he had nonetheless based his hope on the blood of Christ, which purifies from all sins.[11]

None of the above subtracts from the fact that Jean Budé was of great significance, not only for Calvin, but also for the city of Geneva. In the early phase of the French religious wars, he traveled as an untiring diplomat, sometimes along with Beza, to the German princes and the French Huguenots for the sake of the progress of the church. This period was one of extreme anxiety for Calvin because, just when he expected to see a breakthrough of Christ's kingdom in France that would result in the fading of the power of Rome, war had broken out. With prophetic foresight, Calvin understood that this would harm rather than help the cause of the Reformation. In the final years of his life, however, it was a comfort to him that, in the midst of numerous hotheads, he could trust Jean Budé unreservedly and could send him on any mission with full confidence.

We should not fail to note that Jean Budé not only provided his valuable services on his missions outside of Geneva, but he was also far from idle when he was in Geneva. Among other functions, he was a dea-

9. *CO,* 14: 674-78.
10. *CO,* 20: 230-33.
11. Olson, "The Friends of John Calvin," p. 166.

con at the Bourse Française, served on the city council, and assisted Calvin with the publication of his lectures. He never entered the ministry, but as minutes secretary for the church and publisher of Calvin's lectures, his services with regard to the exegesis of the Bible were of great importance in Geneva and far beyond. In this capacity he worked closely with another friend and secretary of Calvin, Charles de Jonvillier, whose sister he had married.[12]

The French Connection — Only Positive?

Was the fact that Calvin was surrounded by so many French friends in Geneva only positive?[13] Though we cannot deny the many valuable aspects, we might nonetheless ask a few questions. We might ask, for example, whether these French friends, who tended to have the greatest admiration for their model and teacher, offered enough balance when needed. They had so much in common with Calvin in their thinking and daily praxis that it would seem to preclude any criticisms of Calvin. And one's friends may be the best persons to point out one's weaknesses. Calvin was aware of the fact that he did not have an easy personality, and his friends undoubtedly noticed that as well. It may well be that reactions from his French friends had a wholesome effect on him, whereas those outside the French circle may not have seen a chance to influence him when he needed it. We do not know how much they tried. But we are left with the impression that his French friends had at least the adverse effect on Calvin of not helping him integrate more fully and naturally with the original inhabitants of Geneva. He remained "that Frenchman," even though he gave his heart and life in the service of God for the church of Geneva.

12. In the preface to Calvin's published lectures on Hosea, Budé and Jonvilliers explain how they worked on the publication of Calvin's lectures.
13. See Olson, "The Friends of John Calvin," pp. 167-68.

A French Family as Friends

HEINRICH BULLINGER

A Swiss Friend

Heinrich Bullinger, from Beza's *Icones*

The friendship between Heinrich Bullinger (1504-1575) and Calvin was of crucial importance for the Reformation.[1] If there had been a rift between the *antistes* (official title of the minister of the main church in Zurich) and the chairman of the Company of Pastors in Geneva, the future of Reformed Protestantism might have looked quite different. And both men fully realized this. Bullinger regularly wrote to Calvin from the depth of his heart: "Let us love each other and thus build the churches." A separation between these leading Reformers, which might have been caused by their differences in temperament or their different theological emphases, could certainly have been fatal for the church in Geneva. Even though there were occasional tensions in their friendship, there was never a split that irreversibly severed their bond. Bullinger and Calvin remained devoted to each other, and in fact became increasingly close as they got older. This was not only because circumstances forced them to remain on good terms with each other,[2] but also because there was a genuine and cordial spiritual bond that was based on their mutual love for the church of Christ.[3]

1. On Bullinger, see Ulrich Gäbler, "Heinrich Bullinger," in Martin Greschat, ed., *Gestalten der Kirchengeschichte: Der Reformationszeit II* (Stuttgart, 1993), pp. 197-209; Aurelio A. Garcia, "Bullinger's Friendship with Calvin: Loving One Another and Edifying the Churches," in *Calvin Studies Society Papers*, 1995, 1997, ed. David Foxgrover (Grand Rapids, 1998), pp. 119-33; Bruce Gordon and Emidio Campi, eds., *Architect of Reformation: An Introduction to Heinrich Bullinger, 1504-1575* (Grand Rapids, 2004); Fritz Büsser, "Calvin und Bullinger," in *Calvinus Servus Christi*, ed. Wilhelm H. Neuser (Budapest, 1988), pp. 107-26; David C. Steinmetz, "Heinrich Bullinger (1504-1575)," in *Reformers in the Wings* (Oxford, 2001), pp. 93-99; De Greef, "Heinrich Bullinger (1504-1575)," in *De Ware Uitleg: Hervormers en hun Verklaring van de Bijbel* (Leyden, 1995), pp. 99-116; Frans P. van Stam, "Das Verhältnis zwischen Bullinger und Calvin während Calvins ersten Aufenthalt in Genf," in *Calvin im Context der Schweizer Reformation,* ed. Peter Opitz (Zurich, 2003), pp. 25-40.

2. We find this view in Gordon and Campi, *Architect of Reformation,* p. 25: "His friendship to the Frenchman was complex, built on necessity and respect more than friendship." This view, however, does not account for the intensity and tone of their extensive exchange of letters.

3. Garcia, "Bullinger's Friendship with Calvin," pp. 126ff.

A Swiss Friend

Men with Beards

Why did most of the preachers of the Reformation have beards, whereas the Roman Catholic clergy did not? One historian gives an interesting explanation of that phenomenon.[4] He suggests that the Protestant clergymen had a need to demonstrate their patriarchal masculinity, while the celibate clergy of Rome did not feel that need. The Reformers married, established families, and grew beards. This also enhanced their authority when they preached, because it made them look like Old Testament prophets, who all were assumed to have beards. No one can be sure of the reason for all these bearded Reformers. We do know that Heinrich Bullinger was one of the most impressive figures among these bearded ministers, as is evident from the surviving portraits of him.

Heinrich was born on July 18, 1504, into the home of a Catholic priest who openly lived with his family. Although the Church of Rome required celibacy of its priests, it was possible in actual practice to make a financial arrangement with the bishop to be married. Many priests thus lived as faithful husbands with a wife and children, even though they had not entered into an official sacramental marriage. The fact that Father Bullinger, as the priest of the Swiss village of Bremgarten, had a wife and five children was evidence that he did not bother too much with the demands that the Catholic Church had made on her servants (without scriptural support).

It seems likely that, from his childhood on, Heinrich inherited his father's healthy independent spirit, which was more interested in biblical authority than church legalities. However, it is noteworthy that, when the senior Bullinger lost his position in 1529 because of his public stand in favor of the Reformation, he had his marriage, which had already existed for decades, formally confirmed on New Year's Eve.

A Born Teacher

The young Heinrich was a precocious child in a family where he received his education with his mother's milk. From the age of five he at-

---

4. Diarmaid MacCulloch, *Reformation: Europe's House Divided, 1490-1700* (London and New York: Allen Lane, 2003).

Heinrich Bullinger

tended the Latin school; when he was twelve, his father sent him away to begin the adventurous life of an international student. He began his studies at the Latin school of Emmerich, which was so close to the Dutch border that he may well have been exposed to the influence of the "Modern Devotion," a theological movement that promoted a scholarly approach to Scripture with the aim of true piety. Though his school had no official link to the "Brethren of the Common Life," it did breathe their spirit.

Student life was a miserable existence. In order to survive, the students had to live more or less like beggars, dependent on the support of others. The reason Heinrich had to live this way was not that his parents were without means. Rather, it was a principle of the school: it supposedly prepared the students to face the real world. After two years, Bullinger registered at the University of Cologne. The years during which he pursued his general scholarly education in Cologne, where he completed his *Magister Artium* (master's degree), proved to be decisive for the rest of his life. From the books that freely circulated among the students he became acquainted with Erasmus, Luther, and Melanchthon. Without having met these scholars in person, he became convinced of the truth of the gospel by studying their writings. This led to his break with Rome.

In 1522, the eighteen-year-old master returned to his birthplace. He had initially planned, after finishing his studies, to enter a monastery and devote the rest of his life to theology. In fact, however, he decided to seek a post as a teacher so that he could serve others with his newly acquired knowledge. The abbot of the Kappel monastery asked him to become the teacher of his monks, to which Bullinger agreed on the condition that he be allowed to continue living according to his reform-minded insights. The abbot did not have a problem with that. For six years Bullinger had ample opportunity to teach, not only the monks but also a much wider circle of interested persons. In order to do all he could to advance the dissemination of the sacred knowledge of Scripture, he taught his lessons in German, the vernacular of that region. The abbot and the monks were thus won over for the Reformation; the result was that the convent school eventually became a training institute for Reformed preachers.

A Swiss Friend

During this period the young teacher also found his life partner, Anna Adlischwyler, a former nun. They were married in 1528, and they were to share more than thirty years of life — as well as eleven children — together in love. In 1560 she fell victim to the plague, which also nearly cost Bullinger his life. Throughout their married life, the Bullinger house in Zurich was like a guesthouse for all those who were in support of the Reformation. Those who visited Zurich — from as far away as England or Hungary — received a warm welcome. And though Bullinger himself liked to stay at home, it became a center for information and the reinforcing of international contacts. After moving back to Zurich in 1531, Bullinger hardly left the city again until his death in 1575. In contrast to other Reformers, he hated traveling. Though Calvin repeatedly invited him to pay a visit to Geneva, arguing that a bit of traveling would be wholesome, Bullinger decided nonetheless to stay near hearth and home.[5] He simply waited for the people to visit him and for the many letters that were brought to him by those who passed through the city on their journeys. He never made the trip to Calvin's city.

Zwingli's Successor

During his years as Bible teacher in Kappel, Bullinger became a devoted student of Zwingli, who was the leader of the Swiss Reformation. During the year when he was married, he succeeded his father as the minister at Bremgarten, the town of his birth. But two years later, we find him inside the city walls of Zurich, where he had to seek refuge after the Roman Catholic cities defeated the cities that had embraced the Reformation. Zwingli's policy, which was aimed at enforcing the Reformation of the Swiss alliance with arms, became a dangerous failure that put the future of Protestantism in all of Switzerland at serious risk. It cost Zwingli his life on October 11, 1531: he died on a battlefield near Kappel while serving as an army chaplain.

Who was to ensure that peace would return during this time of crisis in the troubled city of Zurich? People were convinced that Bullinger, the twenty-seven-year-old exile from Bremgarten, would be the right

5. *CO*, 16: 435-36.

Heinrich Bullinger

person. He was appointed to the position of *antistes,* minister of the Grossmunster church of Zurich, and thus became the formal leader of the Reformation in and around Zurich. He held that position for forty-four years, right up to his death.

In fulfilling this responsibility, he concentrated on the preaching of the Word. For many years he preached as many as six sermons a week, and after 1542 he still continued with at least three a week. It has been calculated that he preached a total of well over 7,500 sermons during his lifetime. He knew how to present the Word in a spiritual and practical manner and how to touch the hearts of simple people as well as scholars. Many of his sermons were published not only in Switzerland, but they were also translated and distributed throughout Europe. He had a profound influence on the Reformation in England and the Netherlands. His publication *Decades,* an exposition of the faith in five series of ten Bible lectures, served ministers and believers as a valuable source of Bible knowledge for many years. The English archbishop even made it required reading for prospective ministers. And it appears that Bullinger's published sermons had even more influence in England than the writings of Calvin did.[6] Hence there is every reason to regard him, along with Calvin, as one of the founders of Reformed Protestantism.

During the years of his leadership in Zurich, Bullinger was not primarily an innovator who shaped the Reformation in new ways; rather, he was the faithful custodian of Zwingli's heritage. He made sure that the significance of his honored predecessor would not forever be lost in Zurich — or beyond, in Switzerland and Europe.

Two Comrades in Arms

Where and when did Bullinger and Calvin first meet? In a letter Calvin wrote years later, he reminds Bullinger of a meeting they had in Basel in early 1536.[7] At that time Calvin was still a young scholar who had escaped from France to find a safe haven where he could finish his *Institutes.* Bullinger had already been the leader of the Swiss Reformation

6. De Greef, *De Ware Uitleg,* pp. 106ff.
7. Letter dated May 22, 1557. *CO,* 16: 490.

for some five years, following in the footsteps of Zwingli. It was probably then that they laid the foundation for a loyal and friendly cooperation, while each one continued to have his own emphases. Was Bullinger impressed right from the beginning with the great gifts of the young Frenchman, gifts that were manifest in his first theological treatise? We do not know whether that was immediately the case.[8] But in any case, we can assume that he understood that he was dealing with a sharp and independent spirit who could not merely be categorized as a follower of Luther. Bullinger appreciated such theologians, all the more because he himself had to do his utmost to keep the heritage of Zwingli alive and pure, particularly in the face of the implicit suspicions of the Wittenbergers. Bullinger suspected that, if he wanted to avoid isolation, he might need Calvin in the future.

Calvin, for his part, could also profit from Bullinger's support in his attempts to improve relationships with the Swiss in Geneva's precarious situation of constantly defending its independence against Bern's interference. From day one, the friendship between Bullinger and Calvin was in part inspired by the situation of these two Reformation leaders, each of whom needed the other as a comrade in arms at the different battlefronts where they had their sentry posts.

A Divisive Issue in the Reformation

One of Bullinger's problems was that Luther, in his later years, was relentless in his efforts to suspiciously caricature Zwingli's doctrine of the Lord's Supper as *Schwärmerei* (the term used in the Lutheran tradition for various Anabaptist groups). He believed that the Swiss were infected by Anabaptism because they denied the real presence of the body of Christ in the Lord's Supper. Bullinger deeply regretted that Bucer, the Strasbourg Reformer, had concluded the so-called Concord of Wittenberg with Luther in 1536, suggesting that the two leaders had come to an agreement. The result was to drive the Swiss more and more into a corner. This was the reason Bullinger had a problem with Bucer,

8. In contrast to others, van Stam does not think so. "Das Verhältnis zwischen Bullinger und Calvin," p. 26.

whom he accused of unforgivable leniency toward Luther. Bullinger feared that the agreement with Luther could become a very divisive issue among the Swiss.

During his early years in Geneva, Calvin was having his own problems. His failure to introduce church discipline had led, after two years of clashes with the authorities, to his exile. But it was not only the uncooperative city council that was responsible for the strained relationships. Matters were further complicated by the patronizing attitude of powerful Bern, which was acting as a protector of the newly won freedom in Geneva. There was no way Bern was going to allow the church in Geneva to develop according to the principles that Calvin and Farel believed were found in Scripture. For the lords in Bern, such matters as the introduction of a confession for all citizens and that of discipline around the table of the Lord were intolerable.

During these difficult times, Calvin sought contact with Bullinger in Zurich, but he did so regarding the issue of excommunication. The opinion in Zurich on that issue was different from that among the ministers of Geneva. Perhaps Calvin was hoping that Zurich would not join its voice to the Bern choir, that is, against Geneva. Did he write in the hope that Bullinger would remain silent about his views and thus not make things even more difficult for the Geneva Reformers? What hope could Calvin have that Bullinger would help him? Perhaps he knew that Bullinger felt very uneasy about the threatening influence of Wittenberg toward the Swiss alliance. Whatever the case, Bullinger knew he had two colleagues in Calvin and Farel who held an independent position in the struggle between the Germans and the Swiss. When Calvin and Farel were eventually forced to leave Geneva, they hastened immediately to Zurich to participate in a theological conference that Bullinger was holding there.

In one of his first extant letters to Bullinger, Calvin says that he understands why Luther's ideas had caused such irritation in Zurich.[9] He refers to the negative character traits of Luther, who, he said, is far too "irritable," and even "embittered," when it concerns the issue of the sacraments. Yet Calvin also defends Luther, saying that, despite his ma-

9. *CO*, 40: 772-75.

A Swiss Friend

jor deficiencies, he remains an "excellent servant of God." "Even if he were to denounce me as a devil," Calvin says, "I would still hold him in a high esteem." He adds: "We must not bite or devour each other."

In this letter Calvin does not define his views of the Lord's Supper, for fear that Bullinger might misunderstand certain things. But he does say that he would like to talk to him face to face for half a day; he believes that the two would soon agree with each other. He ends with the assurances that he believes "a minor disagreement" does not have to obstruct a "brotherly friendship" and signs the letter "your John Calvin." The remarkable thing about the relationship between Bullinger and Calvin is that they both realized how they continued to differ on certain emphases, but that, in the essence of their theology and praxis, they sensed their unity in the Lord. Bullinger sometimes complained to Calvin when — in his hypersensitivity to Lutheran ideas — he believed he had read or heard something from Calvin that he thought was wrong. At times he felt irritated by Calvin's criticism, which he had himself invited by sending Calvin his books for evaluation. Calvin would answer: "What use does it have that we fight with each other? I only do the duty of a friend by giving my opinion. Let us seek the close communion in Christ. . . . We continue to have the same Christ and to be one in Him. Perhaps we will once have the privilege to meet in full unanimity. I have always loved simplicity and have never found joy in sophistries."[10]

The Consensus of Zurich

Calvin's wish was fulfilled in the agreement he and Bullinger reached in 1549 regarding the doctrine of the Lord's Supper, which was a fruit of this brotherly friendship. This agreement received its formal shape in the so-called Consensus Tigurinus, the agreement of Zurich, and it laid the foundation for the communion of all non-Lutheran Protestants around the table of the Lord. This consensus has justifiably been called "a remarkable example of theological statemanship."[11] Bullinger emphasizes how the meaning of the sacrament depends only on the activ-

10. *CO,* 12: 665-67.
11. MacCulloch, *Reformation,* pp. 262-64.

ity of the Holy Spirit, without emphasizing the substances of the sacrament. But for him the Lord's Supper was also more than a pious remembrance, as Zwingli had taught. Calvin passionately believed that Christ truly allows us to become a part of him in the Lord's Supper. The substance of his body is in heaven, but he truly gives his body to those who lift their hearts heavenward. This consensus brought the two views together in one confession of faith.

The agreement was strongly opposed by the Lutheran camp; nevertheless, it was of great service to the Reformed in Geneva and throughout Switzerland, and to all those in Europe who were in the Reformed tradition's sphere of influence. The consensus maintained and strengthened the unity. It also remained the norm that the parties were expected to adhere to, even though at times they continued to look at each other with suspicion. At one point, when Bullinger heard that Beza had spoken too positively about the Augsburg Confession in Germany during his political mission to seek support for the oppressed French, Calvin hastened to assure Bullinger that Beza had been "thoughtless," and that he should have no fear that the agreement was to be annulled.[12]

The Father of Reformed Protestantism

Bullinger and Calvin knew that they were one in Christ. This was the foundation of their friendship, which may not have been primarily a matter of personal affection but rather a brotherly bond in a time of need. Calvin needed Bullinger to acquire and keep the support of the Swiss federation for Geneva and France. Bullinger, for his part, was grateful to have in this friend who was a great theologian and leader someone who understood him and did not want to make the Swiss into Lutherans. They differed in their theology, but not fundamentally so. Although Bullinger's doctrine of predestination was in essence not very different from that of Calvin, he gave it a different weight in ecclesiastical and pastoral praxis.[13] Bullinger's heart was particularly touched by

---

12. *CO,* 16: 564-66.
13. Cornelis P. Venema, "Heinrich Bullinger's Correspondence on Calvin's Doctrine of Predestination," *Sixteenth Century Journal* 17, no. 4 (1986): 435-50.

God's covenantal actions for his people, by God's journey with his people through the ages. Thus he gave human responsibility and obedience in the light of God's sovereign grace its fullest due.

The Remonstrants wrongly tried to make Bullinger their champion during the Synod of Dordrecht. Indeed, Bullinger had strong misgivings about the way he believed the struggle concerning predestination was allowed to escalate in Geneva. And his preaching was full of the breadth and all-encompassing nature of God's promises. But where it concerned God's grace and free will, he was more solidly in the Calvinist camp than the Remonstrants wanted people to believe. It may well be that their attempt to make Bullinger their leader was the reason that, after Dordrecht, he never received the place in the Reformed tradition that he initially had and certainly deserved. When we perceive the far-reaching distribution of his practical and pastoral writings throughout Europe, and survey the extensive Reformational network that surrounded his person, we can justifiably call him — with the same honor Calvin earned — a "father of Reformed Protestantism."[14]

14. Twelve thousand of his letters are extant, more than those of Luther, Calvin, and Melanchthon combined.

Heinrich Bullinger

JOHN KNOX

A Scottish Friend

John Knox, from Beza's *Icones*

A Scottish Friend

227

The Most Perfect School of Christ

It is very interesting to note how the Scottish Reformer John Knox (ca. 1513-1572) occupies a prominent place among the figures on the impressive Monument of the Reformation in Geneva.[1] He is the fourth person, next to the Genevan threesome of Farel, Calvin, and Beza, who are handing the torch to each other. Seen from the perspective of the Reformation in Geneva, a statue of a person such as Pierre Viret might have been more justifiable. But the Reformer from Scotland, who only served for a short time in Geneva as the pastor of the English church, is prominently present with the Geneva Reformers. The reason may be that, when the monument was erected, in the early twentieth century, Knox was regarded as a representative of the international character of the Calvinist Reformation, surely the most famous representative of the Reformation in the English-speaking world.

It may also be that Knox owes his place of honor to the most eloquent description that was ever given of the city of Geneva during Calvin's time. In a letter he speaks about Geneva as a place "that I do not fear and that does not make me ashamed when I say that it is the most perfect school of Christ that ever existed on earth since the days of the apostles."[2] He adds: "There are other places where Christ is faithfully proclaimed, but I have seen no other place where the lifestyle and the religion have been so thoroughly reformed." His appreciation for Calvin's Reformation seems to have assured him a position close to the Reformer, whom he felt privileged to have as a friend. John Knox only

---

1. On John Knox, see Dale W. Johnson and James Edward McGoldrick, "Prophet in Scotland," *Calvin Theological Journal* 33, no. 1 (1998): 76-86; Richard Kyle, "John Knox and the Care of Souls," *Calvin Theological Journal* 38, no. 1 (2003): 125-38; Michael Treschow, "John Knox," in *Encyclopedia of Christianity*, 3: 133-34; E. G. Rupp, "The Europe of John Knox," in *John Knox: A Quarterly Reappraisal*, ed. Duncan Shaw (Edinburgh, 1975), pp. 1-17; Gordon Donaldson, "Knox the Man," in Shaw, *John Knox: A Quarterly Reappraisal*, pp. 18-32; Edwin Muir, *John Knox: Portrait of a Calvinist* (London, 1929); G. Bouwmeester, *John Knox, de Hervormer van Schotland* (Rotterdam, 1964); W. Stanford Reid, *Trumpeter of God* (New York, 1974); Jasper Ridley, *John Knox* (Oxford, 1968); P. J. Kromsigt, *John Knox als Kerkhervormer* (Utrecht, 1895).

2. "Whair I nether feir nor eschame to say is the maist perfyt schoole of Chryst that ever was in the erth since the dayis of te Apostillis" (cited in P. Hume Brown, *John Knox* [London, 1895], p. 194).

John Knox

lived in Geneva for a short period, but it was the happiest time of his life.

A Farmer's Son from Scotland

When he arrived in Geneva for the first time in 1554, Knox could already look back on an eventful life. We do not know for sure how old he was when he arrived: some think he was born in 1505, others say it was closer to 1513. In either case, he was past forty when he set foot in Geneva. He had not known Calvin for many years, nor was he one of Calvin's youthful students. He was a man in the prime of his life, and he had already earned his spurs in the course of the Reformation.

Not much is known about the first few decades of his life. He was a farmer's son, but this did not mean that his background was one of poverty. William Knox, John's father, was an affluent gentleman-farmer who had been born into an ancient and prestigious family. His mother came from the Sinclair clan, and thus was a true Scotswoman. The Knox family lived in Haddington, about fifteen miles east of Edinburgh. John was destined for the clergy from an early age; his parents set great value on a good education and had sufficient means to allow him to study rather than to put him to work on the farm. John's education started at the Latin school of Haddington and continued at St. Andrews, the most famous of the Scottish universities. There he sat at the feet of the theologian and philosopher John Maior, who made certain Knox received a thorough scholastic education that did not lack in elements of renewal.[3] As he studied, the young priest-in-training imbibed criticisms of the abuses in church and politics. He did not really like scholasticism, but it built his knowledge of the church fathers. Scotland could not offer a quality humanistic education centered in the biblical languages; for that he had to wait until his time in Geneva, where he was able to master Greek and Hebrew.

After he completed his education, Knox became a priest and so-

---

3. It was thought for a long time that Calvin had this same teacher in Paris; but it now seems certain that this was not the case. See A. N. S. Lane, *John Calvin: Student of the Church Fathers* (Edinburgh, 1999), pp. 16-25.

licitor in Haddington. We do not know when the light of the Reformation fully broke through in his life, but he probably served for a considerable time as a priest. During the final years, before the dramatic events surrounding the struggle for the Scottish Reformation focused the public's attention on him, he worked as the private tutor of the sons of a nobleman.

One Martyr Is Enough

It is remarkable how little is known of Knox's life before 1546, especially since he himself wrote a *History of the Reformation in Scotland,* in which he provides a great deal of information about what was happening around him. It is an autobiographical account in which he plays a prominent role, yet certain aspects of his life remain rather mysterious. For quite some time he probably remained a loyal son of the Roman Catholic Church, even when the Reformation was already cropping up in Scotland and producing martyrs. The young Patrick Hamilton, who was related to the king and had been taught in Wittenberg, died a martyr's death. In turbulent Scotland the Reformation often involved rather murky political and ecclesiastical factions. John Knox undoubtedly had his opinions about this, but he did not choose sides until he was impressed by the role of George Wishart among the reform-minded.

Scotland had historical ties with France and a constantly precarious relationship with England. These two factors were responsible for a complicated political pattern; and when the Reformation of the church was added to these circumstances, it became even more complex. Henry VIII had distanced himself from Rome because of his marital problems. He wanted his royal colleague in Scotland, James V, to do likewise. But James had close ties with the French monarchy, which was firmly determined to stay with Rome. James was married to Marie de Lorraine, a sister of the duke and Cardinal De Guise, who were to become the leaders of the Roman Catholic camp in the religious wars in France. When James V died, his wife became the regent for her daughter, Mary Stuart. Her main support in the conflict with the reform-minded nobility came from David Beaton, the cardinal of St. Andrews.

During this tense period, George Wishart returned from England to Scotland. He was the son of a country nobleman who had joined the clergy and enthusiastically supported the Reformation. Wherever Wishart went, he openly preached the gospel of free grace, and his preaching was widely accepted among the nobility. However, it was the charge of treason that caused him to end up in the hands of the cardinal, and that brought him to the stake that was erected on the square in front of the cathedral of St. Andrews.

Knox was among Wishart's entourage, but his mentor strongly emphasized that he not seek martyrdom. His counsel became widely known: "Go back to your students — one suffices for a sacrifice."[4] Knox obeyed this command. It almost seems like an affront to his dignity, someone has written, to accuse Knox of timidity or even cowardice.[5] Knox was the man at whose grave Morton would later say, "Here someone rests who feared nor flattered any flesh." Yet his entire life did show a degree of prudence, for Knox understood the value of his life for the cause of the gospel. There were moments when staying at his post would have resulted in martyrdom, for example, when the Roman Catholic Mary Tudor acceded to the English throne. Knox withdrew at those times in order to be longer able to serve his calling. The words of Wishart echoed extensively throughout his life. The image of a man with an unflinching character is not the only picture we may have of Knox.

A Hard Training School

Not long after the death of Wishart, Knox found himself in serious trouble. A Protestant conspiracy against the pro-French Cardinal Beaton had come to nothing. Even when the "bloody wolf" — Knox's name for the cardinal who had burned his beloved teacher at the stake — was in fact murdered, the rebellion did not get off the ground. But the castle of St. Andrews was conquered by the rebels, and Knox was among them. It was the place where he would begin his preaching of the gospel. At first he had planned to leave for the Continent for further study, but circum-

---

4. Brown, *John Knox*, p. 68.
5. Donaldson, "Knox the Man," p. 19.

stances kept him at St. Andrews, where he was urgently called on to serve as pastor. He felt that he could not refuse this appeal.

The people of St. Andrews hoped that the English would come to their aid. But when ships appeared on the horizon, they were flying the French flag. The allies of the Roman Catholic party of Scotland reconquered the castle on behalf of the Scottish authorities. John Knox was taken prisoner and transported to France, and the next nineteen months would be the most difficult period of his life. He was a galley slave on a French warship. Chained to the oars, with a threatening whip always snapping overhead, he was taught in the hard training school of envoys for the cross of Christ. This brutal experience would forever leave the traces of its ravages on his health. But it also reinforced his conviction that, if the Lord was to spare him, another task awaited. At a certain point, when his ship was close to the shore of St. Andrews and he was seriously ill, a friend told him to look toward the shore. Could he not recognize the spire in the distance? "Yes," the greatly weakened Knox replied, "that is the church where I preached my first sermon." And with prophetic conviction he added: "I know that I will once again proclaim the name of God in that church."[6]

En Route to Geneva

In 1549 the galley slave was set free, and he was given a warm welcome when he arrived in England. This was during the brief period when the English Protestants enjoyed a time of freedom: the reign of the young King Edward VI and his Protestant advisers. Knox's capacities and talents for the furtherance of the Reformation were recognized: he was appointed as minister in Berwick and Newcastle (in the north of England), and later he even served as court chaplain. He refused to be promoted to the rank of bishop. Did he still want to keep his options open, for example, for further study on the Continent? Or did he sense a calling to serve in his own country at some future time, when circumstances would permit?

Knox was delighted with the sincere Reformational convictions of

6. Brown, *John Knox,* p. 85.

the young king, but at the same time he deplored the quality of his advisers. It would not be the first time, he once remarked, that "the best and most pious kings were surrounded by perfidious and godless servants and counselors." Knox was also deeply worried about the lack of discipline in the churches. But he would not stay in England for long. King Edward died in 1553, and his half sister, Mary Tudor, succeeded him, setting in motion a radical counter-Reformation effort. As a result, the Protestants in England were unable to continue their work. Hundreds of believers — bishops among them — died as martyrs. Thousands departed for the mainland of Europe, and John Knox was among them.

Where was he to go? He set his sights on Switzerland. There is little doubt that he knew the works of Bullinger and Calvin, for these two Reformers had had many contacts with English believers, and their books were widely distributed and read there. During the six-year reign of a truly Reformed king, Edward VI, Calvin and his colleagues had fostered great hopes that the example of England might have a positive influence on other European kingdoms. It must have been a heavy blow to Calvin when Edward died.

In early 1554, Knox traveled via Dieppe and France to Geneva, where he met Calvin for the first time. Later he would travel through other Swiss cities, invariably receiving a warm welcome, and consulting with the Reformers about a few burning questions. Calvin writes to Bullinger that he was satisfied with the way his colleague, "the Scot," as he called John Knox, had responded. "I have, in a confidential talk, explained my opinion," Calvin writes.[7] Apparently, Knox had asked the two Reformers about the legitimacy of royal succession by women, which was a crucial issue in England and Scotland. Knox had a more radical standpoint in this matter than did either Calvin or Bullinger.

Another question concerned the right to actually defend the gospel with arms. On this point Calvin and Bullinger were also in agreement: one should patiently suffer oppression rather than start a rebellion "without a clear call from God." Calvin left a small opening, but he felt that moderation and prudence ought to prevail. Upon his return from Zurich to Geneva, Knox did not ask Calvin to put his opinion in

7. *CO*, 15: 123-26.

writing. Had Calvin convinced him to drop his more radical ideas? Most likely not. He probably concluded that having a document from Calvin would not help him to legitimate in any authoritative way the resistance in England and Scotland. For that reason he wrote his own pamphlet (Faithful Admonition unto the Professors of God's Truth in England), a passionate appeal to his persecuted fellow believers in England, to encourage them to be steadfast in their resistance.

A Puritan in Frankfurt

Knox's first visit to Geneva did not lead to a long stay in this city. He had wanted to stay and study Hebrew, but he allowed himself to be convinced by Calvin to go to the imperial German city of Frankfurt and minister to the English refugee church there, which had close contacts with the local French Huguenots.[8]

But it did not take long before a conflict erupted in that church concerning the liturgy. Knox and his colleague Wittingham did not accept the Anglican influence on the worship service, which they felt was far too Roman Catholic in character. They fiercely promoted a more austere style of public worship: liturgy as they had experienced it in Geneva. This is why Knox's church appealed to Calvin, with his authority, to help them broker a compromise between Anglicanism and Puritanism. Calvin wrote that he was very upset that brothers who left their own country for the sake of the same precious conviction now disagreed. He clearly shared Knox's view regarding the remaining "follies" in Anglican worship, but in a letter he urges them to use moderation and not to let the transitional situation escalate.[9]

But the fragile compromise that was reached in Frankfurt did not hold when a new group of refugees further strengthened the anti-Puritan party. Knox and his supporters had lost. The matter escalated to the point of an accusation against him of some secret intrigue that had led to *lese majesté* because he was said to have turned against the Ger-

---

8. De Greef, *Johannes Calvijn: Zijn Werk en zijn Geschriften* (Kampen, 2006), pp. 75-78.

9. *CO,* 15: 393-94.

man emperor. He clearly could not stay in Frankfurt. Calvin defends him in a letter to the English church of Frankfurt, saying that his opponents had not treated their minister in a very "brotherly" fashion.[10] In the meantime, Knox was already safely back in Geneva.

Minister of the English Church

It must have been refreshing for Knox to find a safe haven in Geneva after the deep disappointment of the Frankfurt church, where his fellow believers had driven him out. He arrived at a good moment, in 1555, when a period of peace and rest had begun for Calvin, when the influence of his opponents had finally been broken for good. There was now the full opportunity to push for a complete Reformation of the church in Geneva. Knox was appointed as the minister of the English church, which may perhaps be called the first "Puritan congregation."[11] He became a thorough Calvinist, showing the same kind of great admiration for the Reformer as he once had for his spiritual father, Wishart. He was even granted citizenship.

But he would not enjoy the reprieve of ministry in a small church, with ample time for study, for very long. England and Scotland continued to demand his attention. He did not particularly wish to return to the British Isles, but he continued to feel the pull of his homeland. After six months he traveled back to Scotland, and he returned to Geneva from that journey with his wife, Marjory, whom he had married in Scotland, and his mother-in-law, Mrs. Bowes. During his many travels Knox carried on an extensive, lively, and confidential correspondence with his mother-in-law, as well as with other female believers.

Why did he return to Geneva just when the influence of the Protestants in Scotland was increasing? One supposition has been that Knox preferred not to remain in Scotland because, unlike the peaceful atmosphere of Geneva, the cause of the Reformation there was so mixed up with intrigue and violence.[12] Knox knew himself and realized that it

---

10. *CO,* 15: 628-29.
11. Stanford Reid, *Trumpeter of God,* p. 134.
12. Ridley, *John Knox,* p. 236.

would be difficult not to get involved. Geneva was his delightful place of reprieve, but Scotland was his destiny.

A Calvinist in Scotland

His prophetic calling would, inescapably, take him back to Scotland. From 1559 until 1572, he would be the key figure of the Reformed "revolution," which would subject the entire Scottish society forever to the Calvinist "Kirk." But struggle and opposition would not disappear. Scotland, as elsewhere, would ultimately not see a triumphant church. When he was on his deathbed, Knox asked that John 17 (the high-priestly prayer) be read: that was, he testified, "the anchor of my soul." He had not been able to see his wishes realized: a people that would truly live in accordance with God's Word and a society in which the poor received true mercy. These dreams were thwarted by continuous political scheming.[13]

During the final years of his life Calvin must have been looking forward to news from Scotland. Would the Reformation become visible in Scotland among the people and the nobility, just as he passionately hoped it would in France? Would the result of John Knox's work be like "a small cloud the size of a man's hand"?

Knox's fierce opposition to the "unnatural" reign by women, as he expressed it in his book *First Blast of the Trumpet against the monstruous regiment of women,* caused extreme embarrassment to Calvin.[14] Bloody Mary's successor, Queen Elizabeth I, so disliked the "women-hating" Knox that she did not even want to receive an honorable dedication from his friend Calvin when the latter published his sermons on Isaiah. Calvin had to apologize to the queen's councilors, assuring them that he did not hold such extreme opinions, and that he considered the

13. James S. McEwen, *The Faith of John Knox* (London, 1960), p. 5: "Yet here lies the tragedy of John Knox's life — that he coveted peace, but lived and died in strife: that his last years were saddened by tarnished visions and shattered hopes; that he saw with dreaming gaze a Promised Land, but found not the means to lead his people into it."

14. The second and third blast of the trumpeter were never sounded, as originally intended. His indictment of Mary Tudor was never meant for the Protestant Elizabeth.

John Knox

reign of Elizabeth as a blessing under divine providence.[15] Calvin did not always welcome Knox's radical views.

But when we read the letters from Geneva, we can clearly see that Calvin continued to hope for good news from Edinburgh: "Not just I, but all the faithful to whom I communicated the message of joy [the good progress of the Reformation], were pleased to hear about the excellent results of your labor. As we marvel about the unbelievable success in such a short time, we praise God for his extraordinary blessing that is manifested in his glory. This gives us every ground for confidence in the future and must further encourage you towards a blessed continuance of the good fight."[16]

Despite the fact that Calvin at times considered Knox too rigid in his views and actions, he loved him until the end as a dear brother and fellow soldier for the cause of Christ's kingdom.[17] In the midst of all the strife and fear in Geneva, which sometimes utterly distressed him, Calvin continued — partly because of his friendship with John Knox in faraway Scotland — to harbor a prophetic expectation of the breakthrough and victory of the kingdom of Christ.

15. Letter to Lord William Cecil Burleigh. *CO*, 17: 490-92.
16. *CO*, 17: 665-68.
17. *CO*, 18: 433-35.

A Scottish Friend

THEODORE BEZA

A Friend and Successor

Vos docti docta præcingite tempora lauro :
Mi fatis eft illam uel tetigiffe manu.

Theodore Beza, portrait from the *Juvenalia*

Theodore Beza

The Sun Sets

It was a beautiful spring evening, May 27, 1564, and the sun was setting at the very moment that John Calvin was breathing his last. A week earlier, during the meal that the ministers of Geneva had together every quarter, he had said his goodbyes to his brethren in the service of God's Word. This last meal was in his home. He hardly ate anything, and before this meal with his close friends was over, he had already asked to be taken back to his bed in the neighboring room. With a smile he said, "The wall between us does not prevent me from being with you in the spirit, even though my body is elsewhere."

It is Theodore Beza (1519-1605) who tells us about Calvin's last hours.[1] Beza could not be dragged away from the deathbed of his beloved spiritual father. During the last week of his life, Calvin could not leave his bed; he was consumed to the extent that nothing but his breath seemed to remain. Yet the moment of his death came unexpectedly, and Beza was not present. On the day of his death, Calvin seemed to be a little stronger, and he found it a little easier to talk. But this was just the last surge of strength. Beza had left Calvin's home for a moment, so one of Calvin's servants went looking for him with the message that the signs of approaching death were unmistakable. "I returned as quickly as I could," Beza reports, "but could only establish that he had died." He found Calvin in such peace that it was like a sleep and not at all like death. "And, thus, the splendid light for God's church was taken from us to heaven, as the sun was setting."[2]

Executor

A month before Calvin's death, Beza had been elected to succeed him as the moderator of the Company of Pastors of Geneva, and Calvin was

1. On Beza, see Paul F. Geisendorf, *Théodore de Bèze* (Geneva, 1949); Olivier Fatio, "Theodor Beza," in Martin Greschat, ed., *Gestalten der Kirchengeschichte, Reformationszeit II* (Stuttgart, 1993), pp. 255-76; Richard A. Muller, "Beza," in *The Encyclopedia of Christianity* (Grand Rapids, 1999), 1: 231-32; C. Veltenaar, *Beza Herdacht* (Maassluis, 1905).

2. Theodore Beza, *L'Histoire de la Vie et Mort de seu M. Iean Calvin, Fidele Serviteur du Iésus Christ* (Geneva, 1656).

A Friend and Successor

fully confident that his heritage would be in good hands with his younger colleague. During the six years that Beza had been his right-hand man in Geneva, he had been only strengthened in his confidence that this learned countryman, who also was someone with a very kindred mind, would be a worthy successor. He had manifested a passionate desire to promote the kingdom of Christ in Geneva just as he had in France, their common homeland. It gave the dying Calvin an inner peace that enabled him to let go of everything, knowing that the helm would be in good hands. Therefore, he instructed his colleagues to give Beza all the support they could in view of his heavy responsibilities, so that the burden would not become overwhelming. "He has a willing spirit and will do all he can," Calvin assured them.[3]

One of the first things Beza did after Calvin's death was compose a record of the Reformer's life. Did this make him a hagiographer, someone determined to transform Calvin's life story into the history of a saint? Far from it, for Protestants do not recognize any saints. However, he knew that opponents of the Reformation often tried to discredit servants of the gospel by distributing false stories, thereby undermining their teachings. For that reason, Beza considered a reliable biography essential. And the facts of Calvin's life were still easily ascertainable from those who had known him personally. (Another thing Beza did was begin preparations for publishing Calvin's correspondence, which would underscore the key position Calvin had held in the Reformation in Europe.)

Beza wanted to tell Calvin's life story because the man and his truth were so intimately connected, but he was not asking people to venerate him: "We are so far removed from veneration of the dead, as light is from darkness."[4] But there is no reason not to glory in the work God performed by this man. Beza says that he has known Calvin "for the last sixteen years" at very close range. And he refers to October of 1548, when he found refuge in the city of Calvin, as *the* decisive moment of his conversion.

3. Hugh Y. Reyburn, *John Calvin: His Life, Letters, and Work* (London, 1914), p. 316.

4. *L'Histoire de la Via et Mort,* p. 7.

Theodore Beza

From Laurel Wreath to Crown of Life

The portrait of Beza at the beginning of this chapter shows him at the age of twenty-nine. We see a young man with a laurel wreath in his hand, and the Latin caption reads: *Vos docti docta praecingite tempora lauro: Mi satis est illam vel tetigisse manu* ("You scholars adorn your temples with an academic laurel wreath; I am satisfied to have just touched it with my hand"). This was a modest dictum for an ambitious young man, one who was striving for the honor and fame that the muses might bring him. Until his momentous conversion, he was of two different minds. On the one hand, he was impressed by the evangelical movement that was unmistakably present in French humanism. As a sixteen-year-old youth, he had read one of Bullinger's books about the origin of "errors," and had become convinced of the abuses in the Church of Rome.[5] On the other hand, he did not want to break completely with the certainties that the Roman Catholic Church offered, even if these only concerned the ecclesiastical income he received, which enabled him to lead the carefree life of a lover of the liberal arts.

Beza had already come into contact with the influence of the Reformation at an early age. The castle of his father in Vezelay was not the place where his education and spiritual formation took place. As the youngest son of a Burgundian nobleman, the five-year-old Theodore was entrusted to the home of a childless uncle in Paris. His mother was very unhappy to see her youngest son leave home. And, to make matters much worse, after she delivered her son to Paris, she died on the return journey when she fell from her horse. It must have been a traumatic experience for the child, alone in the unknown city of Paris, to be told of his mother's death.

Uncle Nicolas sent the talented boy, when he was not even ten years old, to Orléans, where he could receive a quality education in law. Young Theodore lodged with Melchior Wolmar, and this humanist and Lutheran who taught classical languages in Orléans became his spiritual father. It was in this region of Bourges, where the Wolmar family had moved, that Beza first met Calvin, who was studying with Wolmar.

5. Heinrich Bullinger, *De origine erroris, in divorum ac simulachrorum cultu* (1529).

A Friend and Successor

(Their age difference would mean that, for the time being, the kinship of their minds was not yet really on the same level.) Beza later referred to the moment that he was adopted into this loving family as "the day of my birth." When Wolmar had to flee from France because of his evangelical beliefs in 1534, Beza wanted very badly to go with him; but his father would not allow it.

On completing his law studies in 1539, Beza left Orléans for Paris. But it was not to accept an honorable position; instead, he opted for the carefree life of the literary world. He tried to establish a reputation as a great lover of literature and a gifted practitioner of the art of poetry. Meanwhile, the income he received from church sources allowed him to be financially independent, and he moved enthusiastically within the humanist circles of the French capital. His critical and evangelical posture regarding the conservative Roman Catholic forces in church and society did not yet lead him to a radical choice for the gospel. He moved in circles in which a form of Spiritualism — against which Calvin would warn repeatedly — had so much influence that it did not require a decisive choice for the Reformation and a final separation from Rome.[6]

In 1545 he secretly married a young woman who was beneath his station. A collection of his poems was published in 1548, the so-called *Poëmata,* or *Juvenalia* (literally, "poems of one's youth"). But a few years later, after his conversion, he would openly deplore this publication: he would never again use his poetic talents, he said, in a noncommittal glorification of the arts (in which he did not even shun erotic love poetry). With profound shame, he writes in the preface to his biblical play about Abraham's sacrifice, he is grateful to God that, fortunately, he no longer needs to put his pleasure in poetry and his gifts in the service of "idle and dishonorable phantasies."[7] He would now devote himself to promoting biblical art, for example, by producing a rhymed version of the Psalms.

Shortly after the summit of his fame as a poet, he experienced the

6. H. Meylan, "La conversion de Bèze ou Les longues hésitations d'un humaniste chrétien," in *d'Erasme à Bèze,* ed. H. Meyland (Geneva, 1976), pp. 145-67.

7. Theodore Beza, "Abraham Sacrifiant," in *Four Renaissance Tragedies,* ed. Donald Stone, Jr. (Cambridge, MA, 1966), p. iii.

Theodore Beza

low point of his life when a serious illness brought him to the verge of death. During this illness he became deeply convinced of God's judgment on his life, that God had spared his life as a miracle of grace. At that moment he realized that he was to surrender all his luxuries and privileges in exchange for a life in the service of Christ's kingdom. He replaced his poetic laurel wreath with the crown of life.

Immediately upon his recovery from that illness, he left for Geneva in order to avoid any more temptations in Paris. There he entrusted himself to Calvin's pastoral care, and for the rest of his life he would be a faithful servant of the church of Christ. The first thing Calvin did was publicly confirm Beza's secret marriage in the church, for he believed that all things should take place in an honorable and orderly way.

Son of Three Fathers

This is when Beza's life really began. He was only twenty-nine years old and would still have fifty-seven more years during which he would prove to be a great blessing to the Reformation in France and all of Europe. He was the son of three fathers. He stayed in contact with his biological father as long as that father was alive.[8] However, everything the latter could offer in terms of a noble family's influence no longer counted to Theodore, though he would later occasionally put his noble status to good use in diplomatic contacts for the sake of the Reformation.

His first spiritual father, Melchior Wolmar, the teacher with whom he lived as a boy and the one who brought him in contact with the treasure of the gospel, was of greater importance. But his "third father," John Calvin, to whom he went immediately after his conversion, was of even greater significance to him. Calvin was constantly urging those of kindred minds not to remain in the Roman Catholic Church for the sake of outward appearances while they inwardly cherished an evangelical conviction. At long last, this view found its wholesome mark

---

8. Beza would write his *Confession de Foy* (written in Lausanne and published in Geneva in 1558) as a personal testimony, in which his main aim was to convince his father of his orthodox Christian faith.

in Beza: for the rest of his life he wholeheartedly became the spiritual son of Calvin.

Teacher in Lausanne

By fleeing from Paris to Geneva, Beza had burned all his bridges behind him. The rather carefree existence of a privileged nobleman who could devote himself to poetry and the liberal arts had changed into the life of an exile. After he was tried in absentia, his effigy was burned in Paris, since his departure was by then construed to be his confession that he was a "heretic on the run."

Calvin welcomed Beza with open arms. By way of his contacts in Paris, the former had undoubtedly heard who this gifted humanist was. He may well have been concerned that it had taken this younger brother so long to openly cut the ties that still held him connected to Rome, while in his heart he cherished the evangelical ideals. But now that Beza had exchanged life in Paris for Geneva, Calvin knew that the kingdom of God had experienced an enormous gain. In a 1551 letter to a French lady, Calvin gives his opinion of Beza: "God had endowed him with excellent gifts. And he uses these gifts for the good of the church, so that we might well call him a pearl. . . . All who are interested in the glory of God praise this man as a treasure."[9]

However, the question was how this treasure could be used for the strengthening of the kingdom of Christ. At first Beza planned to start up a print shop where he could produce books along with his friend Crespin, who had been a witness at his secret wedding in Paris. That would be a way of ensuring, from this place of exile, that his oppressed fellow believers in France would have books. But, though Crespin became a printer, it was not to become Beza's profession. Instead, on his way back to Geneva from Germany, where he had visited his second father, Wolmar, he stopped in Lausanne. There he met Pierre Viret, and that was a meeting of lasting significance for him. Lausanne was the only Francophone Swiss city with a theological school where the three classical languages were being taught in the humanist tradition. There

---

9. Letter to Lady de Cany, 1551, cited in Veltenaar, *Beza Herdacht,* p. 20.

was a vacancy in the department of Greek, and who would be better suited to fill this slot than the young French humanist, whose competence was well known? Viret was eager for Beza to be appointed, but he felt that he could not act without asking for Calvin's approval. Did Calvin not have first claim on this talent? Calvin's response was magnanimous and encouraging: "I have faithfully worked toward the goal of pushing Beza in your direction," he says in a letter.[10] But it seems that Beza himself was not immediately excited by the idea. Calvin had to, he admits, urge Beza to accept — almost in "a shameful manner." Calvin promises Viret that he will not stop urging until Beza has agreed to take the position.

What made Beza hesitate to accept an assignment that was so fitting for him? Perhaps he felt that his literary talents did not really qualify him for theology. Perhaps he felt a certain amount of shame; we know that he did feel unworthy because of his past. Perhaps he worried that his Latin poems, which were partly of a sensual nature, would discredit the church if he were to be appointed a teacher. It was honorable of Beza to openly pose that question before accepting the post. However, what he worried about was not considered a hindrance in Lausanne, and later his apologetic candor was to have a positive effect. When some opponents later attempted to reproach Beza by asking whether it was known what kind of poems he had written in his youth, the author could confidently declare that his frivolous past had long been known in Geneva — which nipped that attempt to smear him in the bud.

Beza did accept the faculty appointment in Lausanne, and he experienced great blessings in his work there. He was a gifted exegete whose translation of the New Testament (published in 1556) was to have a major influence. He also proved to be close to Calvin with regard to his views on divine predestination. Because of his publication *Tabula predestinationis* ("Table of Predestination"), he was suspected of having made this doctrine of Calvin into too much of a logical system. Yet his preaching nowhere indicates that this became a constrictive system for him, a system that would narrow the freedom of God's grace. During a

10. *CO*, 13: 376-77.

later stage of hyper-Calvinism, some who were attempting to deal with predestination appealed to Beza and Calvin to limit the element of divine calling in the gospel proclamation. But they failed to realize that Beza's *Table* was in fact only of rather modest significance. It was no more than a preliminary scheme that could play a role in scholarly debates; but it was never meant to be an overarching system in which everything else had to fit. A theologian such as Bullinger — who clearly had different emphases than Calvin and Beza did — admitted, when reading the *Table,* that predestination might indeed be presented in such a scheme in outline, which is a further indication that it should not be given too much weight.[11]

Back to Geneva

Though Calvin had been willing to relinquish Beza to Viret in 1549, he badly wanted him back in Geneva by 1558. And it did cause some friction between the two close friends when Calvin brought Beza back to his city. However, Viret would follow Beza to Geneva very soon himself, because it was becoming increasingly difficult for Calvinist theologians to function in Lausanne. Bern's influence, which ensured that there would be no opportunity for much-needed church discipline — as there was in Geneva — made Calvin's allies leave.

The nine years in Lausanne had been a very valuable training school for Beza: he had changed from a humanist philologist into a Calvinist theologian. Thus could he be of great use to Calvin in the project that, besides the preaching of the Word, was dearest to Calvin's heart — that is, establishing a Reformed academy. He felt the need for this as an institution for the furtherance of the pure Word, and it would serve the kingdom of Christ in Geneva and far beyond.

The question arises why Calvin waited until the year 1559 to request his own rights of citizenship in Geneva. This was not because the city had been unwilling to grant these to him; for example, his brother had been granted that status years earlier — free of charge because of the merits of

---

11. Muller, "Beza," p. 232; C. van Sliedrecht, *Calvijns Opvolger Theodorus Beza* (Leyden, 1996), p. 122.

the Reformer — and it should not have been too difficult for Calvin to also acquire citizenship. Could it be that he did not wish to become a full citizen of the city to which he had come as a foreigner until he saw that long-held dream fulfilled? For the academy that was to be a training institute of preachers for the church in France was the greatest service Geneva would be able to offer Calvin's former fatherland!

Beza, the teacher from Lausanne, became the first rector of the Academy of Geneva. He was chosen to give the rectorial address when the school opened, and in it he passionately emphasized the importance of this institution. It pleases God, by means of a thorough education of the mind, he said, to lead toward a true knowledge of the heart. If blind, pagan philosophers already attached great value to good education, how much more would this be true for those who live according to the light of God's Word. From Scripture he demonstrated that schools are a "benevolent act of God."[12]

The Father of Calvinism

Beza survived his older friend and predecessor by more than forty years, but it could have been different. At one point Calvin was overcome by fear when Beza became critically ill with the plague. How could he cope with the loss of this promising theologian? Calvin wrote to a friend in Paris: "It would be inhumane not to love, in turn, this person who loved me more than a brother and honors me like a father. I was in even greater anxiety from the thought that the church would lose a man, from whom I expected a rich harvest of fruit, if he were to be taken from us through death at the beginning of his career."[13] Fortunately, Calvin was spared such an enormous grief.

Toward the end of his life, Calvin could, with peace in his heart, hand over the function of moderator of the Company of Pastors of Geneva to Beza. During the final years of Calvin's life, when things in Geneva had vastly improved (compared to the years before 1555), the situation in France continued to worsen. It gave Calvin peace of mind

12. Oratio Bezae. *CO,* 17: 542-47.
13. *CO,* 14: 144-45.

that he could in full confidence send Beza to both Germany and France as a representative and diplomat of the Reformation in Geneva. There, in his native country, ten years after he had been symbolically burned at the stake as a heretic, he was treated with so much respect by the queen mother, Catherine de Medicis, that he was even allowed to conduct the service in the court chapel.[14]

Calvin could not have wished for a better successor than Beza, the man who faithfully guarded his heritage. Beza did not forget what Calvin had implored on his deathbed, that "nothing would be changed" after his death. He used the biblical forty-year period to faithfully protect and promote the influence of the Reformation, of which his spiritual father and friend had been the architect. When one walks closely in the footsteps of his predecessor, one will at all times remain somewhat in that person's shadow. Beza always felt much at ease in Calvin's shadow. But more than many perhaps realize, he was the one who kept the light burning in Geneva.[15]

It was largely because of Calvin that Beza became the man he did; but at the same time, we can say that Calvin owes part of what he became to Beza, who continued to honor him until the day of his death. When Beza died, the Calvinist Reformation had become such an important factor in large parts of Europe that Rome, with all its power, could no longer curtail it. Many students from the Academy of Geneva occupied key positions in church and state — in France as well as England, Scotland, Poland, and the Netherlands. Beza, like Calvin, had no surviving physical offspring. But as Calvin's spiritual son, Beza became the father of Calvinism.

14. During the Colloquium of Poissy in 1561, where Beza led the Protestant delegation.

15. The motto of Geneva's freedom was: *Post Tenebras Lux* ("after the darkness, light").

Theodore Beza

Bibliography

Primary Sources

John Calvin

Iohannis Calvini opera quae supersunt omnia. Edited by G. Baum, E. Cunitz, and E. Reuss. Braunschweig, 1863-1900 (cited in notes as *CO*).

Iohannis Calvini Opera Omnia, denua recognita. Series VI, *Epistolae I.* Edited by C. Augustijn and E. P. van Stam. Geneva, 2005.

Calvin's Commentary on Seneca's De Clementia. Edited and translated, with introduction, by Ford Lewis Battles and André Malan Hugo. Leiden: Brill, 1969.

L'Excuse de Noble Seigneur Jacques de Bourgogne Seigneur de Falais en de Bredam. Geneva, 1911.

Lettres à Monsieur et Madame de Falais. Edited by Françoise Bonali-Fiquet. Geneva: Librairie Droz, 1991.

Des Scandales. Edited by Olivier Fatio. Geneva: Droz, 1984.

Writings on Pastoral Piety. Edited and translated by Elsie Anne A. McKee. New York: Paulist, 2001.

Other Sources

Herminjard, A. L. *Correspondance des Réformateurs dans las Pays de Langue Française.* 9 vols. Geneva, Basel, Lyon, Paris, 1878-97 (cited in notes as Herminjard).

Bèze, Theodore de. *Histoire Ecclesiastique des Églises Réformées au Royaume de*

France. Edited by G. Baum and E. Cunitz. Paris: Librairie Fischbacher, 1883-89.

Registres de la Compagnie des pasteurs de Genève. Edited by R. M. Kingdon and J. F. Bergier. Vol. 2, 1553-1564. Geneva: Droz, 1962. English edition: *Registers of the Consistory of Geneva in the Time of Calvin.* Robert Kingdon, general editor. Edited by Thomas A. Lambert and Isaella M. Watt, with the assistance of Jeffrey R. Watt. Translated by M. Wallace McDonald. Grand Rapids: Eerdmans, 2000 (Meeter Center for Calvin Studies).

Secondary Literature

Augustijn, Cornelis. "Bern and France." In *Ordenlich und fruchtbar,* edited by Wilhelm H. Neuser and Herman J. Selderhuis, 155-69. Leiden: Groen en Zoon, 1997.

———. "Farel und Calvin in Bern 1537-1538." In *Calvin im Kontext der Schweizer Reformation,* edited by Peter Opitz, 9-23. Zurich: Theologischer Verlag, 2003.

Augustijn, Cornelis, Christoph Burger, and Frans P. van Stam. "Calvin in the Light of the Early Letters." In *Calvin Praeceptor Ecclesiae,* edited by Herman J. Selderhuis, 139-57. Geneva: Droz, 2004.

Balke, Willem. *Calvijn en de Bijbel.* Kampen: Kok, 2003.

———. "Jean Calvin und Pierre Viret." In Opitz, *Calvin im Kontext der Schweizer Reformation,* 57-92. Zurich: Theologischer Verlag, 2003.

Bevan, Frances. *Het Leven van Willem Farel.* Aalten, 2001.

Bèze, Theodore de. "Abraham Sacrifiant." In *Four Renaissance Tragedies,* edited by Donald Stone, Jr. Cambridge, MA: Harvard University Press, 1966.

Bietenholz, Peter G. *Contemporaries of Erasmus: A Biographical Register of the Renaissance and Reformation.* Vol. 3. Toronto: University of Toronto Press, 1985-87.

Bohatec, Josef. *Budé und Calvin: Studien zur Gedankenwelt des französischen Frühhumanismus.* Graz: H. Böhlaus Nachf., 1950.

Bonnet, Jules. "Calvin à Ferrare." *Bulletin de la Société de l'histoire du protestantisme Français* 41:13.

———. "Idelette, femme de Calvin." *Bulletin de la Société de l'histoire du protestantisme Français* 4 (1856): 636-48.

Bouwmeester, G. *John Knox, de Hervormer van Schotland.* Rotterdam, 1964.

Braekman, E. M. "Sum enim Belga ipse quoque: Calvin et les ressortisants des Pays-Bas." In *Calvin et ses contemporains,* edited by Olivier Millet, 83-96. Geneva: Librairie Droz, 1998.

Brown, Hume. *John Knox.* London: A. and C. Black, 1895.

Burger, Christoph. "Calvins Beziehungen zu Weggefährten in der Schweiz, 1536-1538." In Opitz, *Calvin im Kontext der Schweizer Reformation,* 5-55. Zurich: Theologischer Verlag, 2003.

Büsser, Fritz. "Calvin und Bullinger." In *Calvinus Servus Christi,* edited by Wilhelm H. Neuser, 107-26. Budapest, 1988.

———. *Calvins Urteil über sich selbst.* Zurich: Zwingli Verlag, 1950.

Carpi-Mailly, Olivia. "Jean Calvin et Louis du Tillet, entre foi et amitié, un échange révélateur." In Millet, *Calvin et ses contemporains,* 7-19. Geneva: Droz, 1998.

Cartier, Alfred. *Arrêts du Conseil de Genève sur le fait de l'imprimerie et de la librairie.* Geneva, 1893.

Casalis, G., and B. Roussel, eds. *Olivétan, Traducteur de la Bible.* Actes du Colloque Olivétan, Noyon, May 1985. Paris, 1987.

Cooke, Charles L. "Calvin's Illnesses and Their Relation to Christian Vocation." In *John Calvin and the Church: A Prism of Reform,* edited by Timothy George, 59-70. Louisville: Westminster John Knox, 1990.

Cottret, Bernard. *Calvin.* Paris: J. C. Lattès, 1995.

Croce, Benedetto. *Galéas Caracciolo, Marquis de Vico.* Geneva, 1965.

Dardier, Charles, "Voyage de Calvin en Italie." *Musée Historique de la Réformation Calviania,* 4/2. Geneva.

De Greef, Wulfert. *De Ware Uitleg.* Leiden, 1995.

———. *Calvijn, zijn Werk en Geschriften.* Kampen: Kok, 2006.

De Kroon, Marijn. *Martin Bucer en Johannes Calvijn.* Zoetermeer, the Netherlands: Meinema, 1991.

Dennis, P. "Un combat aux frontières de l'orthodoxie: La controverse entre Acontius et Des Gallars sur la question du fondement en des circonstances de l'église." *Bibliothèque d'Humanisme et Renaissance* 38 (1976): 55-72.

———. "Jacques de Bourgogne, seigneur de Falais." In *Bibiotheca Dissidentium: Répertoire des non-conformistes religieux des seizième et des septième siècles,* edited by André Seguenny, vol. 4: 9-52. Baden-Baden: V. Koerner, 1980-84.

Bibliography

Donaldson, Gordon. "Knox the Man." In *John Knox: A Quartely Reappraisal,* edited by Duncan Shaw, 18-32. Edinburgh: St. Andrew Press, 1975.

Doumergue, Emile. *Calvijn en Genève.* Kampen: Kok, 1986.

———. *Calvijn in het Strijdperk.* Kampen: Kok, 1986.

———. *Calvijn's Jeugd.* Kampen: Kok, 1986.

———. *Iconographie Calvienne.* Lausanne: G. Bridel, 1909.

Elwood, Christophe. *The Body Broken: The Calvinist Doctrine of the Eucharist and the Symbolization of Power in Sixteenth-Century France.* New York and Oxford: Oxford University Press, 1999.

Eurich, S. Amanda. "The Death of Nicolas des Gallars: Evidence from the Notarial Records of the archives départementales des pyrenées-atlantiques." *Bibliothèque d'Humanisme et Renaissance* 60 (1998): 739-40.

Fatio, Olivier. "Theodor Beza." In *Gestalten der Kirchengeschichte, Reformationszeit II,* edited by Martin Greschat, 255-76. Stuttgart: Kohlhammer, 1981-85.

Flood, John L. *Johannes Sinapius (1505-1560): Hellenist and Physician in Germany and Italy.* Geneva: Droz, 1997.

Gäbler, Ulrich. "Heinrich Bullinger." In Greschat, *Gestalten der Kirchengeschichte, Reformationszeit II,* 197-209. Stuttgart: Kohlhammer, 1993.

Ganoczy, Alexandre. *The Young Calvin.* Translated by David Foxgrover and Wade Provo. Philadelphia: Westminster Press, 1987.

Garcia, Aurelio A. "Bullinger's Friendship with Calvin: Loving One Another and Edifying the Churches." In *Calvin Studies Society Papers,* edited by David Foxgrover, 119-33. Grand Rapids: CRC Product Services, 1995, 1997.

Geisendorf, Paul F. *Thédore de Bèze.* Geneva: Jullien, 1967.

Gerstner, Edna. *Idelette.* Grand Rapids: Zondervan, 1963; reprint, Ligonier, PA: Soli Deo Gloria Publications, 1992.

Gilmont, Jean-François. *Jean Calvin et le livre imprimé.* Geneva: Droz, 1997.

Gordon, Bruce, and Emidio Campi. *Architect of the Reformation: An Introduction to Heinrich Bullinger, 1504-1575.* Grand Rapids: Baker Academic, 2004.

Greschat, Martin. "Martin Bucer." In *Gestalten der Kirchengeschichte, Reformationszeit II,* edited by Martin Greschat, 7-28. Stuttgart: Kohlhammer, 1993.

———. "Das Profil Martin Bucers." In *Martin Bucer and Sixteenth-Century Europe.* Actes du colloque de Strasbourg (August 28-31, 1991), edited by

Bibliography

Christian Krieger and Marc Lienhard, 9-17. Leiden and New York: Brill, 1993.

Hazlett, Ian. "A Pilot Study of Martin Bucer's Relations with France, 1524-1448." In Krieger and Lienhard, *Martin Bucer and Sixteenth Century Europe.* Actes du colloque de Strasbourg (August 28-31, 1991), 511-21. Leiden and New York, 1993.

Hillerbrand, Hans J. *The Oxford Encyclopedia of the Reformation.* Vol. 3: 174-75. Oxford and New York: Oxford University Press, 1996.

Hommes, N. J. *Misère en Grootheid van Calvijn.* Delft, n.d.

Johnson, Dale W., and James Edward McGoldrick. "Prophet in Scotland." *Calvin Theological Journal* 33, no. 1 (1998): 76-86.

Kingdon, Robert M. *Geneva and the Coming of the Wars of Religion in France, 1555-1563.* Geneva: Droz, 1956.

————. *Adultery and Divorce in Calvin's Geneva.* Cambridge, MA, and London: Harvard University Press, 1995.

————. "The Galeazzo Caracciolo Case: Divorce for Religious Desertion." In Kingdon, *Adultery and Divorce in Calvin's Geneva,* 143-56. Cambridge, MA, and London: Harvard University Press, 1995.

————. "Calvin's Last Years." In *Calvinus Praeceptor Ecclesiae,* edited by Herman J. Selderhuis, 179-87. Geneva: Droz, 2004.

Kromsigt, Pieter J. *John Knox als Kerkhervormer.* Utrecht, 1895.

Kuropka, Nicole. "Calvins Römerbriefwidmung und der Consensus Piorum." In Opitz, *Calvin im Kontext der Schweizer Reformation,* 147-67. Zurich: Theologischer Verlag, 2003.

Kyle, Richard. "John Knox and the Care of Souls." *Calvin Theological Journal* 38, no. 1 (2003): 125-38.

Lane, Anthony N. S. *John Calvin: Student of the Church Fathers.* Grand Rapids: Baker Books, 1999.

Lefranc, Abel. *La Jeunesse de Calvin.* Paris: Librairie Fischbacher, 1888.

Linder, Robert D. "Brothers in Christ: Pierre Viret and John Calvin as Soul-Mates and Co-laborers in the Work of the Reformation." In Foxgrover, *Calvin Study Society Papers,* 1995, 1997, 134-58. Grand Rapids: CRC Product Services, 1998.

————. *The Political Ideas of Pierre Viret.* Geneva: Droz, 1964.

MacCulloch, Diarmaid. *Reformation: Europe's House Divided, 1490-1700.* London and New York: Allen Lane, 2003.

McEwen, James S. *The Faith of John Knox.* Richmond, VA: John Knox Press, 1961.

Meylan, H. "La conversion de Bèze ou les longes hésitations d'un humaniste chrétien." In *D'Erasme à Bèze,* edited by Henri Meylan, 145-67. Geneva: Droz, 1976.

Muir, Edwin. *John Knox: Portrait of a Calvinist.* Port Washington, NY: Kennikat Press, 1972.

Muller, Richard A. "Beza." In *The Encyclopedia of Christianity,* edited by Erwin Fahlbusch and translated by Geoffrey W. Bromiley, 1: 231-32. Grand Rapids and Leiden: Eerdmans and Brill, 1999-2007.

Naphy, William G. *Calvin and the Consolidation of the Genevan Reformation.* Manchester and New York: Manchester University Press, 1994.

Nauta, Doede. *Guillaume Farel, in Leven en Werken Geschetst.* Amsterdam, 1978.

———. *Pierre Viret (1511-1571): Medestander van Calvijn.* Kampen: Kok, 1988.

Oberman, Heiko O. "Calvin and Farel: The Dynamics of Legitimation in Early Calvinism." *Journal of Early Modern History* 2 (1998): 32-60.

Olson, Jeannine E. *Calvin and Social Welfare, Deacons, and the* Bourse Française. Selinsgrove, PA: Susquehanna University Press, 1989.

———. "Les amis de Jean Calvin: La famille Budé." In Millet, *Calvin et ses Contemporains,* 97-105. Geneva: Droz, 1998.

———. "The Family, Second Marriage, and Death of Nicolas des Gallars within the Context of His Life and Work: Evidence from the Notarial Records in Paris and in Pau." *Bibliothèque d'Humanisme et Renaissance* 63 (2002): 73-79.

———. "The Friends of John Calvin." In Foxgrover, *Calvin Society Study Papers,* 1995, 1997, 159-68. Grand Rapids: CRC Product Services, 1998.

Parker, T. H. L. *John Calvin: A Biography.* Louisville: Westminster John Knox Press, 2006.

Reid, W. Stanford. *Trumpeter of God: A Biography of John Knox.* New York: Scribner, 1974.

Reyburn, Hugh Y. *John Calvin, His Life, Letters, and Work.* London, 1914.

Ridley, Jasper. *John Knox.* Oxford and New York: Oxford University Press, 1968.

Rott, J. "Documents strasbourgois concernant Calvin." *Revue d'Histoire et de Philosophie* 44 (1964): 290-335.

Rupp, G. "The Europe of John Knox." In *John Knox: A Quarterly Reappraisal,* edited by Duncan Shaw, 1-17. Edinburgh: St. Andrew Press, 1975.

Bibliography

Rutgers, F. L. *Calvijns Invloed op de Reformatie in de Nederlanden voor zoveel die door hemzelven is uitgeoefend.* Leiden, 1899.

Schimsheimer, J. F. *Galeazzo Caracciolo, Geschetst als Mens en als Christen.* Amsterdam, 1844.

Schlaepfer, H. L. "Laurent de Normandie." In *Aspects de la Propagande Religieuse,* 176-230. Geneva, 1957.

Selderhuis, H. J. *Marriage and Divorce in the Thought of Martin Bucer.* Translated by John Vriend and Lyle Bierma. Kirksville, MO: Thomas Jefferson University Press at Truman State University, 1999.

Steinmetz, David C. "Heinrich Bullinger (1504-1575)." In Steinmetz, *Reformers in the Wings,* 93-99. Oxford and New York: Oxford University Press, 2001.

————. "Martin Bucer (1491-1551): The Church and the Social Order." In *Reformers in the Wings,* 85-92. Oxford and New York: Oxford University Press, 2001.

Textor, Bernard. *De la Manière de Preserver de la Pestilence & de guerir selon les bons.* Lyon, 1551.

Treschow, Michael. "John Knox." In *The Encyclopedia of Christianity,* edited by Fahlbusch et al., vol. 3: 133-34. Grand Rapids and Leiden: Eerdmans and Brill, 2003.

Van den Berg, M. A. "Calvijn en Melanchthon, een Beproefde Vriendschap." *Theologia Reformata* 41 (1998): 78-102.

Van Itterzon, G. P. "Guillaume Farel." In *Christelijke Encyclopedie.* Vol. 3. Kampen: Kok, 1958.

Van Sliedrecht, C. *Calvijns Opvolger Theodore Beza.* Leiden, 1996.

Van Stam, Frans P. "Das Verhältnis zwischen Bullinger und Calvin während Calvins erstem Aufenthalt in Genf." In Opitz, *Calvin im Kontext der Schweizer Reformation,* 25-40. Zurich: Theologischer Verlag, 2003.

————. "Farels und Calvins Ausweisung aus Genf am 23. April 1538." In *Zeitschrift für Kirchengeschichte,* 209-28. Stuttgart: Kohlhammer, 1998.

Van 't Spijker, Willem. "The Influence of Bucer on Calvin as Becomes Evident from the Institutes." In Van 't Spijker, *John Calvin's Institutes, His Opus Magnum,* 106-32. Potschefstroom, South Africa, 1986.

————. "Bucer und Calvin." In *Martin Bucer and Sixteenth-Century Europe,* Actes du Colloque de Strasbourg (August 28-31, 1993), edited by Christian Krieger and Marc Lienhard, 460-71. Leiden: Brill, 1993.

————. "Calvin's Friendship with Martin Bucer: Did It Make Calvin a Calvinist?" In Foxgrover, *Calvin Study Society Papers,* 1995, 1997, 169-86. Grand Rapids: CRC Product Services, 1998.

Veltenaar, C. *Beza Herdacht.* Maassluis, 1905.

Venema, Cornelis P. "Heinrich Bullinger's Correspondence on Calvin's Doctrine of Predestination." *Sixteenth Century Journal* 17, no. 4 (1986): 435-50.

Walmsley, Lesley. *C. S. Lewis on Love.* Nashville: Thomas Nelson, 1998.

Wellman, Sam. *John Calvin: Father of Reformed Theology.* Ulrichsville, OH: Barbour, 2001.

Wiedeburg, Andrea. "Die Freundschaft zwischen Butzer und Calvin nach ihren Briefen." *Hist. Jahrbuch* 83 (1964): 69-83.

Wiley, David N. "Calvin's Friendship with Guillaume Farel." In Foxgrover, *Calvin Studies Society Papers,* 1995, 1996, 187-204. Grand Rapids: CRC Product Services, 1998.

Wolff, Christian. "Nouvelles Glanes sur la Famille d'Idelette Calvin à Strasbourg." *Bulletin de la Société de l'Histoire du Protestantisme Français* (1991/1992): 137-38.

Illustrations

The portraits and other pictures in this book are taken from the following sources:

Theodore Beza, *Beza's Icones — Contemporary Portraits of Reformers of Religion and Letters.* Facsimile reproductions of the portraits in Beza's "Icones" (1580) and in the Goulard Edition (1581), with introduction and biographies by C. G. McGrie (London: Religious Tract Society, 1906).

G. Berthoud et al., *Aspects de la Propagande Religieuse* (Geneva, 1957).

John Calvin, *L'Excuse de Noble Seigneur Jacques de Bourgogne Seigneur de Falais en de Bredam* (Geneva, 1911).

Benedetto Croce, *Galéas Caracciolo, Marquis de Vico* (Geneva, 1965)

Emile Doumergue, *Iconographie Calvinienne* (Lausanne: G. Bridel, 1909).

Jan Weerda, *Holbein und Calvin: Ein Bildfund* (Neukirchen: Kreis Moers, Verlag der Buchhandlung des Erziehungsvereins, 1955).

Illustrations

Index of People and Places

Heidelberg, University of, 59-60, 70-71, 72-73, 102, 112
Henri II (of France), 16, 158, 163, 172, 213, 248
Henry VIII (of England), 49, 73, 230
Huguenots, 8, 56, 160, 184, 214, 234
Hungary, 70, 220
Hutten, Ulrich von, 60

Italian churches, 198-99, 205n.9, 203-4
Italy, 50, 66, 168, 197, 199, 202-3

James V (of Scotland), 230
Jehannet, 51, 53
Jonvilliers, Charles de, 175, 215
Jussy, 90

Kappel, 219, 220
Karlstadt, Andreas, 71, 74
Keller, Ludwig (Cellarius), 103
Klein, Catharina, 75
Knox family, 229, 235
Knox, John, 227-37
Knox, Marjory Bowes, 235
Knox, William, 229
Kuntz, Peter, 77

La Bresse, 136
Landstuhl, 102
La Rochelle, 184,
Lausanne, 16, 86, 90, 94-97, 127, 137, 138, 162, 243n.8, 244-46
Lescar, 184
libraries, 14, 29-30, 42, 70, 117
Liège, 128
Lieur (Budé), Roberte le, 208, 210-13
Livy, 73
London, 137, 182-83
Lorraine, Marie de, 230
Louis XII, 3, 49
Luther, Martin, vii-viii, 11, 22-24, 40,

71, 81, 102, 105, 112-13, 116n.16, 118n.22, 120-21, 125, 223-24
Luther, teachings of, 12, 20, 42, 105, 199, 219
Lutherans, 60-61, 105, 110, 120, 222, 225
Lucanius, Martianus, 13, 75
Lyon, 18, 26, 136, 162, 171

Macar, 182
Macon, 136-37, 138, 140-41
Maior, John, 229
Manardo, Giovanni, 61
Margaretha, Governess, 187
Marguerite d'Angoulême of Navarre, 14, 21-22, 50, 51, 158
Marot, Clement, 51
martyrs, 32, 158, 162, 181, 191, 230-31, 233
Mary Stuart, 230
Mary Tudor, 231, 233, 236
Maurice I, Elector of Saxony, 113, 120
Medicis, Catherine de, 248
Meaux, 29, 81
Meigret, 172
Melanchthon, Philip, ix, 59, 70-72, 76, 109-22, 126, 219
Metz, 31
ministers, 31, 36, 146, 213. *See also* French ministers; Geneva ministers
Montaigu College, Paris, 92
Montargis, 55-56, 163, 214
Montomor castle, 5
Montomor family, 2-9
Montpelier, 139
More, Thomas, 73, 208
Morel, 55
Morones (Des Galliers), Gabrielle, 177, 182-83
Morton, James Douglas, Earl of, 231

Index of People and Places